Counselling Older Adults

Counselling Older Adults

PERSPECTIVES, APPROACHES AND
RESEARCH

Eleanor O'Leary PhD

Statutory Lecturer, Department of Applied Psychology,
University College Cork, Ireland

With the collaboration of

**Aileen D'Alton, Brian Kelly
and John McCarthy**

CHAPMAN & HALL

London · Glasgow · Weinheim · New York · Tokyo · Melbourne · Madras

Published by Chapman & Hall, 2–6 Boundary Row, London, SE1 8HN, UK

Chapman & Hall, 2–6 Boundary Row, London SE1 8HN, UK

Blackie Academic & Professional, Wester Cleddens Road,Bishopbriggs, Glasgow G64 2NZ, UK

Chapman & Hall GmbH, Pappelallee 3, 69469 Weinheim, Germany

Chapman & Hall USA, 115 Fifth Avenue, New York, NY 10003, USA

Chapman & Hall Japan, ITP-Japan, Kyowa Building, 3F, 2-2-1 Hirakawacho, Chiyoda-ku, Tokyo 102, Japan

Chapman & Hall Australia, 102 Dodds Street, South Melbourne, Victoria 3205, Australia

Chapman & Hall India, R. Seshadri, 32 Second Main Road, CIT East, Madras 600 035, India

Distributed in the USA and Canada by Singular Publishing Group Inc., 4284 41st Street,San Diego, California 92105

First edition 1996

© 1996 Eleanor O'Leary and Aileen D'Alton

Typeset in 10/12pt Times by Mews Photosetting, Beckenham, Kent

Printed in Great Britain by Hartnolls Limited, Bodmin, Cornwall

ISBN 0 412 56140 9   1 56593 123 8 (USA)

A catalogue record for this book is available from the British Library

Library of Congress Catalog Card Number: 95-71857

∞ Printed on acid-free text paper, manufactured in accordance with ANSI/NISO Z39.48-1992 (Permanence of Paper)

To my friend and mentor, Fr Brian Kelly.

Contents

Foreword

Dr O'Leary, Director of postgraduate courses in counselling and psychotherapy at University College Cork and author of books on counselling and psychotherapy, has applied her expertise to the counselling of the older person. In doing so, she has accomplished the rare feat of providing solid information concerning the older adult and setting a new direction for counselling the older person.

Her book gives the satisfied feeling that one has walked through several well-furnished rooms in a well-designed house encountering an expert who talks succintly about a topic of interest to you, answering your questions before you quite ask them. The house that she builds for us is a structure of knowledge about the older adult and about counselling. She starts her building by giving us information about demographic trends among older adults and continues by considering theoretical approaches to ageing. Here, in her emphasis on ageing as part of a life long developmental process, the design of her building becomes discernible. If, as she suggests, ageing is a developmental process, many of the difficulties experienced by older adults are due to impediments in that process, which can be ameliorated by helping those processes in counselling.

Before considering counselling in detail, she discusses the perceptions of ageing of both younger and older adults as well as the perceptions of professionals in the field. Then, after examining the issues and problems that necessitate counselling, approaches which deal with these problems are discussed. We then arrive at the centre of the house. Here she deals with the adaptation of general counselling approaches pertaining to the older adult.

This book has several important strengths. Rather than focusing solely on technique, Dr O'Leary gives us general knowledge about the elderly as well as information about several different approaches to counselling them. She has set a solid base for the consideration of present and future theories of counselling the older person. By setting in order the counselling of older adults in terms of what we know about them, looking at working with them in several contexts and considering several counselling theories, she has created a framework for the reader to examine his or her own theory of counselling. This framework will enable the reader to consider the direction counselling theories should take in the future.

This book will be of value beyond the counselling field. The general reader who is interested in the older adult and what can be changed in the older adult's life, will find much of value here.

This book is more than a scholarly compendium of knowledge about the older adult and about counselling. It urges the counselling field to accept the empowerment of the older person as an important goal. This goal stands in contrast to the more usual one of trying to solve the older person's problems. That is, in seeing the older person as a full person rather than as someone in a declining pathological state, she shifts the emphasis from fixing problems to facilitating the client's effort to live a fuller, more satisfying life. This facilitation greatly increases the possibility of enlisting the client's energy and knowledge in the counselling process.

The emphasis in this book on increasing the personal empowerment of the older person is the forefront of psychotherapy theory. This change has happened as a result of increasing acceptance of the centrality of the self. This leads to an emphasis on the beneficial effect of counselling or psychotherapy resulting from changes in the self rather than from fixing the client's problems.

Professor Fred Zimring
Professor of Psychology
Case Western Reserve University
Cleveland
October 1995

Acknowledgements

The motivation for this book had its origin in my interest in older people which began with my beloved grandparents, John O'Leary and Ellen Murphy. My memories of both are sunfilled ones.

Later, two significant older adults contributed to my store of knowledge: my father, Jack, and Jerry O'Sullivan, both recently deceased.

Outstanding models of a successful old age are my mother, Joan, and Peter Dempsey. Thank you for the many hours of happiness and laughter.

Other older adults I am privileged to call my friends include Margaret Brooks, Granny Flynn, Dympna Conway, Bridie Goggin and Albert Treacy.

An added spur to undertaking the work was provided by the invitation to study older adults in an inner city parish by the Cork Community Development Institute and South Parish Community Association.

I am also indebted to the following:

Professor Dick Page and Puncky Heppner for reading the text, Dr Eddie McHale and Colm O'Connor for commenting on the section on family therapy,
Dr Fionnuala O'Ciardha for sharing her knowledge of biological ageing,
Sharon Burke for co-facilitating groups for older adults with me,
Noreen Keane, Elizabeth Behan, Deborah O'Flynn and David Long for assisting me with the bibliography,
Noreen Moynihan, Joanne Rose and Andrea O'Neill for typing parts of the book,
Dr Art Berger, Noreen Sweeney, Bruno Mulcahy, Triona Histon, Pat Sexton and Eileen Murphy for helping with various tasks,
Jill Lucey and Phil O'Sullivan for securing inter-library loans,

Pat O'Connell for conducting computer searches,
Rosemary Morris and her staff for taking care of the finer points of production,
many others, too numerous to mention, for sharing books and articles.

It is always a pleasure to have the continuing support of my dear brothers, John and Bob, and sister, Joan, while my three nieces and seven nephews offer much fun in my life.

My greatest thanks must go to my three collaborators, Aileen D'Alton, Brian Kelly and John McCarthy. Aileen assisted in the groundwork for the initial chapters before her departure to Thailand, John lent his expertise with appropriate comments on Chapters 2 and 8 while Brian commented on the development of the structure of the book and lent his literary expertise to the task. Furthermore, Brian's pastoral experience was a springboard for far-reaching changes in the approach to older adults. To all three of you, mile buiochas.

Introduction

Counselling, according to O'Leary (1986), may be described as an encounter through which clients are afforded healing help, leading to the diminution or solution of the personal adjustment problems that beset them, as well as to positive growth and actualization of their personality. There are many who would contend that this definition does not apply to those who are old. After all, there is no solution to growing old – it just happens to people. It is widely held that being old is not a time of growth, but of an inexorable decline into mental confusion, physical helplessness and social isolation.

If the foregoing is a true picture of how old age is viewed by a significant number of people – and there is evidence to show that it is – it is not surprising that so little attention has been given to the needs of the older adult in the counselling situation. Counsellors lack experience with older adults who are going through normal ageing processes and who, because of the losses and other traumatic happenings in their lives, would benefit from counselling. A comprehensive counselling and psychotherapeutic approach can be provided by understanding the normal development of people in later life, theoretical approaches to old age, factors that affect the counsellor–older adult relationship and the main issues in the lives of this segment of the population.

In Chapter 1, the demographic trends among older adults in relation to the rest of the population are outlined. The definition of old age is addressed, taking into account chronological, biological, sexual, psychological, social and spiritual dimensions.

Chapter 2 discusses some theoretical approaches to ageing. Recent trends in the literature on ageing have stressed a lifespan perspective. The assumption on which this orientation is based is that development is a lifelong process, beginning at conception and ending in death. This viewpoint has important implications for approaches to counselling the older adult.

Attitudes to older adults are dictated by people's perceptions of them. In Chapter 3 general perceptions of ageing are described, as are the attitudes of professionals and professional trainees; the perceptions of older adults by young people are discussed, and the attitudes of older adults themselves to ageing are considered.

In Chapter 4 the impact of counsellor-related variables, client-related variables and the preparation of counsellors on counselling are explored. Chapter 5 considers counselling issues for the older adult. This chapter concludes on an optimistic note, with emphasis on the possibility of personal growth in older adults in counselling.

Chapter 6 describes counselling approaches that deal specifically with older adults, while Chapter 7 outlines the adaptation of general counselling approaches for use with older adults. Chapter 8 evaluates research findings to date in counselling older adults.

The final chapter deals with research and ethical issues.

Dimensions of later life

1

Our life is 70 years or 80 for those who are strong. (Psalm 89)

The Biblical lifespan was certainly not the norm at the time. In Graceo-Roman times, the average life expectancy was 18 years (Binstock and Shanas, 1985); it had increased to 25 years by the 17th century, and to 30 years in 18th century France (de Beauvoir, 1977). In colonial America, the average lifespan was 16 years and most people died before 40 years (Haber, 1983). Aiken (1989) stated that life expectancy was 45 years in mid-19th century America, 47 years in 1900, 73.3 years in 1978, and the projected life expectancy for the year 2000 is 82 years (Haber, 1983). In Ireland, a baby born in 1900 could expect to live to the age of 50. Current expectations are 70.1 years for men and 75.6 years for women (Irish Department of Health Publication, 1988). Hence more and more people are living out the seventh stage of Shakespeare's ages of life.

Gender is a major variable with regard to life expectancy. Aiken (1989) claimed that the average lifespan of women in pre-Christian times was approximately 25 years, and had reached only 30 years by the 15th century. Death as a result of childbirth was the main cause. That pattern changed only in this century. By 1900, life expectancy was 51.1 years for white American women and 48.2 years for white American men. By 1975, this had increased to 67 years for males and to 75 years for females (Woodruff, 1975). The American Psychological Association (1994) pointed out that ageing is disproportionately a women's issue.

Since 1939, the rate of increase in average life expectancy at birth in western culture has slowed down (Cutler & Marootyan, 1975). There was an increase of 16.4 years from 1900 to 1939 and 7.2 years between 1939 and 1975. There is also a slowing down at 65 years of age. Cutler and Marootyan stated that length of life increased only by an average of 3 years in the over-65 age group between 1900 and 1970. Nevertheless, the percentage of adults who are over 75 has increased in the US from 29% in 1930 to nearly 50% in 1990 (Cavanaugh, 1993). Even though life expectancy prospects are not increasing at the same rate as they did at the beginning of the century, the upper limit for length of life is being conti-nously extended.

Several studies have examined the percentage of the total population who live beyond 60 years of age. In the UK at the end of the last century, the percentage of those over 65 was 4.75% of the total population (Booth, 1980). The UK *Annual Abstract of Statistics* (1974) shows that, in the UK, the proportion of the population over 65 rose from 5.4% in 1911 to 13.2% in 1971. In 1991, 18% of women in Britain and 13% of men were over 65 (Ginn and Arber, 1991). The projections for the UK are that the proportion over 60 will rise to 17.8% for men and 22.7% for women by the year 2000, with a further increase to 21.5% for men and 25.9% for women by the year 2020 (European Demographic Statistics 1991/92).

Similar trends are discernible throughout Europe (European Demographic Statistics 1990/1991). By 1989 Belgium, Greece, Spain, France, The Netherlands, Portugal, Italy and Luxembourg all had more than 20% of their populations over the age of 60. It is estimated that by 2020 the European Union as a whole will have more than 26.4% of its total population over 60. Men over 60 will constitute 23.6% of the total population, while women will make up 29.2%. As a significantly large group, the needs of older adults will have to be addressed specifically.

In 1900 the proportion of the population over 65 years of age in the US was 4% or 3.1 million. This had increased to 30 million by 1990 (Cavanaugh, 1993). In 1983, for the first time in US history, senior citizens outnumbered teenagers (Safford, 1988). Aiken (1989) stated that the percentage increase in the population of the United States during this century has been two and a half times as great in the 65 and over age bracket as in the under 65 age group. This is a direct result of birth patterns and advances in modern medicine. Estimates indicate that the older population will continue to grow in the US, with a figure of 50 million predicted for 50 years' time (Casey, 1994).

Of the 3000 million world population in 1980, approximately 200 million were over the age of 60 (Stanway, 1981). By the year 2000, 13% will have passed their 65th birthdays. In the UK in 1984, 5.1 million women were aged 60 compared to 3.3 million men (Bromley, 1988). Similarly, Bosanquet (1983) found that women in Britain represent 57% of the 65–75-year age group. This proportion increases further with increase in age. Sixty-eight per cent of those over 75 are women, and of those who survive to the age of 85, 76% are women. Bengtson and Haber (1975) suggested that if the tendency for women to outlive men increases over the lifespan, and if the age median for women over 65 continues to rise as it has during the past several decades, the ratio of elderly women to elderly men may increase to 2:1 by the year 2000. If this occurs there are likely to be a large number of widows and unmarried elderly women.

These changing patterns of longevity have led and will continue to lead to the existence of a new and major segment of society. In an attempt to understand this group one must be familiar with the many dimensions of ageing. Chief among these are the chronological, biological, sexual, psychological, social and spiritual.

CHRONOLOGICAL AGEING

How old is old? 'Only the old man [woman] knows when an old man [woman] dies' (Ogden Nash). Growing old is normally a function of time. The demarcation between middle age and old age of 65 was first postulated by Bismarck in Germany in the 1880s, when formulating social policy for that country (Butler and Lewis, 1982). It has since been adhered to as a useful benchmark for the age of retirement and eligibility for social benefits.

Old age can span a period of 30 years, which makes it very difficult to treat as a homogeneous unit. Levinson (1978) identified the early 60s as the period when middle adulthood ends and late adulthood begins. Bromley (1988) distinguished between the 'young-old' (65–74 years) and the 'old-old' (75+ years). This division is quite common in recent literature on ageing, reflecting the pattern of growing old in today's society. Morrison and Radtke (1988) characterized three stages: early ageing, a period of renewed energy; middle ageing, when our world grows smaller; and elder ageing, which brings with it increased dependency.

A different perspective of ageing is offered by Birren and Schaie (1977), who introduced the concept of functional age as an individual's level of capacity to fulfil given roles relative to others of similar chronological age.

The age of 65 has limited relevance as an indicator of functioning, such as general health, mental capacity, psychological or physical endurance, or creativity (Butler and Lewis, 1982). Western society assumes that there is general deterioration in adults in all of these areas of life once the demarcation age of 65 has been reached. Society confuses chronological and biological ageing, with the result that too much importance is attached to the former, thus creating difficulties which do not necessarily exist.

BIOLOGICAL AGEING

Biological age is an estimate of the impact of ageing upon physiological systems (Victor, 1987). It provides a physical basis for ageing. Aiken

(1989) stated that biological age is the anatomical or physiological age as determined by changes in organismic structure and function. It encompasses such features as skin texture, hair colour, strength, mobility and sensory acuity.

Various hypotheses have been proposed to account for biological ageing, such as the 'wear-and-tear' theories (Perlmutter and Hall, 1992). The three most common are the DNA repair theory, the cross-linkage theory (Bjorksten, 1974) and the free radical theory (Harman, 1968). DNA repair theory holds that repair of DNA cannot keep up with the damage from metabolism, radiation or contact with pollutants. Ageing is thus the consequence of damaged DNA. The cross-linkage theory holds that the cross-linking of large intracellular and extracelluar molecules causes connective tissue to stiffen. These highly reactive molecules, or parts of molecules, may connect with and damage other molecules. The free radical theory is based on the fact that free radicals damage membranes by working on unstructured fat in them. Free radicals are created by various foods and tobacco smoke. Their formation is accelerated through radiation and inhibited by antioxidants. Both free radical and cross-linkage theories focus on changes that occur in the proteins of cells after they have been formed. Another theory that centres on these changes is the accumulation theory, which hypothesizes that destructive material in the form of dark-coloured waste material called lipofuscin develops in old age and kills cells.

Four other theories are cited by Busse and Blazer (1989). These include the immunologic theory, which suggests that with time there is a diminishing level of immunoglobin in the human body, which tends to lower immunity to illness and makes older people more susceptible to disease; the exhaustion theory, which suggests that a definite amount of energy is available to the body and that this eventually becomes exhausted; the 'ageing clock' theory, which suggests that a 'clock' resides in the hypothalamus and cell loss in this area results in a decline of homoeostatic mechanisms with age; and the biological programming theory, which suggests that cells are genetically programmed to have a certain lifespan. Busse concluded, however, that a convincing and empirically validated theory of old age does not exist.

Whatever the underlying cause may be, certain biological changes occur in specific body systems in old age. Changes in the skeletomuscular system create a general decline in strength. Muscle cells are replaced by fat cells and bones become thinner. Height can be reduced by up to 2″ owing to atrophy of the discs between the spinal vertebrae, a general atrophy of bones and skeletal atrophy. Yet most older adults have independent movement and reside in the community. Butler (1975a) found that, in the US, 81% of those over 65 years of age are fully ambulatory and 95% of them live in the community.

Changes in the skin, caused by loss of hydration, are often the most obvious manifestations of the ageing process. The skin becomes paler and more blotchy. It takes on a parchment-like quality and dark spots of pigment occur. A change in brain rhythm also occurs in old age. Hultsch and Deutsch (1981) point out that most research shows a decrease in the frequency of the alpha rhythm. Whereas in adolescence this frequency is 10–11 cycles per second (cps), in the 60s it has reduced to 9 cps and a further decrease to between 8 and 8.5 cps occurs after 80 years of age.

As a person ages, metabolic and structural changes occur in the eyes which lead to deterioration in vision and eyeball mobility. The ability to focus at different distances may be reduced owing to loss of lens elasticity (Stuart-Hamilton, 1994): with age, the pupil decreases in size (Perlmutter and Hall, 1992). In a nationwide study of adults over 65, the US Bureau of the Census (1986) found that 90% had some visual impairment and only 10% had good vision without glasses. Most of this latter group retain their good vision into advanced old age. In a study of 1200 adults aged 100 or more, Segerberg (1982) found that 9% could see well without glasses, 62% could see well with glasses, 25% had vision defects that glasses could not correct and 4% were blind.

Impaired sensory perception can cause confusion and stress. Normal activities such as street crossing can become difficult. In an investigation of 189 old people, O'Leary and Kelly (1990) found that 5% had difficulty with pedestrian crossings. Impaired vision also affects driving. The American Psychological Association (1994) pointed out that 'older adults typically characterize driving as the primary source of mobility, so maintenance of driving becomes the primary concern in maintaining independent functioning'.

Increased physical incapacity appears to be age related. Hunt (1978) found that, for each of the three age groups 65–74, 75–84 and 85+, figures for the permanently disabled increased with age for both sexes. When leaving their place of residence for a social visit or on business, 2.3% of the men and 6.6% of the women between 65 and 74 had to be accompanied; 4.2% of men and 14.2% of women aged 75–84 required help; and 30.5% of the females and 16.4% of the males over 85 needed support going out. O'Leary and Kelly (1990) found that 7% of their sample of older adults over 65 were confined to their home and a further 7% needed to be accompanied when they went to town, although half of these were capable of travelling unaccompanied in their own immediate neighbourhood.

Hearing losses are also common in old age. Whitbourne (1985) stated that approximately one-third of older adults have inadequate hearing, while Herbst (1982) estimated that about 50% of adults over 80 have serious hearing difficulties. Corso (1977) studied the question of peripheral versus central deficits in audition. He found that, in old age, when there is a loss in both locations the manner in which these losses interact may vary at different ages. Sadavoy *et al.* (1991) stated that, from the ages of 30 to 85, there is a dramatic decline in high-frequency perception. Perlmutter and Hall (1992) claimed that, by the age of 75, 15% of the population is deaf. Richardson (1964) found that within the 60–69 age bracket 9% had impaired hearing. This increased to 22% for the 70–79 age group, reaching 50% for those aged 80 and over. A gender difference was found in that women were not only more likely to have a hearing aid but were also more inclined to use it. However, for people over 100 years of age only 2% were totally deaf.

The effects of decreasing physical capacities are not as great in familiar surroundings. Older people with failing eyesight are less likely to be afraid in the dark if they know the layout of a house and where assistance may be obtained. It is also easier to engage in an activity if it has been established as a routine. Hence the effects of decreasing physical capacities may be lessened in a familiar and appropriate environment.

Hayflick (1977) concluded that disease rather than biological ageing is the more common cause of deterioration in old age. Hardening of the blood vessels creates circulatory problems in the brain, while the respiratory, digestive and reproductive systems all tend to decline. Butler and Lewis (1982) claimed that severe or even mild organic brain disease can interfere markedly with functioning. Diseases such as osteoarthritis, rheumatoid arthritis and osteoporosis are common in old age.

Biological ageing does not bring about a uniform decrease in functional capacities: this differs from person to person. Woodruff and Birren (1975) stated: 'Older people are less alike than they have ever been, as they have lived through a long life in a particular life style with a unique heredity'. Hence environmental history may be a factor in biological ageing. Although much of the discussion thus far considers particular difficulties that emerge in old age, the general picture is bright, with four out of five older adults being fully ambulatory. The overall physical health of the body plays a critical role in determining the energies and adaptive capacities of older people. Leventhal (1991) stated that 'functional independence can be maintained well into the ninth decade'.

SEXUAL AGEING

There tends to be an accepted stereotype of the 'sexless older years'. Renshaw (1991) stated: 'Disbelief, condescending humour, silence and benign neglect have pervaded the topic of geriatric sexual expression through the centuries'. Of a total of 1700 pages in the two Kinsey reports (1948, 1953), only two deal with men over 60, while women over 60 fare even worse, with just half a page being devoted to this group. Belsky

(1990) observed that negative stereotyping of older adults includes an evaluation of the unattractiveness and inappropriateness of sexual behaviour in this age group. This may militate against older adults disclosing information on their sexual lives. Another possible reason for non-disclosure given by Stuart-Hamilton (1994) was that of a cohort effect: older adults may not be accustomed to speaking about sexual matters.

Sexual desire remains active throughout life, even if only expressed in fantasy. In a cross-cultural study, Winn and Newton (1982) found that, in over two-thirds of 106 different societies, older males had a negligible loss of sexual interest, while the figure for females (84%) was even higher.

An interesting finding was obtained by Brecher (1984) who, in a survey of 4246 older adults, found that they described the characteristics of the 'ideal lover' they would like to have as someone who was about their own age. Yet Clark and Hatfield (1989), in seminars with older individuals, found that they were reluctant to acknowledge anything but an asexual role for themselves.

In a study by Comfort (1974), 25% of adults aged 75 or more were still sexually active. Aiken (1989) pointed out that of the 254 men and women aged 60–94 who participated in the Duke University study, two-thirds of the men and one-fifth of the women had sexual intercourse regularly. Wiedeman and Matison (1975) conclude that where opportunity is regularly available sexual activity is maintained, although with less frequency, throughout late adulthood.

This view is supported by Finkel (1978), who maintained that sexual capacity continues for the majority until extreme old age, and in some individuals can continue into the 90s. Masters and Johnson (1966) found that, although sexual responsiveness weakens for the male after the age of 60, regularity of arousal, adequate physical wellbeing and a healthy mental orientation to the ageing process provide a climate conducive to sexual performance. Such performance may extend up to and beyond the age of 80.

In a study of subjects aged between 60 and 93, Newman and Nichols (1974) found a remarkable consistency in the experiencing of the sexual drive throughout life. They concluded that, given good health and equally healthy partners, older people continue to be sexually active into their seventh, eighth and ninth decades. Aiken (1989) also concluded that, given good health and sufficient practice, men can remain sexually active into their 70s and 80s, and women for as long as they live.

Lidz (1983) confirmed that older people remain sexually active into advanced old age. The male becomes less potent but not impotent. Renshaw (1991) stated that 'every man aged 50 years or over needs to know that, because of general and peripheral arteriosclerotic vascular changes and diminished connective tissue elasticity, partial erections are normal, natural and predictable'. Orgasm occurs in every second act of intercourse (Comfort, 1976) whereas the female continues to achieve orgasm readily. Aspects of sexuality which are important during older adulthood include touching, being physically close to another person and caressing (Starr, 1985). Lidz pointed out that in old age 'an upsurge of deeply felt and rather romantic love often occurs' and 'the elderly are no longer under the sway of sexual impulses unless they need to reassure themselves and counter feelings of ageing by the sexual act'.

A number of studies have been conducted on the sexual response of older males. Solnick and Birren (1977) presented the same erotic film to young and old men. Of the subjects approached, 85% of the young and 70.6% of the older group agreed to participate. It was found that younger men responded rapidly but then partially lost their erection, whereas the older men gradually increased the erectile response, although it never reached the maximum levels attained by younger men. In view of the aforementioned stereotypes surrounding the sexual activity of older adults, the comparative participation rates of the older males in this study are worthy of note.

Each stage of the sexual response cycle in males lengthens after 60 years of age (Perlmutter and Hall, 1992). Older men can maintain an erection much longer before ejaculation. Solnick and Corby (1983) stated that the ability to maintain erection longer may make intercourse more enjoyable for both partners. This is especially true where the woman requires extensive stimulation in order to reach orgasm. The feeling that ejaculation is inevitable lessens in the man, the number of orgasmic spasms diminishes and the refractory period, in which an erection cannot occur, lengthens. The force of ejaculation is reduced, often seeping rather than spurting (Aiken, 1989). Comfort (1978) pointed out that the perception of age changes in sexuality determines outcomes: unanxious men perceive the changes as a gain in control, while anxious males who equate virility with rapidity may experience anxiety.

There is a difference of opinion regarding female sexual response. Corby and Solnick (1980), citing findings by Hite (1976), concluded that the 'vasocongestive increase in clitoral shaft diameter and retraction of the clitoral shaft and glands as the female reached high levels of excitement did not change with age'. By contrast, Masters and Johnson (1966) found that the intensity of physiological reaction and response to sexual stimulation were both reduced with advancing years. Nevertheless, this is of little significance, since they conclude that there is no time limit to female sexuality resulting from advancing years. Aiken (1989) pointed out that the cervix and uterus decrease in size and vaginal lubrication is reduced. However, since the clitoris is still responsive to stimulation, older women may have as many orgasms as younger women.

Porcino (1985) also felt that women's sexuality was not adversely affected in old age. She declared: 'There is no time limit for female sexuality. Women are physiologically capable of full sexual expression until they die...Yet studies show a significant decline in sexual satisfaction'. The reason for this is usually the lack of a sexual partner. Given the shorter life expectancy of men, women are usually left without their sexual partner in old age. This is particularly true since women tend to marry men who are a few years older than themselves. A further reason is the tendency of some older men to seek out younger women as 'stimulants of that waning youthful sexuality'.

Butler and Lewis (1982) viewed sexual activity after 60 years of age 'as the opportunity for the expression of passion, affection and loyalty: it affirms the value of one's body and its functions, it is a means of self-assertion and affirmation of life, it involves the pleasure of being touched and caressed; it defies the stereotype of ageing as the sexless older years and it allows a continuing search for sensual growth and experience'.

Intimacy was defined by Calderone and Johnson (1981) as 'when people delight each other and delight in each other in an atmosphere of security based upon mutuality, reciprocity and total trust in each other'. They held that this is the kind of relationship every human being wants, even if it does not involve physical sex. Renshaw (1981) believed that older adults are 'touch hungry'. This need for touch can be satisfied through a variety of sources, such as physical contact with other family members and friends: grandchildren and pets can be particularly rewarding.

In general, the possibility of a fulfilling sexual life for older adults is high. There is a lengthening of the four phases of sexual arousal and decline (excitement, plateau, orgasm and resolution) for both sexes, but this does not inhibit sexual pleasure (Aiken, 1989). Kimmel (1990) stated that 'most people can expect to be able to have sex long after they no longer wish to ride bicycles'!

PSYCHOLOGICAL AGEING

Psychological ageing is the adaptive capacity of individuals, vis-à-vis their changing environment. It 'involves the study of memory, learning, intelligence, skills, feeling, motivation, and emotions' (Birren and Schaie, 1977). The relevant aspects are intellectual ageing and affective ageing.

Intellectual ageing

One of the earliest investigations of the effects of ageing on intelligence was a longitudinal study by Owens (1966): 127 male freshmen at Iowa State University in 1919 were tested on the army Alpha examination. They were subsequently retested in 1950, and 96 were again tested in 1961. Owens found that the only result that decreased significantly was the numerical score. Allowing subjects longer to complete the tests did not significantly alter the result. Owens found that the decade from 50 to 60 was one of relative constancy in mental ability test performance. The relevance of the study to older adults is somewhat limited in that the average age of the participants was 61 years of age in 1961.

The decrease in numerical ability was contradicted in the Seattle Longitudinal Aging Study (Schaie and Strother, 1968; Schaie *et al.*, 1973; Schaie and Labouvie-Vief, 1974; Schaie, 1983). In an investigation, 161 subjects aged 21–84 years of age were tested on the Primary Mental Abilities test on five occasions in 1956, 1963, 1970, 1977 and 1984. Number scores showed no change at any time. Cohort differences (having been born and grown up under certain socioeconomic conditions) accounted for the decreases in reasoning, verbal meaning and visuo-spatial skills. Schaie concluded that the supposition that intellectual decline occurs with age is not justified. Horn and Donaldson (1976) disagreed with these findings, since Schaie's data showed declines on tests measuring fluid abilities.

Cattell (1971) distinguished between fluid and crystallized intelligence. Fluid abilities are constitutionally or genetically based, while crystallized abilities are derived from cultural experiences. However, the study investigated only those from the early teens to the 40s and 50s. Although Stuart-Hamilton (1994) held that studies show that fluid intelligence decreases with age while crystallized intelligence remains stable, he pointed out that cross-sectional studies usually estimate that the decrease in fluid intelligence is greater than do longitudinal studies.

A study by Blackburn *et al.* (1988) found that fluid ability, namely figure relations and problem solving, improved in older people when they were given formal instructions describing how to solve specific problems, or when they practised generating their own solutions. In the latter exercise gains made were maintained over time. Baltes and Schaie (1982) cited studies which found that 'there is no strong age-related change in cognitive flexibility. For the most important dimension, crystallized intelligence, and for visualization (the ability to organize and process visual materials)...we see a systematic increase in scores for the various age groups, right into old age'. Further, it was discovered that even those over 70 years of age improved from the first testing to the second. They concluded that on at least some measurable dimensions of intelligence, particularly crystallized, older people of average health can expect to maintain or even increase their level of performance.

Memory loss and confusion are often associated with old age. Although some slowing of thought and memory processes does occur, Butler (1984) stated that 75% of the population can expect to retain sharp mental functioning if they live into great old age. Another 10–15% will experience mild to moderate memory loss. Only 5% of the population will be victims of true senile dementia. Brearley (1977) distinguished between 'hold' and 'don't hold' tests. 'Hold' tests involve the capacity to reproduce well-learned information, and this skill, he found, remains constant throughout adult life. 'Don't hold' tests, on the other hand, show a gradual decline with ageing. Kimmel (1990) claimed that older adults maintain competency in areas where they have developed relatively high levels of expertise. This was borne out in a study of nearly 2500 subjects by West (1992). They found *inter alia* that female subjects were better than male subjects at memorizing grocery lists!

More central than the discussion of increase or decrease is the relevance of intelligence test scores to the measurement of intelligence in old age. Labouvie-Vief (1985) differentiated between these scores and real-world intelligence. He believed that people who possess the latter are sensitive to the many perspectives involved in issues, and integrate them in obtaining solutions. Additionally, they are socially aware and empathic and include both affective and cognitive factors in their decision-making. Labouvie-Vief's distinction closely resembles Egan's (1975) differentiation of general and social intelligence. Schaie (1977–78) proposed a four-stage approach to intelligence: in childhood and adolescence, the essence of intelligence is ease of learning; in young adulthood it is reflected in the achievement of life goals; during middle age, cognitive competence is seen in responsibility and decision making and the ability to integrate complex relationships; in old age personality and attitude contribute to intelligence as individuals evaluate the relevance of knowledge to life.

Certain variables influence the outcome of testing in older adults, but have little to do with the intrinsic ability of the ageing person. Older adults are especially susceptible to fatigue, particularly the 'old-old'. They may become tired much more easily in experimental situations than those in younger age groups. Impaired vision or hearing, as well as intellectually and socially impoverished environments in family settings and institutions, can also alter outcomes. Birkhill and Schaie (1975) found that performance on four of the five factors of the Primary Mental Abilities test could be significantly increased in older adults by changing situational factors in the standard form of administration of the tests. This study provides evidence that reported decreases in intellectual ability may be due to situational factors.

The outcome of testing in older adults may be further influenced by the use of cross-sectional studies. Some of these have failed to control for relevant factors. First, older adults when younger may not have received the same stimulation, either in advanced schooling at second- and third-level education or through the news media. Apparent decreases in intelligence in old age in these instances may be due to a cohort effect, hence in studying the older adult it is important that longitudinal studies be used where possible. Cox (1988) pointed out that differences in education level explain much of the decline in intelligence test scores for the older age group in more recent longitudinal studies. Intelligence is frequently measured on only two or three occasions, often at widely separated ages. For example, the first two tests carried out by Owens (1966) had a 31-year time interval between them. Secondly, these studies may suffer from selective drop-out effects. Older adults are survivors and a bias related to intelligence may have been introduced into the sample through the effects of either death or unwillingness to participate, which may have distorted the nature of the sample. Thirdly, longitudinal studies are costly and time-consuming, particularly in the case of older adults, where a comprehensive study may take from half to a full century. These studies might be interrupted by the death of the main researcher and become dependent for their continuation on the group dynamics of the research team. Fourthly, Schaie's (1977–78) stage approach to intelligence suggests that measures of intelligence used with younger age groups may not be as relevant to older adults.

Another factor which needs to be taken into consideration in the context of intelligence is the presence or absence of illness. Health factors appear to be closely related to decrease in intelligence. Having reviewed the available literature, Botwinick (1977) suggested that decline in intellectual ability is part of the ageing picture. High blood pressure and reduced cerebral blood flow seem related to this decrease. Disease rather than ageing is responsible for both of these factors. Another aspect of intelligence, namely vocabulary, was found to be a significant indicator of altered health status as well as a predictor of non-survival (Eisdorfer and Wilkie, 1973; Jarvik et al., 1973). Wilkie and Eisdorfer (1973) found that high blood pressure is negatively correlated with Wechsler IQ subtest scores in individuals aged 60–79 years. According to Botwinick, the decline in intellectual ability begins later in life than previously thought and may be smaller in magnitude, involving fewer functions. In a review of the literature, Botwinick (1970) concluded that good health and high intelligence reduce age-related differences in verbal learning, whereas greater task difficulty increases these differences. Kalish (1975) concurred, and stated that although older people experience slight losses in a number of areas where speed is required, poor health is probably the single most important cause of these losses.

In summary, it can be stated that older adults for the most part retain their intellectual ability as measured by intelligence tests throughout life. Poor health is the most likely contributory factor to deterioration. New conceptions, definitions and tests of intelligence are needed based on Schaie's (1977–78) model of intelligence. The American Psychological

Association (1994) stated that with young-old adults (aged 60–75 years) 'there are age-related changes in learning and problem solving. Research on other psychological factors, however, such as personality or knowledge-based cognition (e.g. vocabulary), often show little change with time'.

Affective ageing

Affect is an important dimension of the psychological persona. Its significance in old age was touched upon by Cicero in *De Senectute*. In accepting ageing as natural and inevitable, he believed that one's attitude to it was most important. Emotional adjustment is of great importance in old age, as change in different forms becomes the reality of the older person's life.

Emotional reactions in old age are very much an individual process based on how a person has coped with previous life experiences. Maladjusted older people, according to Curtin (1972), had usually been uninvolved, passive or unhappy at an earlier period. Neugarten (1971, 1972) found that broad predictions can be made as to how a person will adjust to old age if the individual's personality in middle age is known. Butler and Lewis (1982) agree.

In a study of 87 men aged 55–84, Reichard *et al.* (1962) identified five possible approaches to dealing with problems in later life. These are termed constructive, dependent, defensive, hostile and self-hating. Constructive older adults possess a range of socially desirable attributes, including self-sufficiency, tolerance of others and optimism. The dependent group is well adjusted and satisfied but life is relatively passive and lazy. The defensive tend to be self-restrictive, obsessively hard-working, self-contained and disinclined to face up to the problems associated with ageing. Hostile older people are aggressive and suspicious, afraid of growing old, and have a history of poor social adjustment. Self-hating types are socially inadequate, with low self-esteem and little feeling of control over their life. Reichard *et al.* found that the latter are comparatively few in number. These patterns seem to be consistent in the histories of the men in the sample.

Gitelson (1948) identified six patterns which occur in maladjustment to old age: a decreased memory for present events; a sharpening of memory of the past, especially for a time when life was successful; a feeling of insecurity; a mild depression; introversion and increased sensitivity, and a free-floating anxiety.

Affective ageing depends, to a great extent, on the interaction between the individual and the culture (Woodruff and Birren, 1975). Kastenbaum (1971) claimed that the behaviour of the young and old tends to be similar if their environments resemble one another. It is unlikely that maladjustment will develop in old age if there is stability in one's environment. Gitelson (1975) stated that there is increasing anxiety in new and untried situations. Anxiety can manifest itself in many forms, such as rigid thinking, fear of being alone, and deep suspicion of others. De Beauvoir (1977) argued that marriage did not protect couples from this anxiety: 'The anxieties of each merge with and reinforce those of the other: each feels a double burden of care, both for oneself and the other'. Loss in its many forms, loneliness, depression and fear of death form part of the affective experience of most older adults, and will be considered in more detail in Chapter 5.

In a study designed to determine age differences in relation to emotional experience, Matatesta and Kalnok (1984) interviewed 240 adults aged 17–88, and found that older subjects did not differ from middle-aged subjects in the degree of importance placed on emotions. Furthermore, negative emotions were experienced no more frequently in old age than in the younger groups. An important task of ageing, according to Brearley (1977), is to accept increasing dependence in a way that will still permit functioning as an independent individual. Serious frustration occurs when a persistent, stressful, insoluble situation emerges (Bromley, 1988). The institutionalized elderly are likely to be frustrated if they lose their ability to influence events and circumstances in their environment.

The elderly in rural Ireland were studied by Daly and O'Connor (1984), who found a high level of passivity and fatalism in this group. They considered these factors to have both positive and negative effects. Passivity and fatalism cushion older adults from the harsh reality of life, helping them to maintain a positive outlook and thus preventing feelings of self-pity. On the other hand, 'because they are quite passive in the face of what is happening in their lives, they become somewhat immobilized and are prevented from taking specific action to change their situation' (Daly and O'Connor, 1984).

Emotion does not decrease in significance in old age and adjustment patterns appear to be related to adjustment patterns in earlier periods of life. Personal growth in the emotional life of the older adult is discussed in Chapter 5.

SOCIAL AGEING

Social ageing is the changing pattern of interaction in relation to other members of the community. Aiken (1989) stated that it is determined by the social activities of a person and whether society considered these to be appropriate or inappropriate at a particular age or stage of maturity. It is in the social aspect of an older person's life that the most clearly age-specific patterns can be seen (Butler and Lewis, 1982).

Role theory holds that successful social ageing is dependent on appropriate role transitions and substitutions. The taking on of new roles in old age may occur when the support network of friends is diminished by death. Butler and Lewis (1977) pointed out that older adults often lack the appropriate role model of a healthy older adult. The experience of being a grandparent or even a great-grandparent is a new role, which emphasizes that one is part of the older generation. However, in a study of 70 sets of grandparents, half maternal and half paternal, Neugarten and Weinstein (1964) found that this role may be viewed in five different ways: formal, maintaining clearly demarcated boundaries (22% grand-mothers, 23% grandfathers); fun-seeking – self-indulgence by the grand-parent and mutuality of pleasure (20% grandmothers, 17% grandfathers); surrogate parent (10% grandmothers, 0% grandfathers); reservoir of family wisdom (1% grandmothers, 4% grandfathers); and distant figure (13% grandmothers, 20% grandfathers). However, the grandparents in this study were in their 50s and 60s. Further studies need to be conducted with grandparents in the 70+ age group in order to see if these roles are maintained.

The symbolic interaction approach holds that older people create their own old age (Marshall, 1980). Individuals interact with the social world to construct their own self-concept. Hence, if retired older executives are invited to be on the board of directors of a company, they will see themselves as capable of fulfilling such a position and carrying it out effectively. If, on the other hand, these individuals are not offered such roles, they may assume that this is an indication of incompetence.

Health is the single most important factor determining the older person's social lifestyle (Daly and O'Connor, 1984). In Ireland, people over 65 years of age account for approximately 40% of acute admissions to hospitals, although they represent only 11% of the total population (Irish Department of Health, 1987). Carey and Carroll (1986) found that 5% of the elderly are resident in long-term institutional care, not always for medical or rehabilitative purposes: 28% of these were there for 'social reasons'. Carey and Carroll estimate that between 20% and 30% of the institutionalized elderly could live in the community, given adequate housing and services.

O'Leary and Kelly (1990) found that 53% of older adults were free of ill-health or any physical disability, whereas 40% suffered from a variety of complaints. Sixteen per cent had a yearly holiday and the two most popular sources of entertainment were the local public house and day outings: 19% made use of both of these outlets very often.

As with psychological ageing, there tends to be continuity in a person's social activities from middle adulthood to old age. Rose (1965) suggested that social adjustment is best served by maintaining effective relationships within one's own age group. Social class may influence ageing. The fact that major events in the lower socioeconomic classes, e.g. parenthood and grandparenthood, tend to occur at an earlier stage may lead to its members perceiving themselves as older at earlier chronological ages than members of the middle and upper classes (Woodruff and Birren, 1975). Furthermore, older adults from lower socioeconomic classes are less likely to be involved in community activities and more likely to live with their children than the middle social classes (Bengston *et al.*, 1977). Cutler (1977) found that older people in the middle and upper social classes have more friends outside the family than older people of lower-class status. They also take a more active part in social organizations. The sense of identity and personal satisfaction thus obtained can enhance social ageing. Further studies are required in order to determine whether these patterns are widespread.

Most of the changes and problems associated with old age have social implications. Chronological ageing brings with it new experiences, such as being a grandparent, and other changes in social roles. A loss of social identity can occur due to retirement and death. Patterns of interaction with work colleagues can disappear completely. Loss of spouse also involves loss of a significant role within the family. Older individuals can find themselves in a vacuum when both of these life events occur. Unlike unemployment, old age does not bring with it the possibility of future work roles. Blau (1973) pointed out that if the morale of people under 70 is compared with that of those over 70, taking into account whether or not they are still married or employed, cessation of roles, particularly retirement, is a far more significant cause of demoralization than chronological age. Social roles which may serve as substitutions have to be found by the individual. George (1988) suggested that major sources of formal social participation include political involvement, voluntary organization membership, religious participation and living arrangements, while friendship networks and family support systems are sources of informal social participation. Keating and Cole (1980) found that for most couples retirement brings very little change in domestic roles, as the pattern is based on that set during the early and middle years of marriage. Consequently, if the female has worked full-time in the home while the male has worked outside, retirement may be particularly difficult for the male.

SPIRITUAL AGEING

The lessening degree of activity common to other aspects of growing old does not apply to spiritual life. Old age can bring new possibilities for spiritual growth. According to Erikson (1982), integrity can overcome despair only if a person finds meaning in life. Whitehead and Whitehead (1982) spoke of the following realizations: 'that my life has a significance that transcends my death, that my value is not limited to my achievements, that apparent "losses" may, in fact, be "gains".' Although these meanings need not be discovered in a traditional religious setting, for the majority it occurs within such a framework. Tellis-Nayak (1982) investigated religiosity, which he defined as a combination of religious attitudes, beliefs and practices, and found that in a group of older white rural residents of upstate New York, religiosity correlated strongly with an individual's sense of meaning and purpose in life. It bore no relationship to health, marital status or happiness.

More recent studies have found that the type of religiosity may have differential effects on outcomes. Subjective religiosity, but not organizational religiosity, significantly affects self-esteem (Krause, 1993), whereas organizational religiosity significantly affects depressive symptoms in older adults (Idler, 1987). Of the three dimensions, organizational religiosity, subjective religiosity and religious beliefs, only subjective religiosity was related to life satisfaction (Krause, 1993). In a study of 165 adults 60–100+ years of age, Courtney *et al.* (1992) found that religiosity was significantly related to neurological and musculoskeletal problems, whereas ritualistic religiosity was positively related to almost every physical health area.

In a study of older adults in Minnesota, Stotsky (1968) found that more than half of the men and almost 70% of the women regarded religion as the most significant aspect of their daily living. He stated: 'A sense of serenity and decreased fear of death tended to accompany conservative religious beliefs which stress the reality of the afterlife'. Pratt (1992) found that older adults were more likely than middle-aged or younger adults to adhere to traditional Christian doctrine.

Involvement in church services is high among older adults. Bibby (1993) found that approximately 80% of older American adults had attended services in the previous 12 months compared to 70% of younger adults. In an Irish study Fogarty *et al.* (1984) found that the 'young-old' (65–74 years) had a weekly church attendance rate of 93%, while 90% of the "old-old' (75+) attended weekly. Percentages were high across most age groups, the lowest being 72% for the 25–34 age group. In a study in the US Schick (1984) found a difference between the age groups: 56% of adults under 65 viewed religion as very important, while 82% of those over 65 years did so. With respect to church attendance, 48% of adults over 65 attended church weekly compared to 31% of those under 65 (Schick, 1984). Greater church attendance by the older adult may be the result of the stronger emphasis on religion in their youth rather than the anticipation of death. However, such attendance provides an opportunity to meet friends, a source of support in time of stress and an opportunity to meet individuals with a common world view and philosophy. Although wide variations occur within and between differing social groups, Vayhinger (1980) asserted that studies have consistently revealed that nine out of every ten people aged 60 and over participated in some way in churches and other places of worship. This was particularly true in smaller communities and away from the larger urban centres.

However, some difference of opinion exists in this area. Perlmutter and Hall (1992) found that church attendance in the US declines with age, although this is principally due to problems relating to health, transportation or finance. In a national sample of Mennonites, Ainley and Smith (1984) discovered that church attendance decreased with growing old, although private religious activities increased. Vayhinger (1980) showed that older adults are more involved with religion than with any other social activity. This factor appears to have changed for the older adult since the 1920s. Hall (1922) found that people did not necessarily show an increase in religious interest as they grew older. Although no firm conclusion can be drawn as to the role of religious activities in old age, Bromley (1988) claimed that 'most religions enable believers to come to terms with death, through beliefs and ritual practices ... but people with no firm beliefs either way may not be able to make sense of what is happening or to reconcile themselves to the idea of death'.

Four studies in the US in the 1980s found evidence that religion was a commonly used resource among older adults. Rosen (1982), in a study of 148 people 65 years of age or older consisting of 71 whites and 77 blacks, discovered that religion was most frequently mentioned as a coping behaviour (40%). However, a difference existed between the two groups in that a larger number of blacks (51%) than whites (28%) used this response. Conway (1985–86) investigated coping behaviours with respect to stressful medical conditions in a sample of 65 women aged 65 or over living in Kansas. He found that prayer was the most frequently used action-oriented behaviour (59); thinking about religion tied with realizing that they were better off than most people (56) in the cognitive-oriented behaviours, while more people (55) mentioned God rather than any other source as the person who assisted them. In a sample of 65–79-year-old participants in a senior centre in Rhode Island, prayer was listed among the ten most frequently used behaviours (Manfredi and Pickett, 1987). The final study (Koenig et al., 1988) dealt with three stressful periods in the lives of 100 participants aged 55–80: 45% of the sample reported using a religious coping behaviour in at least one situation. Hence the evidence suggests that religion is an important element in the lives of some older adults.

A HOLISTIC VIEWPOINT

Old age is a time when many changes take place in each of the dimensions outlined so far. Despite some biological and intellectual decline development can continue to the end of life, bringing with it opportunities for enrichment, growth and satisfaction. Waters *et al.* (1980) outlined four basic characteristics of normal age-related changes. First, these changes are universal: they affect all older adults. However, each individual is influenced differently. A person can be a 'young' 85-year-old in a physical sense or an 'old' 60-year-old. Secondly, the onset of change is gradual: it happens very slowly, so that there may be little awareness of what is occurring. Thirdly, these changes are progressive. Fourthly, normal age-related changes occur from within. But there are many outside elements which affect the ageing process: the relative influences of internal and external factors are not yet clear.

The genetic, social, environmental and health history of individuals influences normal age-related changes (Waters *et al.*, 1980). It is therefore important to view ageing from a holistic point of view. For example, the social isolation of an individual can lead to psychological and physical breakdown. Morrison and Radtke (1988) cited a study by Spitz, who discovered that if human beings did not get significant recognition from others their spines literally shrivelled and they became increasingly withdrawn from relationships. The *Vienna International Plan of Action on Ageing* (1988) recommended that care should go beyond a disease orientation and should involve the total wellbeing of the older adult, taking into account the interdependence of the physical, mental, social, spiritual and environmental factors.

The need for such a holistic approach has been pointed out by Scrutton (1989). Physical decline may have an emotional side which is less easily recognized. Scrutton also pointed out that there are social class differences in life expectancy, health and physical incapacity of people generally, and of older people in particular. He cited a survey carried out by Age Concern in the UK which found that 35% of people in the more affluent social groupings were considered 'very fit' compared with 19% of those doing unskilled or semiskilled manual work. He concluded that issues for older adults arise as much from social organization as from the nature of old age, and that the social, emotional and economic realities of life need to be a normal part of the counselling agenda.

Consideration of the various dimensions of ageing allows a greater understanding of personal change in old age, since there are no clear markers to indicate transition into this phase of life. Ageing is not a unitary process. Viewing old age biologically allows the consideration of bodily functions; the psychological aspect deals with mental and emotional processes; social ageing considers attitudes in old age, interpersonal relations and roles; and the spiritual aspect reflects the continuous search for meaning in life. All of these dimensions interact in the lives of older adults.

Theoretical approaches to ageing

Until recently the majority of psychologists confined their attention to the early years – childhood, adolescence and early adulthood. Growing old and the problems arising therefrom received little attention. Ageing was not viewed as a process in which development occurred but rather as a state which 'was characterized by decay and deterioration' (Bromley, 1988). Bromley reflected the general attitude when he regarded the ageing process as postdevelopmental: all latent capacities for development had been realized. But already some psychologists were beginning to buck the trend. In a review of the literature on adult development and ageing, Birren *et al.* (1983) found that the topic was showing an explosive growth in research and published literature. This is borne out by the increasing attention devoted to distinct theories of ageing, such as disengagement, activity, subculture, phenomenological and lifespan developmental approaches. A detailed study of these theories is necessary if counsellors are to acquire an insight into the patterns of old age.

DISENGAGEMENT THEORY

For some people growing old means disassociating themselves from people and activities. Disengagement theory asserts that the process of disengagement is a mutual one between the person and society, and may be initiated by the older individual or by others. Propounded by Cumming and colleagues (1960) and by Cumming and Henry (1961), it holds that old people voluntarily withdraw from many of the connections and obligations in which they were previously engaged. The process of growing old alters the manner in which individuals view themselves. The consequent adjustment arises from a lessening of responsibility and participation owing to the presumed decrease in physical and psychic energy.

Berger (1994) outlined four steps in the process of disengagement:

1. The social sphere of individuals contracts owing to a variety of factors, which include the death of relatives and friends and changing parental and work roles.
2. Individuals accept this change in their social interactions.
3. Their interactions become more passive.
4. Because of this passivity, it is less probable that they will be offered new roles. Hence disengagement is more likely.

The effects of disengagement on older adults are likely to vary depending on their individual orientations. Those who are socially or work orientated are more likely to be unhappy with withdrawal from their roles than are reflective inward-looking people. Central to disengagement is the question of the voluntary or non-voluntary nature of decisions made.

Disengagement can be seen in a positive light if it is something desired. It can bring a freedom from pressures such as work productivity. Withdrawal from the marketplace, one aspect of disengagement, can open the door to other forms of social engagement, such as the cultivation of interests and the development of new roles and relationships. These are likely to be satisfying if they are interesting to the individual. In such a context disengagement becomes a re-engagement.

Havighurst et al. (1968) pointed out that disengagement is often forced on older people as a result of society's failure to enable them to continue making a positive contribution. Disengagement may also be a response to the constraints imposed by society through stereotyping. Rose (1968) criticized disengagement theory on three counts: he believed that disengagement in old age reflects a continuation of an earlier lifestyle; secondly, he held that active socially involved individuals are essentially happier than those who have disengaged; thirdly, changes in societal conditions are more likely to result in more active lives on the part of older adults.

Disengagement does not take into account individual and cultural differences and the enormous variations that occur in response to the onset of old age. Many people in their 60s and 70s are involved in society. Rather than being a natural part of ageing, disengagement is only one of many possible reactions to it. Mandatory retirement for a 65-year-old does not necessarily lead to disengagement, but may lead to uncertainty and insecurity. An important issue is whether disengagement occurs as a gradual process or as an abrupt transition. Although retirement from work is frequently determined by chronological age, preparation for this event can significantly change its impact on the individual. Psychological growth can occur if it is viewed as part of the older person's continuing emotional and social development.

The main contribution of disengagement theory was in providing a theoretical framework for old age which led to much discussion and debate. According to Bromley (1988), disengagement brings about 'a policy of segregation of, or even indifference to, the elderly, and the nihilistic attitude that old age has no value'. Estes *et al.* (1982) argued that an attitude of disengagement leads to a policy of non-intervention which results in the separation of the older person from society. Scrutton (1989) evaluated disengagement theory as providing 'younger relatives with a convenient explanation for any guilt they may feel about their role with ageing relatives'. The equation of worth with productivity in society often means that disengagement may mean an abrupt transition for males, since work has been their major role. In the case of females it is more likely that they have been significantly involved in the nurturance of either immediate or extended family members. Where substitute activities are not engaged in, the older person can become preoccupied with self.

Research evidence relating to disengagement is mixed. Larson *et al.* (1985) investigated 92 retired adults over a 1-week period. Each participant carried an electronic pager and was asked to fill in reports on their company and internal states when they were randomly paged by the researcher. In all, 3412 reports were obtained. Results indicated that the participants voluntarily spent approximately half of their waking time alone. While alone, they were involved in activities that required concentration and challenge. However, Hultsch and Deutsch (1981) observed that while some individuals do disengage, it is not useful to associate withdrawal from activities with successful ageing.

ACTIVITY THEORY

Activity theory is in direct contrast to disengagement theory. Proposed by Havighurst (1972), it views older adults as active and involved even when their major work role has been lost. It holds that they should maintain their work activities for as long as possible and then replace them with others.

The theory assumes that active, productive people are happiest in old age. Continued productivity and social interaction are essential to satisfaction and a sense of wellbeing, according to Maddox (1968, 1970). He found that 79% of individuals who had retired still showed a high-activity lifestyle pattern, which was accompanied by high satisfaction. Only 14% showed the disengagement pattern and high satisfaction. Finding substitute activities for those which have terminated is central to adjustment. The pioneer of the study of older adults, Lillian Martin, held that 'The really happy old ... are going from level to level of achievement in that which gives them joy, mastering life with enthusiasm, and so life seems good and zestful to them until the end' (Martin and DeGrunchy, 1930).

Interesting findings on activity levels in nursing homes for the aged in Connecticut were obtained by Langer and Rodin (1976). Although the homes were well run and provided many benefits for the residents, much of the environment was controlled by the staff. They devised an experiment based on two floors, one floor constituting an experimental group, the other a control. On both floors physical conditions were similar. The experimental group chose the movies they saw and selected and cared for plants, whereas the staff chose the movies and cared for the plants in the rooms of the control group. The experimental group, not surprisingly, maintained a much higher activity level than the control group. What was unexpected was that there were far fewer deaths in the experimental group than in the control group. However, level of disability was not taken into account in the study.

Activity theory corresponds closely to popular commonsense notions about successful ageing (Sherman, 1981). The major problem with extreme forms of activity theory is that they do not take into account the need for reduced activity among some aged, especially those markedly affected by declining health. Sherman reported research findings which are contrary to those of Maddox (1968, 1970). He found that general activity level is not significantly associated with life satisfaction.

An interesting variation of activity theory called the consolidation approach was proposed by Atchley (1976). He stated that older adults who are involved in a variety of roles may not need to find new roles when they lose some. Rather, they can redistribute their energy and time across the remaining activities. However, the effectiveness of such an approach is likely to depend on the importance of the lost roles to the individual. Furthermore, the consolidation approach is not applicable when people have so few roles that loss of them means non-involvement. This is likely to occur if opportunities for developing new activities are curtailed by the environment. For example, an inner-city older adult may not have the opportunity a rural dweller possesses to engage in gardening.

Activity must be meaningful to the individual. Ogilvie (1987) asked 33 older men and women to rank a variety of roles in order of importance to them. He then questioned them on the extent to which each role brought out their 'best' or 'worst' self, and how much time they spent in each role. Older adults who spent most time in the roles they considered most important to them were the most content. The investigation offers some support for a relationship between meaningful activity and contentment in older adults, although owing to the small sample size further replication studies are needed.

Further distinctions need to be made as to the kinds of activities older adults engage in and the level of satisfaction they experience. It is likely that the amount of choice and control they exert over these activities may be significant. Activity theory does not take biological factors such as the slowing of behaviour into sufficient consideration. It needs further research on its major tenet before any firm conclusions can be made on its validity. A limitation of both activity and disengagement theories is that they offer a single direction in which older adults may move in order to experience a satisfying old age. Yet individuals rarely, if ever, behave in a linear manner. They may disengage and be active alternately. Subculture theory, on the other hand, offers a greater choice to the older adult.

SUBCULTURE THEORY

Subculture theory was developed by Rose (1962) and Rose and Peterson (1965). It originated as a partial remedy for the dysfunctional aspects of old age, e.g lack of status, role and security. This approach maintained that the elderly form a subculture within society. Sherman (1981) defined a subculture as 'a group within the larger society that shares many of society's cultural characteristics but also exhibits characteristics that are unique to itself and are not generally found in other segments of society'. Within this subgroup, older adults can meet their needs for status and new roles can be defined.

Rose (1962) held that a subculture develops within any category of a population when its members interact with each other more than they interact with people in other categories. He viewed this as occurring under two sets of circumstances: when members have a positive affinity for each other, or when they are excluded from interaction with other groups to a significant extent. Positive affinity among older adults emerges partly from physical limitations and rejection by younger age groups. Retirement often means exclusion from interaction with the working population. The factors that minimize the development of a subculture include contact with family, continued employment and an unwillingness to accept stereotyping.

Cox (1988) pointed out that the great majority of older adults reside in age-integrated communities. In an investigation of county and city politics in Florida, Rosenbaum and Button (1989) found that, although older people were active politically, they did not organize themselves to either advance their own concerns or oppose other interest groups. Sherman (1981) stated that there are dramatic differences among elements in the aged population that challenge the idea of a single subculture. For example, a subculture formed by the wealthy aged would be vastly different from one formed by the poor, for whom financial need would be ever present. Yet being a certain age is used by society to classify all groups across the lifespan. Hence reference is made to the child, the teenager, the adult.

Subculture theory offers a view of older adults which allows them to find fulfilment in any of several directions within their own age group. Its limitation emerges from the view that such positive affinity emerges because of exclusion by younger age groups. Optimally, subculture theory should be one component in the lives of older adults. Belonging to a strong subculture while not segregating oneself from other age groups allows for greater communication with others, shared activities and possibilities for further friendships.

THE PHENOMENOLOGICAL APPROACH

The phenomenological approach holds that to comprehend human behaviour it is necessary to do so from the point of view of the individual. This approach is based on the existential philosophy of Husserl. When applied to the ageing process, older adults will react and respond differently to events in their lives, such as bereavement, poor health, retirement and other changes.

This approach has not gained much prominence in the gerontological literature, largely because of the difficulty in conducting scientific research appropriate for its testing (Sherman, 1981). With the increasing emphasis on qualitative research it is likely that it will come more to the fore in the future. In this area, according to Datan *et al.* (1987), researchers are moving away from testing theoretical hypotheses and towards more basic descriptive work. This involves 'a more systematic use of autobiography, biography, storytelling and conversation, diaries, literature, clinical case histories, historical fiction and the like, with a new emphasis upon the person's reconstruction of the "life story", rather than upon what might be considered a more objective account of what happened'. Although useful in its application in counselling psychology practice, scientific confirmation of the phenomenological approach is unlikely to occur owing to the individual nature of its hypotheses.

The theories of disengagement and subculture emphasize the apartness of the older person, whereas the activity and phenomenological theories acknowledge their contribution. The latter are more supportive of continuing individual development, whereas the former tend to explain segregation and in the process tend to further isolate the older person.

LIFESPAN APPROACHES

The focus of lifespan approaches is on the challenges and changes that occur throughout adulthood. Danish (1981) outlined four basic suppositions in the lifespan developmental approach:

- development is a continual process, not limited to any one stage of life;
- change occurs in various interrelated social, psychological and biological areas of human development;
- change is sequential and therefore it is necessary to place any 'stage' of life within the context of that which preceded and followed it;
- changes in individuals must be considered within the framework of the prevailing norms of the day, as well as the historical time within which one lives.

Within the developmental perspective, the tasks of one stage must be completed before individuals can move to those of the next stage. Individuals are understood within the context of their lives to date and encouraged to find patterns and themes in order to better understand the developmental sequence.

The lifespan approach challenges the assumption of an inexorable downhill course in old age. While acknowledging the changes and losses that occur as one advances in years, it emphasizes the ability of the individual to change and develop. Butler and Lewis (1982) point to the lifetime gathered potential of older people for a richer emotional, spiritual, intellectual and social life. The developmental approach connects current behaviour to past development and views old age as a continuing development based on previous experiences. Hence older adults will not deal with old age in a uniform manner, but with a variety of responses that depend on their personality and previous experiences. However, these theories do not consider in depth what happens for those who have dealt with the developmental tasks of previous stages unsuccessfully. Cox (1988) stated that 'Failure at any level implies inability to move on in the expected pattern'.

The developmental perspective on ageing tends to underemphasize individual variations (Kimmel, 1974). It stresses general developmental trends that are believed to refer to most people, but which do not apply equally to everyone. However, once the developmental themes are recognized, individual variations may then be considered to allow concentration on a particular individual, in a specific place, at a specific time.

Jung, Adler, Erikson, Peck, Neugarten and Havighurst are the better-known proponents of lifespan psychology. Each suggests different methods through which older adults may attain full potential.

The Jungian approach

The original lifespan approach was outlined by Jung, who described the age of 40 as the noon of life and stressed the importance of understanding the afternoon and evening of life in their own right. A key concept in his approach was that of balance. He distinguished between two major orientations: towards the external world or towards inner subjective experience. He believed that in the first phase of life individuals learn to deal with instinctual drives, and are caught up in the emotional involvements of childhood and adolescence. As young adults they focus largely on the outside world as they cope with the demands of family, work and society, and with establishing an identity. However, their need for balance emerges as they approach middle age. In the second phase of life they assess their lives and develop an increasing awareness of the self and the inner life. Neugarten (1964) found that there was an increased inward orientation from the mid-40s onwards.

The search for meaning takes place in the face of inevitable death. The death of parents lessens the need for success in children and causes them to turn inwards. Coming to terms with the conclusion of life on earth is part of the task of the older adult. The process through which this is accomplished is called individuation, in which individuals become conscious of the self. Older adults turn their energy towards the undeveloped aspects of their personality, which are usually the neglected intrapsychic realities.

Jungian theory postulates that there is a tendency in old age for men to attend to the more feminine side of the personality, and for women to concentrate on their more masculine characteristics. This allows a greater sense of balance to develop in the individual. Well-adjusted men may accept the nurturing side of their personality, whereas well-adjusted women often begin to use their assertive side. Prior to this, behaviour is largely determined by sex role stereotypes.

Jung (cited in Hall, 1986) believed that growth occurred as a result of the creative choices individuals make. It is not how things really are that is significant: it is how they are perceived. Fordham (1966) considered that the experience of the second half of life could also be formulated as the finding of the God within. Jung stated that the correct way to approach death was to carry on as if one had a thousand years to live. He used the term self-actualization to express the ability of individuals to enrich their inner lives and to better their appreciation and understanding of themselves. Accepting death and living life as fully as possible are the two major tasks of the older adult. It is during the later years of life that self-actualization reaches its zenith.

Jung's approach helped to direct attention to the second half of life at a time when Freud held that personality development ended in adolescence. One of the major drawbacks of his approach is the limited educational background of some older adults. His work abounds with examples taken from classical literature and modern anthropology, and requires a high level of sophistication. Its complex symbolism and explanatory concepts account for its lack of popularity with older adults. However, research studies by Neugarten (1964) confirm that, with increasing age, preoccupation with the inner life becomes greater, emotional attachment to people and objects lessens, and there is a movement away from the outer world towards the inner.

The Adlerian approach

Adler (cf. Ansbacher and Ansbacher, 1956) did not deal extensively with old age. When he did he considered mostly the younger old who, he felt, would be much happier if they had an opportunity to work. Adler believed that mental health depended on social involvement and satisfactory lifestyle. He believed that people define themselves in relation to other people. Decreased social involvement can occur due to retirement, loss of spouse and friends, and lack of mobility. Satisfactory lifestyle refers to modes of perception that allow the individual to organize, understand and control experiences. It is relatively constant from birth to death.

With increasing age older adults find that they are less significant to others since they are no longer actively fulfilling their old social and occupational roles, and many of their friends die. Yet they want to be significant to somebody since, according to Adler, those who have contributed nothing will disappear completely from the world. He also believed that both community feeling and social interest were central to the solution of difficulties in old age. Community feeling involves being part of a larger community, and includes parental love, filial love, sexual love, love of one's country, love of nature, art, science and humanity, while social interest denotes active interest in others. Although both involve self-transcendence, community feeling involves a spiritual state. Many of the problems of older adults relate to a loss of a sense of belonging in their social structure, leading to a loss of self-esteem and meaning in their life. Adler believed that successful ageing was dependent on a person's conviction of spiritual survival, which arose from having children or from one's cultural contribution. Adler's approach closely resembles activity theory in that it stresses the impact of social involvement and meaningful lifestyle.

The Eriksonian approach

Erikson (1963) highlighted the developmental conflict of old age as ego integrity versus despair. Ego integrity is the acceptance of one's life to date and responsibility for how it has turned out, whereas despair derives from the non-acceptance of one's life and the feeling that it is now too late to make up for missed opportunities. Erikson believed that right up to the end of life individuals either grow and develop or stagnate and wither. The manner in which individuals deal with old age depends on personality development throughout life. The awareness that little time remains and that death is approaching heightens the basic conflict.

Regret and guilt are manifestations of despair. Resentment towards others or self-hatred may accompany this state of mind. In ego integrity, on the other hand, one lives 'hopefully rather than helplessly' (Aiken, 1989). Ego integrity involves an emotional integration of all that has gone before, whereas loss of this integration results in a fear of death. Erikson says that ego integrity is only possible for individuals who have cared about others and who have experienced and accepted the triumphs and disappointments of life. Included in ego integrity is 'a new different love of one's parents, free of the wish that they should have been different' (Erikson, 1980). In a study of 29 octogenarians, Erikson *et al.* (1986) found that ego integrity involved the incorporation of legitimate feelings of despair concerning a past that older adults wish could have been different, aspects of a present that can involve pain, and a future that can be uncertain. In ego integrity this despair is integrated into the life of the older adult as a component of old age.

The acquisition of integrity brings a sense of closure to life. Brearley (1975) saw this as the ability to 'look back on life and see a clear, logical pattern in which good or bad events each have their place in the final order'. This involves seeing the present as a development of the past and finding meaning in both. A person with ego integrity possesses wisdom, which includes knowledge, accurate judgement and understanding and an active concern with life in the face of death. Achieving ego integrity involves reflection on one's life. Ryff and Heincke (1983) found that older adults considered themselves to be more reflective than when younger.

Butler (1982) advocated caution in accepting Erikson's theoretical framework. He regarded Erikson's studies with middle-aged and older adults as meagre, and stated that his views of 'integrity versus despair do not hold up well in my clinical and research experience with patients in ... later life'. Pratt and Norris (1994) concurred when they stated that there is very little empirical work to substantiate Erikson's stages, despite their wide usage. Cavanaugh (1993) pointed out that the reasons individuals deal with certain issues at certain times in life is not clear, nor are the transitions from one stage to the next fully explained. Stuart-Hamilton (1994) held that successful ageing according to Erikson's theory may be seen as a passive preparation for death, whereas Erikson's emphasis was on learning in such a manner that individuals are able to deal with death from the standpoint of integrating all that has gone before.

By using the polarity of ego integrity versus despair, Erikson (1950) heightened the positive and negative aspects of old age. In this respect his approach provides a contextual framework for which the methodology of gestalt therapy is particularly suitable. Dialogue work between the poles, with the use of an empty chair, may result in more integration for the older individual than adherence to the either/or proposition of Erikson. Erikson's work, although a modification of the psychoanalytical approach, went beyond it. He facilitated serious consideration of the hitherto largely neglected topic of old age by psychiatrists and psychoanalysts.

The approach of Peck

Peck (1968) developed Erikson's global thinking by distinguishing three stages of old age, namely, ego differentiation vs. work role preoccupation; body transcendence vs. body preoccupation; and ego transcendence vs. ego involvement. The process of ego differentiation is likely to emerge at retirement. Finding a sense of identity apart from the job is essential to continuing satisfaction with life. This may involve the acquisition of new activities or the development of other attributes that having more leisure time allows. Retirement brings opportunities to travel for longer periods, to spend greater amounts of time with one's friends, or to become involved in community activities. Ego differentiation involves the acquisition of a range of valued self-attributes that relate to alternatives other than the work role.

Body transcendence reflects the older adult's capacity to invest energy in human relationships and creative mental activities despite physical deterioration. Where there is a greater emphasis on bodily preoccupation during early life, the less likely it is that body transcendence will be achieved. For these individuals inner preoccupation with their bodies is likely to be the focus of their old age. Body transcendence is most likely to occur in individuals who have invested time and energy in mental activities, relationships and community endeavours. Although physical powers may decrease, emotional and social powers may increase.

Ego transcendence means that older adults transcend self concerns and accept that they will eventually die. This occurs when they live generously and unselfishly. They are interested in the lives of others, concerned about their families and culture, and emotionally involved in their relationships. Hence older adults who have achieved ego transcendence may be concerned with providing for those they will leave behind and may try to improve the environment of loved ones. The author experienced a vivid example of this when her 54-year-old uncle became aware that he had cancer. In the 2 years from that point until his death he personally redecorated his house. Thus the final stages outlined in successful ageing can come into play when death is imminent. Peck (1968) suggested that success in ego transcendence can be measured by the degree of contentment or stress experienced by older adults, and by the impact on others around them, whether constructive or stress inducing.

Peck emphasized the use of developmental criteria rather than age criteria for looking at the later stages of life. There is great variability in the chronological age at which any of the stages arises. E.M. Brody (1982) claimed that 'older people are even more heterogeneous than younger people. Not only do they carry their own unique personalities into the ageing phase of life, but they also have had longer lives and more varied experiences that produce a high degree of differentiation'.

The approach of Neugarten

In contrast to Peck, Neugarten (1964) stated that the development of the ego is, for the first two-thirds of the lifespan, outward toward the environment, and for the final third inward toward the self. In old age there is a withdrawal of investment from the outer world and a new preoccupation with the inner self. This process is referred to as the 'interiority' of the personality. Neugarten held that the individual's social framework is important for understanding the older adult. The age structure of a society, the internalization of age norms and age-group identifications are dimensions of the environment within which the individual life must be placed. Hence Neugarten and Datan (1973) held that the stress associated with an event is less intense when the change is an expected one at a specific age, rather than when it is not appropriate at that particular life stage.

Neugarten and Peterson (1957) found that adulthood was seen in terms of transition points, namely young adulthood, maturity, middle age and old age. Each period had its distinctive characteristics and psychological flavour. Progression from one period to another was seen to be related to psychological and social changes rather than biological changes. They suggested that a time clock can be superimposed over the biological clock: the use of both assists in the understanding of the period of adulthood under consideration.

The approach of Havighurst

Havighurst (1972) viewed the developmental task of old age as involving change in a social–psychological context. He did not believe that either activity theory or disengagement theory was sufficient for explaining patterns of ageing, and proposed that personality organization and coping style were the main factors involved in adjustment to old age. He listed three adjustments which might have to be made: to decreasing physical strength and health, to retirement and reduced income, and to the death of one's spouse. Decreased physical vigour often means retirement from work. In professional organizations and social clubs the older adult may have to assume positions of less importance and even withdrawal. The death of a spouse can cause a crisis of identity or lead to loneliness.

Adaptation frequently takes place within the context of diminished bodily strength and negative environmental circumstances. Havighurst (1972) stated that adaptation is maximized when the personality is strong and flexible, the social environment is supportive and the body is vigorous. He held that these three factors are important in predicting life satisfaction, but one must also take into account the norms and expectations of the subculture in which the person lives, economic security and societal provisions to assist adaptation. Inability to adapt to the developmental tasks of old age can lead to feelings of low self-worth or anger towards life. This can rob older people of the opportunities for growth and pleasure that are possible as they advance in years.

Havighurst (1972) believed that three tasks are necessary in old age: establishing an explicit affiliation with one's age group; adopting and adapting social roles in a flexible manner; and establishing satisfactory living arrangements. Association with one's own age group can occur through engaging in a new hobby or becoming involved in a social or political group. People may expand their social roles through involvement in community or church activities. Finally, it is important that older adults live in an environment which enables easy access to shops, church and recreational activities: living on a steep hill is not facilitative to optimal development in older adults. The key to development, then, is adaptation to changes in the structure and functions of the body and changes in the social environment.

The adjustments and tasks outlined by Havighurst (1972) are more or less relevant to older adults, depending on whether they are young-old or old-old. The healthy old-old will have adjusted to retirement and reduced income almost a decade previously, although different financial difficulties may become the focus of concern, such as the ability to pay for nursing-home care or an extended stay in hospital. Physical decline is more likely to occur among the old-old than the young-old. Given that old age can span a period of 30 years or more, the adjustments and tasks outlined by Havighurst could be considered more appropriately if viewed within the two different contexts of young-old and old-old.

CONCLUSION

The theories of old age outlined in this chapter vary from viewing older adults as victims of social forces to seeing them as inner-directed and capable of change. Different theories may apply to different individuals. The assumption that any theory fully describes old age rests on the premise that development is fixed and linear. Yet development by its very nature is dynamic, a fact often forgotten when dealing with older adults.

The goal of counselling - the development of the individual – is usually framed in self-actualization terms within the humanistic–existential tradition. Although not usually associated with this orientation, Jung's theory of old age supports it since its goal is realizing oneself. Concepts such as interiority (Neugarten) and ego integrity (Erikson) contribute to the process. Lifespan developmental theories of ageing highlight the older adult's ability to change and grow in the later stages of their lives. They draw attention to the difference between developmental and chronological criteria in assessing the process of ageing, and the tasks of coming to terms with one's life and its conclusion while continuing to grow. These theories view old age as a normal phase of development, with its own tasks. Smyer (1984) points out that they contradict previous therapeutic pessimism, which equated old age with rigid defences, lack of therapeutic motivation, poor prospects for change or growth, and a stage of life not worthy of therapeutic investment of time and energy. They stress that optimal growth can occur throughout the lifecycle of the individual, thus providing a positive context in which to examine old age. Viewed from this perspective, old age can be a time of exciting possibilities. Much potential in older adults remains untapped. This is partly due to the attitude of society. Chapter 3 deals with this topic.

Society and older adults

3

The perception of older adults varies from one culture to another. In Japanese society, for example, increased age brings increased status. A big celebration takes place on a man's 60th birthday, symbolizing a rebirth into the advanced phase of life (Kimmel, 1988). In western culture, however, this change is viewed negatively. The older generation is seen as having less to contribute to the succeeding generations because rapid social and scientific changes have made their experience irrelevant.

In the United States, Crocket et al. (1979) concluded that negative attitudes far exceed positive attitudes towards older adults. Americans believe that age brings an inevitable decline in health, intelligence and sexuality; that people become dependent on others; that they become locked in their opinions; that they suffer from depression and the fear of death; and that they become grouchy, passive and childish. However, the authors did find that younger people recognized some positive qualities in older adults. They perceived them as wise, experienced and kind.

In Israel, different age groups from three-generation families were compared on their attitudes to the concept 'old person', among others (Netz and Ben-Sira, 1993). Forty young people, 48 middle-aged and 42 older people participated. All three groups had an overall negative attitude to ageing.

The quality of life of older people is influenced by the attitudes and values of society. The market contribution of any segment qualifies society's attitude to that group of people. This is reflected in ageism and stereotyping of the old, which leads to a lowering of self-esteem.

AGEISM

Ageism is a salient feature of society's perception of the older adult. Butler (1969) coined the term to describe discrimination based on age, especially discrimination against middle-aged and older people. Ageism is distinct from all other forms of discrimination because it cuts across all of society's traditional classifications: gender, race, religion and national origin (Nuessel, 1982). Butler (1969) states that ageism reflects a deep-seated uneasiness on the part of the young and middle-aged, a personal revulsion to and distaste for growing old, to the onset of disease, disability, powerlessness, 'uselessness' and death. He sees cultural attitudes in society as reinforcing these feelings: 'We have chosen mandatory retirement from the workforce and thus removed the elderly from the mainstream of life'.

Arie (1981) contended that it is common to distance oneself from the very old, to assume that they do not know and that they do not notice, and consequently that they do not suffer. According to de Beauvoir (1977), if old people show the same desires, the same feelings and the same requirements as the young, the world looks upon them with disgust: 'in them love and jealousy seem revolting or absurd, sexuality repulsive and violence ludicrous'. By definition, ageist terms are deprecatory and demeaning because they depict older adults as possessing largely undesirable traits and characteristics. Nuessel (1982) gave examples of ageist words which, he says, are insidious in their impact because they demean people on the basis of age and gender. Such words are codger, geezer, fogey, fuddy-duddy, dirty old man, biddy, crone, hag, old maid, little old lady. Terminology for the state of being old, such as declining years, second childhood, over the hill and twilight years, also imply decadence, decline or foolish behaviour. More recently, Covey (1988) suggested that as change in the role of older adults occurred over time, so did language to describe them. Moving from an agricultural society to an industrialized one meant that the position of power held by the elderly in the transfer of land to the younger generations became less important as younger and older adults vied for the same jobs, financial rewards and positions.

The debate over the 'correct' label for older people reflects the importance of stereotypes about old age. In a US study conducted for The National Council on the Aging by Harris et al. (1975) there was considerable disagreement among older people on the implications of using terms such as 'elderly', 'an older American' and 'an old timer'. The term 'old' was to be avoided as implying a stigma attached to the process of ageing. Cicero (*De Senectute*, 44 BC) asserted that everyone hopes to attain an advanced age, yet when it comes they all complain! 'Age takes hold of us by surprise' (Goethe). According to de Beauvoir (1977), when old age seizes upon our own personal life we are dumbfounded. She continued:

'The fact that the passage of universal time should have brought about a private, personal metamorphosis is something that takes us completely aback'. Given the generally negative attitudes held by society about old age, it is not surprising that the experience of ageing can be difficult.

Ageist practices permit people to dehumanize older people, thereby oppressing them. This oppression can take many forms. People look past them in the street, conversation goes on around them, and they are no longer included in various activities. Ford and Sinclair (1987) described Freda, a 69-year-old woman, as follows: 'Her family now take decisions for her, and indicate that her competence is in doubt. She is defined in terms of the stereotypes of her age, but says nothing, because she knows that any complaint will be seen as "her being difficult"'.

Scrutton (1989) stated that ageism in our society is being increasingly recognized as a powerful influence, developing a stereotype of 'old people' which diminishes and undermines their social status. It consists of several unhelpful myths outlined by Scrutton, based on Dixon and Gregory (1987):

- the myth of chronology – that elderly people are a homogeneous group by virtue of their age alone, i.e. once a person's age reaches an arbitrary number of years they automatically become old and part of the group 'the elderly';
- the myth of ill health – that old age automatically involves physical deterioration and that illness in old age is part of normal ageing, not the result of disease processes;
- the myth of mental deterioration – that elderly people automatically lose their mental faculties, slow down and become 'senile';
- the myth of inflexible personality – that personality changes with age to become more intolerant, inflexible and conservative;
- the myth of misery – that elderly people are unhappy because they are old;
- the myth of rejection and isolation – that society rejects its elderly people and is uncaring towards them, and that elderly people accepting this prefer to 'disengage' from life;
- the myth of unproductivity and dependence – that elderly people are not productive members of society because they are not engaged in paid employment and are inevitably dependent upon others.

There is also a myth that older people lose their sexual drive. This myth, according to Shura (1974), views old people as arid and biologically unproductive and robs them of sexual identity. Although some decline in sexual performance does occur with ageing, both the desire and the capacity for sexual activity are lifelong. Scrutton (1989) believed that much depression in older people can be caused by the lack of essential physical contact.

Positive myths can also be damaging. Shura (1974) cited the 'tranquillity myth', which holds that old age is a time of peace and tranquillity. This is also known as the 'myth of the golden years'. This extreme, Shura declared, 'overlooks the reality that old age is a time of substantial stresses, especially those related to poverty, illness and isolation'.

Shura (1974) summed up the problems created by such myths: if society focuses only on the problems, it may well realize all the stereotypes through self-fulfilling prophecies, reinforcing the hopeless view of ageing as a dependent, arid phase of life. On the other hand, he feels that if society focuses only on the positive potentials, without a clear assessment of need, it is 'led down the primrose path of the "Golden Years" myth'. He concluded that what society really needs is a soberly balanced view of people growing old, with a clear understanding of both their assets and their needs.

Examples of stereotyping abound very often in unconscious expression. Richman (1977) found that 66% of a sample of jokes about older people were negative or critical, whereas 70% of jokes about children were positive. Davies (1977), who examined six anthologies of jokes, found that the majority of jokes about ageing were negative, particularly with respect to physical, social, sexual and, to a lesser degree, mental changes. Male ageing was considered much more positively than female ageing. The author concluded that interventions in education could counteract the negative stereotyping expressed in popular humour.

The assumption of negative attitudes was labelled by Schonfield (1982) as a 'social myth' which has been perpetuated by gerontological literature. His view may appear extreme, although there is a danger that constant reiteration in the literature can overstress the negative aspects of attitudes towards the older adult. In an examination of 139 undergraduate psychology textbooks, Whitbourne and Hulicka (1990) found that older adults were described in a condescending tone, as suffering from personality deterioration, rigidity, inevitable biological decline, senility, loss of psychological functions and social losses. This study contradicts Tibbitts' (1979) assertion that since older people are assuming vital social roles in the United States, a better understanding has developed of the capacities of people to lead full lives in their later years. Tibbits further suggested that older people themselves have improved self-attitudes that influence the views others hold towards them.

Brubaker and Powers (1976) analysed 47 research reports on stereotypes of old age in order to consider the relationship between a negative stereotype of old age and a person's subjective definition, and to determine the extent of empirical support for a negative stereotype of late life. The review revealed that positive as well as negative elements characterize the extant stereotype, and that the assumption that the aged accept a negative stereotype of old age may not be valid. Viewed from the framework of cognitive dissonance theory, the authors argue that the self-concept formed at an earlier age mediates between the definition of self as old and the acceptance of a stereotype of old (positive or negative). They propose that researchers should distinguish between a 'generalized old' stimulus and a 'personalized old' stimulus.

A negative aspect of ageism is that both older people themselves and society in general come to view deterioration in old age as inevitable. The consequences of this can include referrals to doctors only in emergencies; non-referral by doctors to appropriate consultants; reduction in periods of hospitalization; non-attendance to the complaints of older adults; and non-provision of psychological and counselling services. Ageist attitudes also promote the notion of compulsory retirement.

ATTITUDES OF PROFESSIONALS AND PROFESSIONAL TRAINEES

Attitudes of health care professionals and professional trainees to older adults have been the subject of investigation in the medical, educational and pastoral fields. Within the medical field, research by Perlick and Atkins (1984) suggested that elderly patients who present a combined clinical picture of deficits in intellectual functioning and depressive symptoms are more frequently seen as suffering from senile dementia rather than being regarded as clinically depressed, which would be the normal diagnosis if they were younger. This bias may lead to an underdiagnosis of potentially treatable depression among older patients.

Rodin and Langer (1980) found that clinicians showed a greater propensity to diagnose the same psychotic behaviour as organically based when the individual was old rather than young. When the pathology was less serious, the older and younger clients received the diagnosis of depression with more or less equal frequency, but the treatment prescribed for the two varied in many cases. More long-term therapy was prescribed for the younger people. The authors concluded that age does influence both the diagnosis and recommendations for treatment of the older individual.

Butler (1980) estimated that from 10 to 30% of all treatable mental disorders in older people are misdiagnosed as untreatable. The relevant physician assumes that such impairment is to be accepted with advancing age and makes no special effort to rule out reversible disorders. These findings have serious implications for the health care of the older adult.

Kiyak et al. (1982) examined dentists' attitudes and knowledge of the elderly. Questionnaires were mailed to 439 Washington State dentists in private practice and 332 returns were received (76% response rate). The mean age was 46. None of the participants had received any formal training in geriatrics while studying dentistry. It was found that dentists generally have inaccurate perceptions of older adults. However, their feelings towards the elderly were generally favourable. More experienced dentists, and those who had greater numbers of self-paying patients, held fewer stereotypes.

Within the pastoral field, the stereotypical attitudes of parish clergy in the US towards ministering to the elderly were examined by Longino and Kitsen (1976). Reanalysing data from a national study of American Baptist clergymen, the authors found that (a) a majority of clergymen enjoyed their pastoral contact with their older parishioners; (b) the enjoyment was on a par with that for other pastoral activities; (c) relative to other age groups the aged were not the least enjoyable to minister to; and (d) ministers who most enjoy expressive role activities derive greater satisfaction from pastoral care of the elderly.

The attitudes of university administrators were the subject of a study by Nidiffer and Moore (1985). They found that older respondents viewed older people more favourably. Knowledge of the field of gerontology was related to positive attitudes to older people, while neither the amount of time spent with older adults or the level of degree obtained were significantly related to positive attitudes.

The attitudes of medical students toward the older patient were the subject of a study by Spence (1968). Responses from 92 out of a possible 117 freshmen students and 46 out of 102 senior students with two pre-clinical and one clinical year of formal medical schooling at the University of California School of Medicine were obtained. The participants perceived older adults as having more political power than their soundness of judgement warranted. They considered them to be more emotionally ill, disagreeable, inactive, economically burdensome, dependent, dull, socially undesirable, dissatisfied, socially withdrawn and disruptive of family life than youths or other adults. Other characteristics associated with old age by these groups included less anxiety about the future and a lack of desire to work. When asked to rank a preference for work in a choice of wards, both groups of students answered as follows: (1) surgery, (2) paediatric, (3) obstetrics, (4) psychiatry, (5) eye clinic and (6) chronically ill old people. When asked to rank a given list of medical cases freshmen gave the following preferences: (1) a patient with heart disease, (2) a patient with kidney disease, (3) a mentally ill patient, (4) a fatally ill child, not expected to recover consciousness, (5) a patient recovering from an appendectomy and (6) an old person in a terminal coma. Seniors responded similarly, with the exception that (4) and (5) reversed positions. Given that the future older population will be dependent for medical care on the medical students of today, it is vital that replication studies in the 1990s be undertaken to assess such preferences and the quality of this care.

A further study of medical students' attitudes was undertaken by Intrieri et al. (1993). They investigated the effectiveness of a programme in gerontology and geriatrics on medical students' knowledge, attitudes and interview skill behaviour. Ninety-six third-year medical students volunteered to participate in the study. Forty-five were assigned to the experimental group and 51 to the control group. Both groups were similar in age range. The programme lasted 6 weeks. The students were tested on a set of questionnaires before and after the programme. Four weekly 90-minute group sessions to provide information and social skills training were led by three medical school faculty and a research assistant in psychology.

Results revealed that the programme group participants developed more positive attitudes and more socially skilled behaviour towards older adults. They used clarifying statements more often than control group members, and patients talked for longer periods when interviewed by them. Since the programme was only of six hours' duration, the results provide evidence for a cost-effective measure in educating medical students to provide a more effective and skilful service to older adults.

The picture emerging from research with professionals is one of generally positive feelings towards working with older adults. The age of the professional is an important mediating factor. The provision of a programme in gerontology to trainees produces positive attitudes towards working with older adults.

PERCEPTIONS OF YOUNG PEOPLE

Research on the attitudes of young people towards the aged has produced varying results. Within the educational field, Schmidt and Boland (1986) examined the structure and organization of stereotypes of older adults among 86 university students. They found that older people were seen not only as quarrelsome and set in their ways but also as wise, loving and generous. They were viewed either as frail and incompetent, or resilient and tough. The authors concluded that the students had a number of stereotypes of the older adult; those stereotypes were organized in a hierarchical structure; the stereotypes encompassed positive and negative traits; and attitudes towards older adults depended on the specific stereotype(s) held by an individual and on which stereotype was salient when the attitude was assessed. The authors suggest that ageism may be directed more at older adults who are perceived to represent negative stereotypes than towards those who represent more positive stereotypes. The study points to the contradictory views of older people held by college students. It offers hope that traditional negative stereotypes are gradually being replaced by positive perceptions.

Wingard et al. (1982) investigated the effects of contextual variations on attitudes toward the elderly. The study evaluated Kogan's hypothesis that conflicting evidence from investigations on attitudes towards older adults may be explained by the instructional format used with participants. Two hundred and sixty-three volunteered to participate in the study, 109 males and 154 females. The mean age of participants was 26 years.

All participants completed a version of the Tuckman–Lorge Attitudes toward Old People Questionnaire (1953) which was modified to ensure that all items were evaluative attitude statements. The questionnaire comprised 137 items but had three different instructional formats. The first two versions used counterbalanced ratings, in that comparative ratings of old and young people were sought, with the order of the ratings being reversed on the second occasion. The third version asked participants to rate old people only. The questionnaires were randomly administered in either a group or an individual format. The two comparative versions were both distributed to approximately the same number of male and female participants as the isolated-judgement instructional format. Results showed that adults in the comparative context evaluated old people more negatively than adults in the old-only context, thus confirming the importance of context in evaluating attitudes towards older adults.

In an experimental study, Levin (1988) presented approximately 170 undergraduate students in regular classroom meetings in San Francisco, Tennessee and Massachusetts with one of three photographs of a male at 25, 52 and 73 years of age. They were asked to read a bogus résumé of the person which was constant for the three groups. They then evaluated personal characteristics of the person on 19 seven-point semantic differential items. The older person was evaluated more negatively by the subjects in all three groups, the number of characteristics being evaluated negatively ranging from 14 to 17 in the three groups. The only characteristic on which more negative evaluations were not obtained was generosity. The study provides data that the same individual was judged more negatively in later life on several characteristics on the basis of a photograph. A similar study using a female stimulus subject is desirable. The study provides strong evidence for the continuance of negative stereotypes among undergraduate students towards older adults.

Ivester and King (1977) found that adolescents' attitudes towards older adults were positive, regardless of the age of the adolescent and the frequency of contact with grandparents. A study by Austin (1985) of college students between the age of 18 and 40 indicated that more positive perceptions of older people were developing. When urged to make judgements about specific individuals, Green (1981) found that young people did not form more negative impressions of elderly people than of their own age group.

In a survey carried out by the Irish National Council for the Aged (1987) on the attitudes of postprimary school pupils aged 15–19 years to older adults, predominantly negative images prevailed among more than half the young people interviewed. A majority also believed that the disregard was mutual. A possible explanation for these negative attitudes was offered by Rodin and Langer (1980). Drawing on research into the effect the presence of people from relatively unfamiliar groups has on others, such as feelings of discomfort, avoidance and negative stereotyping, the authors point out that younger adults and children spend their time in settings that are unlikely to have a large number of older people present, e.g. school, sports activities, work, which can result in negative reactions towards adults on the part of the young. This negative attitude is compounded by the virtual disappearance of the extended family, where contact between young and old would have been a normal feature.

However, Miller et al. (1984–85) found that frequency of contact did not significantly affect the attitudes of young children to older people. This conclusion was based on the attitudes of 68 3–6-year-old children: 33% had contact with older adults over 70 at least once a week, while 55% had contact at least once a month. No figures were given for the remaining 12%. Based on these figures, Miller et al.'s conclusion seems hardly justified. Nor is it surprising that these young children preferred young people to old people.

The attitudes or perceptions of young people towards age was the subject of investigation by Thomas and Yamamoto (1975). Two data-gathering devices – story writing and the semantic differential – were administered to a large sample of students from grades 5, 7, 9 and 11. The results of the story writing were analysed in terms of age estimates given, selection order and stereotyping in story content. With the semantic differential, subjects were asked to rate a young person, a middle-aged person and an old person on 12 seven-point bipolar scales.

The age estimates proved sharply focused, the stories displayed an understanding of the lifecycle, and the old person was presented as a loving grandparent type. Scores from the semantic differential revealed that all three groups were perceived as good and wise; as adult age increased, the characterization became less happy, less pleasant and less exciting; and the older group compared less favourably on the dimension of power, position and activity. Except for the latter the overall findings revealed favourable attitudes to adults of all ages, but showed discrimination by the subjects on different attributes of adult age.

Literature is a possible factor influencing childrens' attitudes to older people. From an investigation of 656 books suitable for children aged 3–9, Ansello (1977) concluded that the cumulative stereotype of the older person is that of a boring and non-creative individual. This concurred with Ward (1979) who, on the basis of studies of childrens' books by Seltzer and Atchley (1971) and Peterson and Karnes (1976), concluded that old people are either seldom depicted or are portrayed as inert and limited.

Fillmer (1984) examined whether children used the same stereotypes of the elderly that are portrayed in the literature. Subjects included 74 boys and 70 girls from fourth, fifth and sixth grades, and the investigators worked with the subjects in small groups of four or five. They were exposed to a picture of a young man (age range 22–28 years), an old man (age range 60+), a young woman (age range 22–28 years) and an old woman (age range 60+). Participants were asked to indicate on their answer sheets whether they thought the person in the picture was sick/healthy, ugly/attractive, rich/poor, happy/sad or friendly/unfriendly, on a five-point scale. Five questions were asked to assess the attitudes of the participants towards the person pictured.

Results indicated that both boys and girls rated old people more favourably than young people in their choice of adjectives. An overall sex difference emerged which favoured women over men in the adjective ratings. Higher ratings of women by boys were found to be responsible for this effect. Answers to the questions favoured young people. This was found to result from the high rating of the young men by both boys and girls. Overall, men were given much more favourable responses than women. The study provides interesting data on sex differences in the perceptions of young people towards older adults, an area which has not received much attention in the research literature to date.

ATTITUDES OF OLDER ADULTS TO AGEING

The attitude of older adults to ageing is very much influenced by their personalities and attitudes to life. De Beauvoir (1977) quotes Yeats who, in his old age, gives a graphic description of his feelings: 'Being old makes me tired and furious; I am everything that I was, and indeed more, but an enemy has bound and twisted me so that although I can make plans and think better than ever, I can no longer carry out what I plan and think'. On the other hand, Walt Whitman, who suffered much in his old age, was full of life and optimism, and despite having a series of strokes was able to say: 'The old ship is not in a state to make many voyages. But the flag is still at the mast and I am still at the wheel' (de Beauvoir, 1977).

The perception of oneself as old was the subject of a 10-year longitudinal study by Bultena and Powers (1978) of 235 people over the age of 70. Four factors were important in the process of identifying oneself as old: health, physical independence, need for help, and interaction with siblings. Comparisons of themselves with older people on these four factors determined whether the study participants viewed themselves as middle-aged or old.

In an interview survey of a cross-section of 4250 American adults, the National Council on the Aging (1975) found that more than half expected poor health, insufficient money to live on and loneliness to be very serious problems in old age, while less than one-quarter of older adults actually reported these as problems. Three-quarters stated that they were pleasantly surprised to find that old age was better than they expected it to be.

In a study of the elderly in sheltered housing, O'Connor et al. (1989) found that 28% felt that life gets better as one gets older, while 12% believed that life is no different with increasing age. The majority view, however, was that things got worse, at least to some extent, as one gets older (53%). Loneliness (mainly through bereavement) and poor health were the main reasons given for being unhappy in old age. Even though many felt that their lives were not as good as when they were younger, 61% stated that life was better than they had expected. Hence the indications from these two studies were that between three fifths and three quarters of older people experienced old age favourably.

In a study of the rural elderly, Daly and O'Connor (1984) found that the elderly felt that they had little to contribute to society. As the authors see it, this view reflects society's attitude towards older adults, especially that of the young: 'As a result, they have a low self-image in terms of their usefulness and contribution to the community'. The main issue emerging in the study was the difficulty older people find in remaining integrated in the mainstream of life in their community.

A more positive picture was painted by Fogarty et al. (1984). They found that older people are in many ways content with the world around them: 'They express as much satisfaction as anyone else with their life in general, their home life, their jobs ... and even their household's financial situation ...'. The writers found that the over-75s feel as much in control of their own lives as anyone else, although interestingly they state that this is not true of the young-old on the edge of retirement or just over it: 'The relatively very low index on choice and control for the 65–74 age group could point to retirement shock, from which, however, the oldest of all appear to recover'. It could be that retirement brings with it an uncertainty that dissolves with the passage of time, as people discover that retirement is not as traumatic as they had anticipated. Fogarty et al. point to flaws in the contentment of the elderly, with the incidence of such negative phenomena as depression, loneliness and health problems.

In a study of adjustment to old age, Livson (1981) found that favourable attitudes toward ageing were closely related to good adjustment. Respondents who saw themselves as old and viewed older people unfavourably were less well adjusted than older people who had an optimistic view of the social value of old age. The better adjusted older people were also less envious of younger people, and placed less emphasis on the advantage of youth. The well adjusted had lessened their level of anxiety as they grew older, while the poorly adjusted had become more anxious.

The more favourable perception of middle-aged adults in comparison to other age groups by older adults was proposed by Dowd (1975) and Williamson *et al.* (1980) to be an inverted U-curve of status and power across the lifespan. In a study of 198 older individuals (mean age 67), Graham and Baker (1989) found similar evidence. However, declining status stopped at the age of 80 and began to rise thereafter. The description of the sample in the study as older adults needs to be borne in mind, since the participants had an age range of 45–92 years.

In order to confront the realistic difficulties of late life, older people must first recognize their age, accept it and even take pride in it. Butler and Lewis (1982) expressed the view that when one is old there is really no effective way to escape the effects of a culture that denigrates age: 'The most effective defense is a united challenge that combines practical, direct action with psychological support – both from others and from each other'. According to Arie (1981), the voice of old people themselves is heard neither often enough nor loudly enough.

INTERGROUP STUDIES

Thorson *et al.* (1974) studied the attitudes to old age of 61 undergraduate and graduate students and 59 practitioners in the field working with the aged. Using Kogan's (1961) Attitudes Toward Old People Scale, the authors found a more negative attitude to the aged with increasing age, although subjects with a higher level of education exhibited a more positive attitude. The generalizability of the findings is questioned by the authors, who suggest that the composition of the subjects in the study – i.e. undergraduates and practitioners in the field – may have had an undue influence on the research findings. A similar study using a random sample of the general population would be desirable.

Leszcz (1986) argued that previous research (Bell and Stanfield, 1973) had found few differences in attitudes to older adults when a between-group design was used, while large differences were found when within-group designs were employed (Ryan and Capando, 1978; Weinberger and Millham, 1975). Consequently she used three groups of female volunteers to describe a real, typical or ideal person of their own age and of the other two age groups on four dimensions: autonomy, acceptability, integrity and instrumentality. Sixty adolescents, 60 middle-aged adults and 60 older adults were used. Not surprisingly, ideal people were characterized more positively than real or typical people. Adolescents were viewed as most instrumental or adaptable, the middle-aged were most autonomous, and older people were the most integrated. On three of the four dimensions adolescents were viewed more negatively than the other two groups, while on instrumentality older adults were viewed more negatively than adolescents. However, the volunteer nature of the sample limits the generalizability of the study.

The formation of impressions of older adults and young mature adults by older adults themselves and college students was investigated by Bassili and Reil (1981). They hypothesized that in forming impressions, individuals base their perceptions on a variety of category membership (e.g. race, sex, occupation) in the case of younger people, but that they describe older adults on the basis of age only. They administered a questionnaire in which each category contained one of two age designations (35-year-old or 70-year-old) and one of six other labels (male, female, engineer, bus driver, Canadian Indian, white Canadian) to 180 college students and 180 older adults. The results confirmed the hypothesis, with one exception: college students' ratings of engineers, whether 35 or 70 years old, were as scientific, industrious and efficient. The stereotype of old age characteristics included traditional, conservative, moral centred and present centred.

CONCLUSION

The studies reported in this chapter are useful in providing initial knowledge of the attitudes of groups of individuals who are likely to relate to old people in a helping capacity. Initial indications are that clinicians (Rodin and Langer, 1980; Kucharski *et al.*, 1979), medical students (Spence, 1968) and undergraduate students (Levin, 1988) could all benefit from a raising of awareness and eliminating negative attitudes towards older adults. The attitudes of younger people betray intergroup tension which arises from a different perception of life. For younger people achievement is still to come, while for older adults many of these achievements are in the past. Consequently they do not resonate with the enthusiasm of the young. It is heartening that the indications are that parish clergy enjoy working with the elderly (Longino and Kitsen, 1976). Most of these findings are based on studies that have not been replicated.

With respect to the attitudes of old people themselves to old age, the findings are mixed. Indications are that, despite problems, they find old age to be a better experience than anticipated (O'Connor *et al.*, 1989). A development of research in this area could include an examination of Wingard *et al.*'s (1982) proposal that demographic variables are 'distal' measures of more specific variables, such as individuals' prior experiences and role relationships with older adults.

The value attached to older people differs according to culture. Within a culture a variety of factors combine to produce stereotypes: variables associated with the perceiver, e.g. age; variables relating to the perceived, e.g. race, sex, occupation; contextual variables, e.g. frequency of contact and training in gerontology; and images in literature. Professionals and professional trainees are not immune to the influence of stereotypes and myths, and professional practice can be directly influenced by them.

Overcoming ageism, correcting the myths and stereotypes associated with growing old and taking on board older adults' self-perceptions are major tasks for society generally, and particularly for those who work with older adults, including counsellors. It is imperative that stereotypes do not result in either inappropriate referral or non-referral by physicians.

The counselling factor

4

The effect of counselling intervention in old age depends on many factors: the attitudes and response of counsellors; the perception of older adults of counselling; the preparation of counsellors for work in the particular field; the client's problem; and the counselling approach used. The first three factors will be dealt with in this chapter and the last two will be considered in Chapters 5, 6 and 7.

COUNSELLOR-RELATED VARIABLES

Freud (1905, in Scrutton, 1989) did the older adult a disservice when he pronounced on three separate occasions (1898, 1904, 1905) that analysis was not suitable for adults over 50: that ' ... Psychotherapy is not possible near or above the age of 50. The elasticity of the mental processes on which the treatment depends is as a rule lacking'. Life expectancy has increased so much since 1905 that Freud's belief would seem to consign a much larger proportion of the population to the same oblivion, i.e. an irredeemable psychological state. It is unfortunate that opinions such as Freud's, which are based on anecdotal accounts and uncontrolled case studies, should have been so significant in the mental health treatment of older adults.

Ageist attitudes on the part of psychiatrists and physicians can militate against appropriate referral to counsellors and psychotherapists. Ray *et al.* (1985) studied ageism in psychiatrists and found that, because of negative attitudes on the part of psychiatrists only a limited number of aged people received psychiatric treatment, despite the fact that such individuals are the most likely to develop mental illnesses (Butler and Lewis, 1977). When older people are seen by psychiatrists in private practice, they most often receive consultation concerning institutionalization rather than psychotherapy (Butler, 1975b).

Kucharski *et al.* (1979) examined differences in the referral rates for psychological assistance of young and old patients by physicians. Old patients were referred for psychological assistance less frequently than young patients, although both groups were described as presenting identical symptomatology in a structured experiment that sought the referral responses of physicians to eight vignettes. The results of the study provided partial support for the view that physician bias against the referral of elderly patients for mental health assistance may contribute to the neglect of the psychological problems of the elderly.

Stereotypical beliefs were found in a survey of the attitudes of psychotherapists at a New York city mental health clinic. Garfinkel (1975) found that the therapists agreed that old people usually do not talk much, a finding which can serve as a convenient justification for concentrating solely on the needs of younger people.

Little research has been carried out on the response of counsellors to older adults (Poggi and Berland, 1985). However, Butler and Lewis (1982) listed six reasons for negative attitudes on the part of psychodynamic counsellors towards treating older people. First, older individuals may stimulate fear in some counsellors of their own old age. Secondly, they may arouse conflicts in counsellors concerning their own relationships with parental figures. Thirdly, counsellors may believe they have nothing useful to offer older people, because they regard their problems as arising from untreatable organic brain diseases (a viewpoint which reflects the authors' psychodynamic background). Fourthly, counsellors may consider that their psychodynamic skills will be wasted if they work with older adults, since they are near death and not really deserving of attention. Fifthly, older individuals might die while in treatment, which could challenge the sense of importance of counsellors; and finally, colleagues may be contemptuous of their efforts on behalf of older individuals. Furthermore, involvement with older people may enkindle in counsellors the western taboo against facing death's inevitability. In a youth-oriented society the prestige and power of senior status is declining, producing ambiguity in the relations between generations.

It is worthy of note that the six reasons given by Butler and Lewis (1982) had already been cited by Cohen in 1977. In addition, Cohen mentioned the fear of therapists that they will be overwhelmed by the presenting problems, the ageist attitudes and beliefs of therapists, which can adversely affect the counselling process, and economic considerations which result in no treatment.

In 1982 Lewis and Johansen viewed the situation from a slightly different angle. Reluctance to work with older adults, they felt, was due to cognitive misunderstanding of the nature of old age or to lack of empathy. Cognitive understanding of old age requires the counsellor to grasp essential features of ageing such as interiority; reminiscence; alterations in the perception of time in terms of time left to live; increased personalization of death; diminished capacity for the spontaneous expression of warmth; changes in gender roles, with men becoming more nurturing and women more assertive; increased preoccupation with physical health; and partial grief arising from physical losses. Lewis and Johansen hold that lack of empathy may arise from counsellors engaging in countertransference, projecting their past emotional experience on to older adults; placing emphasis on differences between the clients and themselves; experiencing anxiety about their own failures as they listen to the failures of the older adults; experiencing unresolved feelings about the ageing and death of their own parents; and anticipating loss from the death of clients.

Three countertransference reactions which may occur in counsellors when working with older adults were identified by Nemiroff and Colarusso (1988). These consisted of the therapist's reaction to ageing, to the sexuality of older people and to their dependency needs. While admitting that countertransference contributes to the lack of empathy, it is more therapeutically useful to regard it as the unfinished business of the counsellor. Originally discussed by Perls *et al.* (1951), unfinished business refers to experiences in the past that were not completed. The concept helps to clarify what precisely is projected in countertransference. Of particular relevance when working with older adults is unfinished grief and conflicts with parents. If counsellors ignored these in their past, they are likely to re-emerge in their interactions with older adults. O'Leary (1992) states: 'It (unfinished business) obscures present experience and hinders the investment of energy in current events'. Third-party direction in the form of supervision is essential for counsellors to deal with unfinished business.

Lack of empathy can also arise if the counsellor and client are from different age cohorts. A young financially secure counsellor may not understand the preoccupation with money of older people who lived through the great depression or the second world war. Further difficulties in the establishment of empathy can include the counsellor being insensitive to or unaware of what may appear to be little fears in older adults, such as sitting with strangers at the dining table in a residential unit, or not making an appropriate referral when necessary. Empathy may not be established if the counsellor sits at too great a distance from older adults who have impaired hearing or sight. In the former case too gentle a voice on the part of the counsellor will also militate against empathy.

A lack of structuring can also create difficulties. In structuring clients are orientated to their own role and that of the counsellor in the relationship. Formal structuring is not necessary if clients are aware of the purpose and format of counselling, but it is essential if older adults have misperceptions of counselling, or have no idea of the purpose or nature of counselling. In this way, the readiness of clients is increased.

Three different types of thinking can hinder the estabishment of empathy: thinking for, thinking about and thinking against (O'Leary, 1992). Thinking for includes interrupting or putting words into clients' mouths; giving advice prematurely or in a paternalistic manner; changing the emphasis of what clients are saying; or directing the interaction. In thinking about, counsellors may analyse the motivation of older adults; give theoretical pronouncements which indicate that everyone feels that way; or give 'pat' answers of a 'popular psychology' type. Finally, counsellors think against older adults when they argue or disagree with them; imply or state that they should not feel the way they are feeling; threaten them or are defensive and justify themselves.

A counsellor may encounter further difficulty in working with clients because of conflicts arising from differences in counsellor–client value systems. In old age these are likely to become a central concern of therapy, as the work environment changes and retirement and approaching death become realities. Counsellors may be restricted by non-exploration of their own values in those areas. The values of older adults may pose personal conflicts for the counsellors which hinder progress in counselling.

Familiarity with the central values of the client's religion enhances the counselling relationship (Bergin, 1980; Lovinger, 1984; Spero, 1985; Worthington, 1988). Cox (1973) viewed religion as including a system of beliefs, practices and customs rooted in a culture, a view of the individual's relationship to the universe, a moral and ethical code and a community of adherents providing social relationships. Bergin and Payne (1991) pointed out that counsellors should not attempt to alter the value system of the client.

However, counsellors often see spiritual and religious matters as a minefield in which they tread carefully if at all. Henning and Tirrell (1982) suggested that counsellors are fearful of their own personal unresolved doubts and of emotion which they might arouse if they consider their own mortality. Counsellors may also have a negative attitude to religion in general, or to a specific denomination which may hinder the development of empathy. Irrespective of their own value system, counsellors need to be able to understand the older person's spiritual and religious values if they are introduced by them as part of their concern.

Lewis and Butler (1974) mentioned that an interesting fringe benefit for counsellors and therapists in working with older adults is the acquisition of a rich supply of information and models for their own eventual old age. Rubin (1977) also found that this experience embellishes the skill of the counsellor. In working with a 69-year-old man, he worried that the client's problems might result in dependent behaviour and identified this problem as a fear of losing independence himself in the future. Working with the client allowed him to accept his fears instead of reacting defensively.

Ray *et al.* (1985) strongly supported the view that, through being exposed to both ailing and healthy older people, practitioners will develop more realistic and optimistic attitudes. They cited a study by Tuckman and Lorge (1958), which suggested that individuals who associate more with old people tend to ascribe fewer negative characteristics to them.

CLIENT-RELATED VARIABLES

Older people are often averse to the intervention of a counsellor. Negative stereotypes regarding mental illness and emotional problems may prevent them from seeking appropriate assistance. Many older people equate attending a counsellor with attending a psychiatrist, and presume that it signifies mental disturbance. This is particularly true in the case of the lower socioeconomic groups, where there has not been an opportunity to come in contact with a counsellor. Many older adults are reluctant to admit to problems and prefer to deal with them on their own (Roybal, 1988). Scher (1981) pointed out that some individuals, particularly males, think that it is a sign of weakness to need help to solve problems.

How clients dealt with problems in the past may influence their present approach. Ineffective problem solving has been linked to stressful outcomes and maladjustment (D'Zurilla and Goldfried, 1971; D'Zurilla, 1986; Heppner and Hillerbrand, 1991). In particular, how individuals appraise their problem-solving efforts in terms of confidence, personal control and approach or avoidance, was found to be related to a range of cognitive and affective variables, which are considered to be important in coping as well as psychological adjustment (cf. Heppner, 1988). Specifically, those who appraise themselves as having confidence and personal control and who approach problems, as opposed to their counterparts who lacked the foregoing, reported:

- fewer personal problems (Heppner *et al.*, 1982; Nezu, 1985);
- more positive self-concepts and fewer dysfunctional thoughts and irrational beliefs (Heppner *et al.*, 1983);
- less social anxiety (De Clue, 1984);
- less trait anxiety and more interpersonal assertiveness (Larson, 1984; Neal and Heppner, 1982);
- fewer physical symptoms (Tracey *et al.*, 1986);
- better psychological adjustment as measured by the MMPI and SCL-90 (Heppner and Anderson, 1985; Heppner *et al.*, 1987);
- less depression (Heppner and Anderson, 1985; Heppner *et al.*, 1985; Nezu, 1985), particularly with stressful situations (Nezu *et al.*, 1986; Nezu and Ronan, 1988);
- fewer suicidal thoughts (Dixon *et al.*, 1994).

There are also cultural differences in coping behaviour for problems. McGoldrick and Pearce (1981) stated that Irish-American adults rarely seek therapy of their own volition, since the process of disclosing themselves to others would be both a sign of moral weakness and an embarrassing experience. Some support for this was obtained by O'Leary (1990), who found that avoidance of problems or keeping problems to themselves was characteristic of Irish people, while a problem-solving orientation, a willingness to discuss problems and the acceptance of professional help characterized the American attitude. Yet problem-solving style may vary from individual to individual within each culture. Most likely problem-solving style will affect how people respond to counselling, including how problems are presented, what kind of solutions might be accepted, whether individuals try to solve the problem independently, avoid it, or ask for help (Heppner and Krauskopf, 1987).

It is not surprising that some older adults may be reluctant to seek counselling since most did not have counsellors available to them when younger. It is only 40 years since counselling for personal problems was spearheaded in the US (Nelson-Jones, 1982). Furthermore, it is likely that for many older adults the different reasons for visiting a psychiatrist, psychologist, therapist or counsellor are not clear.

Help-seeking behaviour on the part of older adults, as with other age groups, is likely to be a function of their self-concept. Insecure individuals may feel threatened in exposing themselves to another person. A method of defending themselves against such threat is to label counselling negatively. Hence self-concept filters and colours the experience of older adults.

A possible hindrance in seeking help is the emphasis in western society on independence and autonomy. Emphasis is placed on assisting individuals to move from dependence on others to self-support. In addition, maturity is often viewed by society as involving this ability to be self-supporting. The 'old-old' are caught in a cultural lag between their old behaviour patterns and the problems of today (Sargent, 1980). There is a need in them to be seen as strong and self-sufficient, as they were in their younger days. Brought up in a culture of independence, where independent problem solving was valued, a previously strong asset may militate against them considering counselling as an option. Rogers (1980) puts it strongly when he states: 'We in the west seem to have made a fetish out of complete individual self-sufficiency, of not needing help, of being completely private except in a very few selected relationships ... But we pay a price ... From our private middle years, we "progress" to a very lonely "senior citizen" status'. Fortunately, this trend is gradually being replaced by an emphasis on self-support and interdependence (O'Leary, 1992).

Butler and Lewis (1977) listed five reasons why older people may resist the intervention of a counsellor: a desire for independence; fear of change; suspicion based on past experiences; realistic appraisal of the inadequacies of most 'helping' programmes for old people; and clumsy, insensitive or patronizing intervention techniques on the part of mental health staff and other helpers. Sargent (1980) stated that older people may sense a lack of interest in them on the part of professionals, which increases their resistance to help and at the same time reinforces any negative impressions held by these professionals. To compound the problem, some older adults are victims of their own earlier stereotyping, of which they have now become part.

In discussing psychiatric care, Sparacino (1978) pointed out that older people, like their doctors, may all too readily attribute many correctable conditions to what they consider the normal ageing process. Butler and Lewis (1982) concurred, and stated that older people will tenaciously hold on to what little they have rather than risk the unknown. They concluded that pride and desire for self-reliance, as well as depression and mental confusion, must be considered as factors in resistance.

Transference can also occur. This is the projection of unresolved issues – which may include irrational feelings and unrealistic demands from the person's past – on to the therapist. Older adults feel and act as they did towards significant people in the past. If they experienced difficulty with authority figures, such as their parents, they may experience hostility towards the counsellor, whom they perceive as an authority figure. Alternatively, they may comply excessively with the counsellor from a habit of doing so with authority figures in the past (Patterson and Eisenberg, 1983). In such a situation clients may forget what brought them to counselling in the first instance, as they develop a special interest in the counsellor.

Watkins (1983) spoke of five different kinds of transference reactions, where the counsellor is viewed as the ideal, the seer, the nurturer, the frustrator and the nonentity. In the ideal, the counsellor is viewed as the perfect individual; the seer is expert and powerful; the nurturer is the carer; the frustrator is the one who hinders, and the nonentity is inconsequential.

Dealing effectively with these transference phenomena involves taking their specific nature into account. Watkins made the following suggestions: in the counsellor-as-ideal transference, the counsellor should provide ongoing ego support to clients and understand their feelings of anger and disappointment when confronted. Attention to the self-effacement characteristics of clients is also desirable. In the counsellor-as-seer phenomenon, older adults do not trust themselves or their decisions and thus do not have to bear the consequences of any decision. The counsellor explores these characteristics with them. When the counsellor is viewed as nurturer, older adults need to explore their dependence and underlying terror of being on their own. Unlike the previous three transference reactions, the counsellor-as-frustrator can naturally lead to feelings of uneasiness in the counsellor. However, the counsellor needs to be aware that older adults experiencing this phenomenon need to rework the issue of basic trust versus mistrust (Erikson, 1963,

1980). Finally, in the counsellor-as-nonentity transference the counsellor needs to be firm and persistent in working with older adults.

In group counselling the older adult may transfer feelings to other members of the group or to the group as a collective entity. In such circumstances the different individuals in the group may represent the different people around whom the unfinished situation originally developed, or the group itself may do so. However, it is important not to label all the affect of the client towards the counsellor as transference. Older adults may have a genuine feeling of like or dislike for the counsellor based on the counsellor's actual behaviour.

Some older adults participating in group counselling may remain silent and rationalize their non-participation by stating that they are acquiring insight into themselves. Insight, however, deals only with the cognitive dimension of the individual, whereas awareness involves both the cognitive and the affective dimensions. Another method of rationalizing their non-participation may be through describing the group as an unreal situation. Manthei and Matthews (1982) made the following suggestions for dealing with a client's silence; counsellors could try to understand the possible meanings of silence: counsellors could share their observations of the non-verbal behaviour of clients as a means of involving them; counsellors could use writing and drawing in endeavouring to elicit a response from clients; and counsellors could mirror the body language of clients.

Practical considerations, such as availability of counselling services, lack of knowledge of the services, cost and transportation, must also be taken into account when considering client reluctance. However, there are indications that the attitudes of older people to counselling may be changing. Wellman and McCormack (1984) found that older people have become more sophisticated and open, and are able to take advantage of available services. King (1980) listed six phase-specific reasons for older people seeking counselling: fear of a decrease in sexual potency; fear of diminished competence at work; anxiety about retirement; issues relating to the marital relationship which emerge when the children leave home; awareness of ageing, illness and dependence on others; and an increasing realization of the finality of one's own death.

PREPARATION OF COUNSELLORS

Adequate training of counsellors is vital to their success in counselling older adults and for the elimination of prejudical concepts of the counselling factor. K. Rubin (1973) highlighted this neglect in psychiatric settings.

Whether specialized training for counselling older adults should be provided or not rests on the perspective in which one regards older adults.

Two polarized positions are possible: older adults are unique psychologically and counselling them requires special training, or older adults are like other adults and can benefit from similar counselling approaches. The latter suggests that there is no need for specialist training for older individuals. Many of the problems encountered by older adults, such as bereavement and retirement, are common to other age groups. However, many lifespan psychologists (discussed in Chapter 2) have allocated specific psychological tasks to old age.

A case can be made that counsellors should follow a specific course in gerontology as part of their training. Seltzer (1977) found that exposure to such a course clearly changed the stereotypes and attitudes held by participants regarding older people in the decreased use of categorical approaches. A positive relationship was found between acquisition of information and change in attitude. Similar positive change is reported by Porter and O'Connor (1978) for participants in a psychology of ageing course. Their experimental study was unique in that each participant was matched with an older person (over 60) who acted as a 'consultant' for the duration of the course. Such an experiential method of teaching would fit easily in a counsellor training programme. Ideally the general and specific need to be combined.

Whichever alternative is chosen it is important that all trainee counsellors of older adults, as indeed all other counsellors, undertake experiential group work. The focus of this work is to assist trainees to achieve personal affective and cognitive development. Although many training courses recommend individual counselling, and certain progress can be made in this context, increased learning can occur in a group context. A valuable instrument in achieving personal growth in a group is the Johari window (Table 4.1) in that it helps to identify issues and problem areas in the counsellor's life which would diminish their effectiveness in counselling the older adult. Named after Joe Luft and Harry Ingram, its originators, it was originally used in T-groups.

Table 4.1 Johari window

	Known to others	Unknown to others
Known to self	A OPEN AREA	B HIDDEN AREA
Unknown to self	C BLIND AREA	D UNKNOWN AREA

Source: Luft and Ingram (1955)

Area A is an area of common knowledge, known to the self and others. Feedback from others in a group context can lead to the enhancement of previously accepted behaviours by crystallizing personal attributes. Area B contains those aspects of themselves known to individuals but which they keep hidden from others. It may be described as the secret area of a person's life. Shlien (1984) held that keeping secrets prevents change, while revealing them initiates it and allows movement out of a frozen position. Individuals do not usually reveal experiences which are difficult. Secrecy is a form of self-protection against exposure. Egan (1973) stated that individuals who find their behaviour unacceptable must conceal their identities from others, but the energy invested in this process prevents them from considering their own experiences. Secrecy may be temporarily necessary for individuals who rely on environmental support and are not yet ready to be self-supporting. Hence it is important to devote careful consideration to the selection of trainee counsellors to ensure that such individuals are not accepted into training, particularly when self-development is encouraged in a group format.

Area C refers to those aspects of individuals which are known to others but unknown to themselves. Egan (1973) proposed an interesting hypothesis when he suggests that the avoidance of self-revelation may occur through fear of contact with oneself. The advantage of group work is that, through feedback from others, individuals are enabled to increase contact with themselves.

Area D includes those aspects of individuals of which neither themselve or others are aware. In psychodynamic terms it is known as the unconscious. This area can become known to individuals through new situations, such as that which an experiential training group provides.

In experiential group work, Area A becomes more clearly defined through focusing on personal characteristics and experiences. Area B expands as individuals become more self-supporting, interactive and interdependent, and ready to share their secrets with others. Area C decreases as feedback from other group members leads to an increase in awareness. It is in this particular dimension that opportunity for personal growth in a group context is greatly enhanced, as individuals can obtain feedback from a number of individuals. Area D may emerge as individuals engage in new experiences. This is particularly true when working with experiment in gestalt therapy (cf. O'Leary, 1992).

Participation in an experiential group allows trainees to communicate more effectively with themselves and others. Canter and Canter (1983) emphasized the necessity for psychologists to have competence in the latter area, as they form part of an interdisciplinary team. In working with older adults it is likely that counsellors and counselling psychologists may need consultation skills in order to enhance communication with staff and to set up effective programmes in residential units and in the wider community. Hence a course in consultation skills would be a desirable asset to any programme which seeks to provide enhanced services to older adults. These skills could subsequently be used to provide expert knowledge to administrators of centres or residential units for older adults.

The counsellor of older adults needs to be involved in a variety of activities, including individual and group counselling; liaison activities with outside contacts; and coordinator of activities such as pastoral care. Since the goal of intervention by counselling psychologists and counsellors is to improve the quality of life of older adults, particularly in the emotional, social and spiritual area, different modes of intervention must be used.

In terms of training equal emphasis needs to be given to group interventions such as reminiscence therapy (see Chapter 6) as to basic individual counselling skills such as listening, responding and questioning. It is also desirable that trainees undertake a supervised practical placement with an elderly group. Assessment skills are also essential to enable the future counsellor either to refer those who may be suffering from Alzheimer's disease or senile dementia for appropriate consultation, or to arrange suitable activities for them. Finally, a knowledge of research skills needs to be acquired which will enable them to evaluate their work and continually acquire more information from their experience on the job.

A study by Lopez and Silber (1981) examined the effectiveness of a training programme designed to teach mental health professionals information and skills specific to counselling the older adult. The programme was offered twice, with 25 mental health professionals registering for each programme. Only information from participants who completed all pre and post measures and attended all sessions was included for data analysis. The final group consisted of 28 women and four men, with a mean age of 37 years. The same trainers, a clinical psychologist and a graduate student in clinical psychology, met with both groups. The training programme consisted of four 3-hour sessions.

A number of measures were administered both before and after the programme. The major assessment instrument was composed of eight brief descriptions of situations commonly encountered in the psychological treatment of the elderly. This was called the 'counselling situations' measure. Trainees' descriptions of their preferred treatment plan, including options and alternatives, for each problem situation were rated by the experimenters.

Four other instruments were used: a 10-question mental health information test designed to measure general background knowledge concerning the mental health of older people; a 10-point Likert scale to assess their level of preparation for their current job positions; a measure of job satisfaction, the Job Description Index (Smith *et al.*, 1969), and Kogan's

(1961) Attitudes Towards Old People Scale. Participants anonymously completed questionnaires designed to evaluate programme content and method. Two months later they were retested on all the instruments except the counselling situations test.

Participants showed a statistically significant improvement on both the counselling situations measure and the mental health information test, after completion of the training programme. They also showed trends toward gains on job satisfaction and preparedness, which were maintained 2 months later. Pretraining scores on the counselling situations measure were the best predictors of success on this measure after training. Less significant were scores on the mental health information test. The other variables such as attitudes toward the elderly and job satisfaction were not significant predictors.

The results are interesting in that the training programme may be an effective method to improve participants' knowledge of mental health and ability to devise suitable interventions for older adults. A replication study is desirable. Behavioural measures by peers and supervisors could be used, and it would be preferable if the trainers were different individuals from the researchers.

CONCLUSION

Negative attitudes on the part of professionals can prevent appropriate referral of older adults. This problem is compounded by the reluctance of older adults to seek help. It is important that trainee counsellors explore their own attitudes to this segment of the population. Experiential group work is an effective means of achieving this. Subsequent to training, supervision can further monitor any such negative reaction. To achieve success in counselling, counsellors must be aware of the problems that older adults present.

Counselling issues affecting older adults

5

The psychological consequences of growing old are frequently over-looked by society, being regarded simply as part of old age, but older people have essentially the same needs as everyone else. Many of these can be addressed by adequate counselling. Counsellors have a major role to play in improving the quality of life of older adults. To identify this contribution one must first identify the issues facing older adults to which counselling may make a therapeutic contribution. Seven such issues can be identified: loss, retirement, loneliness, depression, psychosexual diffi-culties, anticipation of death and insomnia. These are not all negative: there is also the possibility of positive personal growth. Both sides of the coin will be discussed in this chapter.

THE PROBLEM OF LOSS

Loss is a universal experience in the older age group. Scrutton (1989) identified it as the most significant contributory factor to distress in older people. There is the loss of significant people; a loss of close contact with offspring; a loss of physical abilities to varying degrees and a diminution in financial independence.

Loss of significant people

Loss of significant people such as relatives, friends and colleagues, whether through life's changing circumstances or through death, occurs at every stage of life, but in old age it is very much increased. Such loss can be more final and have major implications for the older adult. Opportunities for forming new relationships are limited, and secondary losses such as a drop in income and change of house may occur.

The greatest challenge facing older adults may be the loss of intimate relationships through death. In a US study in 1984, Belsky (1990) reported that two out of three women over the age of 70 were widows, whereas two out of three men had wives who were still alive. Bernardo (1968) noted that the ratio of widows to widowers was 4:1. Thus because of the greater longevity of women, spousal mourning is a problem more likely to be found in older women.

There are a variety of factors that may affect the nature of loss. In a study in Chicago, Lopata (1973) found that widowhood meant the loss of the wife's social role. A consequence of this was that only a quarter of the widows saw their husband's relatives and associates with any frequency. Their social interaction was often curtailed, due to a limited budget or their inability to drive. However, half of Lopata's widows had reorganized themselves and were benefiting from the independence and reduction in workload.

The death of a husband may result in both emotional and social losses. It can bring about an overriding sense in the bereaved person that life has no further personal meaning. In Lopata's (1973) study older widows showed limited involvement within their communities (except for religion). Satisfaction of physical and sexual needs, emotional closeness and self-identity may have been intertwined with one's spouse. A spouse is often a partner in many of life's activities. Lowy (1979) suggested that the absence of a confidant appears to be far more devastating to the morale of older people than does the lack of social or work roles. Widows and widowers emerged as having the greatest difficulty with loneliness, which was closely related to their loss of a companion in O'Leary and Kelly's (1990) study. Loss of this significant person may overshadow all other events and experiences, even those that had been sources of pleasure in the past. However Breckenridge et al. (1986) found that older adults coped with the loss of a spouse better than younger adults, expressing less intense distress during the first months.

A notable effect of widowhood for many people is psychosomatic in nature (Brink, 1979). Visits to the doctor and hospitalization increase significantly in the 6 months following bereavement. However, Stroebe et al. (1988) and Stroebe and Stroebe (1989) found that men accept fewer opportunities to discuss their bereavement and form fewer interpersonal relationships. They seemed to suffer more than the women, although this was not usually recognized by the people in their environment. Stuart-Hamilton (1994) pointed out that the evidence as to which gender suffers the most is contradictory. However, everyone mourns for what is lost. The consequent grief and its effects will be considered in Chapter 6.

The paradox is to be able to live and enjoy life in the face of loss and still remain open to new and meaningful relationships. Belsky (1990) considered that the possession of inner qualities such as emotional resilience, ego strength and adaptability, when combined with a recovery-inducing environment, assists adaptation to loss. When the death of a spouse occurs, older adults need to let go of their image of themselves as married individuals and begin to behave as single people. Such a process may require considerable time, depending on the closeness of the relationship with the spouse.

Loss of contact with children

The loss of close contact with offspring is another element of loss. Older adults have outgrown the normal parent–child relationship: their children no longer see them as 'Daddy' and 'Mummy' and the knowledge that they are no longer depended on by their children is often a difficulty. With increasing frailty the roles are gradually reversed, with adult children taking on the caring function. Lidz (1983) noted that, in the Fiji Islands, the ageing man who ceases to be responsible for the family is no longer called 'father' by his children; rather, he addresses his eldest son, who is now head of the family, as 'father'. Wiedeman and Matison (1975) pointed out that family members can find this change of roles difficult to handle. The adult child can have difficulty in letting go of the all-powerful parent of childhood.

Four patterns of ageing parent and adult child relationships were identified by Shulman and Berman (1988), namely status equality, status quo, status conflict and status reversal. In the status-equality pattern, both function as interdependent adults. This is likely to occur as long as the older adult is healthy and financially secure. When the older adult retains considerable control, and the adult child remains under the parent's influence, the status quo pattern is maintained. A status-conflict pattern emerges when older adults experience difficulty in transferring power to their adult children. To be effective, transfer of power involves a maintenance of status and a sense of belonging by the older adult. The status reversal pattern has already been discussed.

In some European countries, such as Austria, Germany, France and Ireland, where three-generation households are common, changed circumstances affect development in parent–child relationships. Grandparents frequently take over the childminding responsibilities and contribute to the life of the family while the mother pursues her career. This pattern was found to exist in new urban areas in the UK (Anderson, 1972) and in parts of the New England region of the US (Chudacoff and Hareven, 1978). The role of the grandmother is well described in a quotation from a study by Kornhaber and Woodward (1981) on the practice of grandparents: 'Grandma has got a bad leg, so she can't walk around without her cane. I can sit on her lap, though, and she tells me stories about when she was young and I can cuddle up with her … She is so cozy.

She can't walk too well, but she can talk. And she is the best back rubber in the world.' In family environments such as this one the sense of loss which may occur when the family leaves home is replaced by the nurturance of grandchildren.

Loss of emotional support from their children may be particularly distressing for older adults. Hill (1970) found that 62% of older adults viewed emotional gratification as the greatest assistance received, 61% mentioned aid during illness, and 52% spoke of help running their households. This concurred with Treas (1975), who found that older people value their children's love and respect more than they regard their assistance. Perlmutter and Hall (1992) cited studies showing that most old people have frequent contact with their grown children, and the family provides them with consistent emotional and social support as well as aid in times of crisis. Daly and O'Connor (1984) found that, in rural Ireland, those with close relatives have frequent contact with them. However, Carey and Carroll (1986), in a study of the needs of the elderly in Dublin, reported that although 48.7% of the elderly had daily visits from relatives and 32% weekly visits, 12.3% were rarely visited and 7% never had visits. Hence approximately 20% lacked support in an urban context.

Loss for older adults can also occur through a gender-stereotyped pattern of caring. Evandrou et al. (1986) found that, for elderly people living alone, sons and daughters provided the most help. Most of this help was furnished by females. Shulman and Sperry (1992) found that 72% of carers were women. In an investigation of older adults in south Wales, daughters were three times more likely to be identified as carers than sons (Jones et al., 1983). Victor (1987) stated that only one-third of all carers of the elderly are men. Walker (1981) commented: 'care will be provided within families by women ... men are not ... expected to look after elderly or infirm relatives'.

Similar evidence of the gender-specific nature of caring was provided by Charlesworth et al. (1983), who discovered that daughters and daughters-in-law constitute the largest group of carers for elderly people. Cultural patterns determined which of these two groups provided help. In a study of elderly Chinese and Irish in Boston, Ikels (1982) found that although the offspring living nearest was most likely to become the main caretaker, this was usually the daughter-in-law in the case of the Chinese and the daughter in the case of the Irish. Woodruff and Birren (1975) drew the following conclusions with regard to contact with parents: 'It seems daughters keep in touch more than do sons, unmarried offspring more than married ones, own children more than sons-in-law and daughters-in-law, and nearby children more than distant ones'. Hence diminished contact for older parents is more likely to occur with sons and married children. The question that arises is, does this gender imbalance accentuate the sense of loss in older adults?

Where family support for older adults is inadequate it is frequently due to economic factors, causing older adults to be placed in institutions for the elderly. But there is no support in the literature for the view that the majority of older adults are consigned indiscriminately to such institutions. Perlmutter and Hall (1992) cite studies showing that, contrary to popular belief, the elderly are not isolated from their adult children. Only 5% of the elderly population of Europe and the United States are in institutions at any particular time. Older people who have no families, and who are ill and feeble, often are admitted to institutions because there is nobody available to care for them.

Although dependence on family is important, it is also true that older adults still see independence as a major value. The desire to remain independent is reflected in the findings of a study by Shanas *et al.* (1968), who found that only 8% of older adults were living with their families; 83% preferred their own homes. Living alone can be a choice for many elderly people. Well-adjusted elderly people who have a number of satisfying personal relationships with others, family or otherwise, may enjoy being alone at times. O'Leary and Kelly (1990) found that more than 90% of those who lived alone were not lonely. It is less likely for loneliness to ensue from living alone if people have lived in the same area for most of their lives, as was the case in the latter study.

Decline in physical abilities

Declining physical abilities and poor health, and the social changes that accompany them, were identified as the greatest areas of loss in the lives of older adults (Working Party on Services for the Elderly in Ireland, 1988). As the person grows old, vitality lessens and vulnerability increases. Daly and O'Connor (1984) found that the main anxiety of old people living in rural areas was centred around health. Good health ensures independence and an ability to look after oneself. They state that for the very old, ill health is an ever-present threat. 'In old age, a fall, a chill, a small injury may quickly result not only in incapacity, but in loss of independence and choice.'

However, declining health contributes more to the sense of loss in the very old rather than those under the age of 75. Woodruff and Birren (1975) stated that 40% of adults between 65 and 74 have some type of impairment, while 60% of those over 75 have similar difficulties. Aiken (1989) estimated that if cancer was eradicated in older adults, the average lifespan would rise by only 1.2–2.3 years. However, if all cardiovascular and kidney diseases were conquered, the average lifespan would increase by approximately 10 years (Butler, 1975a), thus confirming Belsky's (1990) assertion that serious physical losses in old age are due to age-related illness.

Loss may be experienced because of the emphasis society places not only on being young but also on appearing youthful. Symbolic interactionist theory hypothesizes that the manner in which individuals are labelled by others has a significant impact on self-concept and behaviour (Cox, 1988). Nowak *et al.* (1976) noted the relationship between physical appearance and stereotypes of old age: 'Researchers concerned with interpersonal attraction, but not with attitudes toward ageing, have independently discovered a set of characteristics used to describe unattractive people that are remarkably similar to those descriptive of people who are old'. Traxler (1971) found that firm, smooth, unwrinkled skin is associated with the impression of youthfulness and attractiveness. However, the impact of changing physical appearance in the form of grey hair and wrinkles can be more stressful for a woman, whose self-esteem is likely to be related to it.

The degree of decline in physical abilites in old age may be moderate. Studies in Ireland show that approximately 80% of adults over 65 are fully independent in the sense of not being in need of care (Blackwell *et al.*, 1992; O'Connor *et al.*, 1989; Moane, 1993). Both the contemplation and the reality that they may become dependent on others to meet their most basic personal and physical needs may cause considerable emotional turmoil to older people, and can be deeply distressing to individual pride. Scrutton (1989) stated: 'Dependence, imminent or actual, should therefore constitute an important agenda in the counselling of older people'.

Economic independence

Loss of or decrease in income frequently poses an additional problem for older adults. The US Bureau of the Census (1982) found that after age 65, per capita income is 26% less than it is between the ages of 55 and 64. Espenshade and Brown (1983) estimated that single older adults need from 51 to 79% of their normal income, and married couples need 55–86%.

This decrease of income is usually accompanied by a fall in the standard of living, a loss of status in the community, and a preoccupation with making ends meet. All these factors can create feelings of anxiety. Working-class people are often the most affected, as many are dependent on fixed state benefits which do not usually allow for inflation.

The extent of this financial insecurity was identified by the Irish National Council for the Aged (1984), who estimated that in 1980 30% of older adults had an income which placed them in the lowest 20% of all household incomes. More than half of this group were dependent on social welfare pensions or lived alone. Of these, about 12% of social welfare recipients and 18% of those who lived alone were deemed by the

Council to be in 'absolute' poverty. The majority were women. However, O'Leary and Kelly (1990) found that two-thirds of their sample of older adults felt that they had enough money, while 18% considered that they could use more and 3% thought that they could use a lot more.

RETIREMENT

A further instance of loss is retirement. The loss of employment and the habitual activity and satisfaction of their working years is frequently an occasion of distress for the older adult. Berghorn and Thompson (1994) pointed out that for most of human history people only stopped working when ill-health occurred. Johnson (1985) stated that in Britain, 73% of the male population over 65 were at work in 1881, but by 1981 this had reduced to only 11%. Townsend (1981) cited the International Labour Office in confirming that this is the international trend.

For many people forced retirement at a fixed age implies a sudden passage from full activity to relative inactivity. The impact of such a transition depends on a number of factors: its voluntary or compulsory nature; the associated level of anxiety; loss of income; the extent of pre-planning; and adjustment for the future to a changed daily routine. It is likely that voluntary retirement is not harmful to morale but that forced disengagement, whatever the reason, can affect social interaction. In the US the National Council on the Aging (1975) found that 86% of older people believed that mandatory retirement should be abolished. Aiken (1982) pointed out that a US federal statute in 1979 raised the mandatory retirement age from 65 to 70, since a fixed retirement age of 65 was not based on any scientific finding and was against the public interest. Hertzog et al. (1990) found that wellbeing for older adults who were working or semiretired was not related to the amount of work they did, but rather to its voluntary nature. Hence the voluntary nature of either work or retirement in the lives of older adults is central.

There is a great deal of anxiety about retirement, especially on the part of those for whom it is imminent. Such anxiety may centre around the fear of getting old, loss of status and loss of income. Swan et al. (1991) found that retirement means not only loss of employment but also separation from sources of status and social support. In a 1993 Eurobar survey on attitudes to ageing, financial concerns relating to having enough money were the most frequently mentioned difficulty. In the UK, a basic state retirement pension provides an income of between a third and a half of average earnings (Scrutton, 1989). A decrease of 33–45% was found by Parnes and Nestel (1981) when they compared incomes before retirement to those after retirement.

Streib and Schneider (1971) noted that people with low incomes did not wish to retire, and found other employment if they were fit enough, which supported Palmore and Maeda's (1985) finding that enjoyment of retirement is linked to financial circumstances. Further support was obtained in studies by Bengtson and Treas (1980) and Ward (1984), where white-collar workers were happier with retirement than blue-collar workers, probably owing to better health and financial security. Without adequate financial means it is unlikely that old age can be what Belsky (1990) saw as a 'time of liberation, a healthy and happy reprieve from the stress of having to work'.

Retirement is more likely to be accepted, and even enjoyed, if there is careful planning for it. The switch from full-time work to the leisure of retirement can involve a complete change in the person's pattern of living. The Irish National Council for the Aged (1982) asserted that specific help in preparing for retirement can dispel uncertainties, reduce uneasiness and provide useful information. This assistance encourages a positive attitude, stimulates a higher level of social participation and improves health and wellbeing. Individuals nearing retirement should ask themselves the following questions:

1. When will I be retiring?
2. Will I lead a life of leisure or continue to work?
3. What is my present financial situation?
4. Will it mean a change of residence?
5. How much money do I need in retirement?
6. When can I start drawing social security and my other pension benefits?
7. What precisely are my benefits under my company's pension plan?
8. Will I have enough health insurance?
9. What kind of investments can help me obtain additional retirement income?

Retirement brings with it a change in daily routine: a new meaningful pattern has to be created. Disruption of customary habits often occurs for wives who do not work outside the home, when their husbands retire. The couple as a unit, whatever their individual circumstances, has to adjust to the changed conditions, which may be a cause of stress. Honest feedback needs to take place so that the disadvantages can be explored and alternatives created. Retirement can be greatly ameliorated if the family can provide substitute satisfactions for those that have been lost. Aiken (1989) suggested that a combination of activity and interpersonal contact is necessary for wellbeing during retirement. A sense of usefulness and involvement helps in adjustment, whereas feeling useless leads to low morale. While recognizing that retirement is a transition that affects the whole family, it is especially important that the retiring person chooses their new pattern of living themselves.

Adjustment to retirement was viewed by Atchley (1976) as a series of two pre-retirement and five retirement phases. The two preretirement steps are referred to as remote and near. Transition between these occurs when individuals change their perception of retirement as a remote event to a near one. The five states associated with retirement are labelled honeymoon, disenchantment, reorientation, stability and termination. At the outset individuals may experience the freedom to engage in all the activities or pastimes that work did not allow them to pursue. However, for some a feeling of letdown occurs as they become disenchanted with it. They may reorientate themselves and develop a realistic sense of alternatives, in which case their lives then become stable.

The response to retirement varies. A survey carried out by Whelan and Whelan (1988) found that almost 40% of their respondents feared retirement when it happened. A smaller number – 32% – had some trouble in settling down. However, the researchers found that at the time of the survey less than 30% indicated that they continued to experience problems in adjustment. Victor (1987) held that ease or difficulty of adjustment to retirement depends on five factors: type of job, health, income, family and purpose in life. The National Council on the Aging in the US (1975) gave the following figures for the seven aspects of their jobs that people over 65 miss:

- the money it brings in (75%);
- the people at work (73%);
- the work itself (62%);
- the feeling of being useful (59%);
- things happening around you (57%);
- the respect of others (50%);
- having a fixed schedule every day (43%).

In an era of increased female participation in the workforce, there is a need for the counsellor to know whether the effects of retirement differ for men and women. Research needs to be conducted in this area, since as Calasanti (1993) pointed out, those researchers who considered gender differences in retirement used a male model.

Since the majority of people will retire without any formal support (Scrutton, 1989), it is likely that the counsellor will be involved with those who are experiencing problems in the post-retirement period. At this stage, problems with which the counsellor may have to deal include the feelings associated with retirement, decrease in social support, ways of coping with the change in lifestyle, drop in income, decrease in status and a new daily routine.

All the dimensions of loss discussed so far can be explored in either gestalt therapy or reality therapy, since both are based on the present experience of the individual (see Chapter 7).

LONELINESS

Loneliness is a cause of concern for many older adults. In the USA 12–40% of the total population over 65 suffer from loneliness (Creacy *et al.*, 1985). In a national survey there, Harris *et al.* (1975) found that older adults considered it to be the fourth most serious problem in their lives after poor health, financial difficulties and personal security. In a study of 256 older adults in Ireland, O'Leary and Kelly (1990) found that 12% experienced loneliness.

Loneliness is the perception of isolation emphasized by apartness or an inability to bridge the gap existing between oneself and others (Landau, 1980). Walton *et al.* (1991) described loneliness as an emotional response to the difference between desired and actual relationships. It can manifest itself in an unnoticed inability to engage in activity while alone (Peplau and Perlman, 1982). Another indicator is overplanning: some individuals make extensive lists of what they have to do in order to avoid the emptiness they experience. Loneliness is often accompanied by feelings of boredom, emptiness, exclusion and self-pity. Statements that 'the days are so long' may be one sign of it.

Loneliness can be first experienced, and sometimes with great intensity, in adolescence (Mijuskovic, 1986). It usually occurs as a result of external circumstances. Loneliness may arise from the loss of significant people in one's life, causing deprivation of emotional gratification. This emotional as well as social isolation was identified by Creacy *et al.* (1985) as a cause of loneliness. Social isolation occurs when the person has an inadequate social life. Scrutton (1989) held that the morale and happiness of the older adult are more deeply affected by loneliness than any other single factor.

The existence of a close friendship can serve as a buffer against loneliness (Rokach, 1989). Lowy (1979) pointed out that, as people age, the loss of a confidant appears to be far more devastating than does the loss of social or work roles.

Females complain of loneliness more than males, and those who have lost their spouse within the previous 5 years appear to suffer most (Ryan and Peterson, 1987). In a research study involving 107 adults over 65, Watson and Ager (1991) found that higher scores for age-related losses and hopelessness were associated with higher loneliness scores. O'Leary and Kelly (1990) found that almost one in four of older adults were without close friends. A possible explanation is that many of their peers have died. Physical debility, such as failing sight, deteriorating hearing or decreased mobility, may also be a factor in that it lessens the ability to make new friends. From a review of 30 000 surveys on loneliness, Rubenstein and Shaver (1982) concluded that the only lasting remedy was mutual affection and participation in a genuine community.

Living alone may also contribute to loneliness. In 1981, 39.5% of all individuals living on their own in the US were over 65 (US Statistical Abstract 1982/83). Carey and Carroll (1986) discovered that 45% of older adults living alone said that they were lonely. Living alone reduces the availability of an immediate source of social support and interaction. As old people gradually feel themselves to be more isolated, they become more introspective. O'Leary and Kelly (1990) reported a higher frequency of loneliness among those living on their own. However, in the last study, the least likely group to be lonely were widows or widowers. This may be due to the fact that 59% lived with either a son or daughter. Where older adults did not reside with their offspring, 9% of sons and 10% of daughters visited their parents weekly, while 11% had a sister who visited daily or monthly and 9% had brothers who did so.

It is worth noting that, by deduction, 55% of older adults living alone in Carey and Carroll's study did not report being lonely. This bears out Rubenstein and Shaver's (1982) view that solitude can be a form of positive aloneness, which can be a corrective for feeling lonely: 'In solitude we are intimate with ourselves in a way that enhances our intimacy with other people'. The ability to be inner directed is central to the enjoyment of solitude. Martin discovered that the extent of self-determination was positively correlated with higher life satisfaction. This association was maintained even when controlling for other variables, such as income and self-rated health. It is probable that it is the quality rather than the quantity of the time one spends with others which is most important. Positive aloneness is more likely to result if living alone is by choice rather than by fate. This state of positive aloneness is important in the lives of older people, since a study of 92 retired older people by Larson et al. (1985) found that approximately 50% of their active time was spent alone. Married and unmarried reacted differently: the married reported greater concentration and challenge than the unmarried, who became drowsy, passive, tired and bored. In a study of 64 healthy and 64 chronically ill adults, Miller (1985) found that loneliness decreased as spiritual wellbeing increased.

The ability to travel unaccompanied would appear to assist the prevention of loneliness in the elderly. Power (1980) discovered that 56% of older adults in the Republic of Ireland believed that socializing with neighbours was very important. Leaving one's residence to meet or just to observe other people helps to alleviate the feeling of aloneness. Amenities such as community centres and social events, including bingo, card drives and concerts, further assist this process. Weeks (1994) pointed out that although lonely people initially look for any form of contact, loneliness is lessened only by a reciprocal trusting relationship.

In their study of the rural elderly in Ireland, Daly and O'Connor (1984) discovered that loneliness is a commonly reported experience.

Bereavement rather than isolation was its most frequent cause. This is not surprising, given the open nature of households in rural Ireland.

Indications are that loss, hopelessness, bereavement, emotional and social isolation and living on one's own are related to a greater sense of loneliness, whereas spiritual wellbeing, socializing with neighbours and the presence of a confidant decrease loneliness. If the quality of life of older adults is to improve, research needs to consider the predictors of loneliness in this segment of the population. Such research would enable appropriate counselling programmes to be devised which would assist in the prevention of loneliness. Although not specifically devised for older adults, one approach to counselling loneliness is that by Natale (1986) (see Chapter 6).

DEPRESSION

Depression often accompanies the losses and changes associated with old age. Research has consistently found that the highest rate of symptoms of depression is in the 65+ age group, with La Rue *et al.* (1985) giving a figure of between 30 and 65% for those over 60. Butler and Lewis (1982) and Comfort (1980) pointed out that depression is one of the most common of all reactions to stress and change in advancing years: 10–20% of all older people are depressed (Aiken, 1989). Stanway (1981) concurred with this estimate when he claimed that about one in ten people over 65 will suffer from depression at some time. These figures appear to refer to minor depressions, as Casey (1994) pointed out that only 2–5% of adults over 65 meet the criteria for major depression as defined by DSM III (1978).

Cross-cultural variations exist in the prevalence of depression. Older Japanese adults have a lower rate of depressive symptoms than older adults living in the west (Hasegawa, 1985). This finding was confirmed in a large-scale study of older adults across four cultures, which included 1094 white Americans, 464 black Americans, 2041 Japanese and 3865 Taiwanese (Krause and Liang, 1992). They found that overall depressive symptoms were lowest for the Japanese, followed by the Taiwanese, white Americans and black Americans. However, caution must be exercised in interpreting these findings since there is no evidence that accepted measures of depression are equally pertinent in all cultures.

Different theories exist as to the origin of depression. A biological explanation was proposed by Hippocrates, who believed that it resulted from too much black bile in the body. The modern biological explanation proposes that neurotransmitters, which enable the transfer of electrical impulses from one neuron to another, mediate depression. The level of neurotransmitters and the body's response to stress are altered with ageing (Finch, 1977). Changes in the endocrine system, which occur as a result of stress, may be responsible (Blazer, 1982).

Psychoanalytical explanations are based on childhood experiences such as losses and separation, which create the basis for depression. Freud (1917) proposed that loss was central to depression, or melancholia as he called it. In melancholia there is an extraordinary lessening of self-regard, as the internal world becomes poor and empty. Events in the lives of older adults recall previous unresolved losses.

A cognitive explanation of depression was proposed by Beck (1967, 1976), who hypothesized that cognitive thought patterns were possibly learned in childhood. He stressed the significance of these patterns in determining subsequent behaviour and emotion. Older adults may hold unfavourable views of old age, acquired during an earlier period of their lives, and consequently develop a negative self-image leading to depression.

A behavioural explanation was offered by Lewinsohn *et al.* (1976, 1978). The lack of involvement of the person in activities which are positively reinforcing results in depression. Closely related to this is the absence of social interaction usually found in depressed individuals. Older adults with lessened physical capacity caused by a variety of events, such as hip replacement operations, may find that they have to give up activities which gave them the greatest enjoyment.

Brown and Harris (1978) identified four factors which increase a person's vulnerability to depression. Two of these are particularly relevant to the older adult, namely the absence of a confiding relationship with a spouse or partner and the lack of employment outside the home. Gallagher and Thompson (1982) found that depression is often the result of the loss of a spouse, which supports Wiedeman and Matison's (1975) definition of depression as a 'clinical syndrome reflecting a patient's response to loss and his/her attempts to cope with it'. Although negative reactions to retirement are common until a new equilibrium is established (Lidz, 1983), depression occurs when a person continues to brood and feels displaced or neglected.

Various medications or drugs may also contribute to depression in older adults. Chief among these are histamine blocking agents, antihypertensives, betablockers and digitalis preparations (Casey, 1994). Some medical illnesses, such as endocrine disorders, neurological disorders, chronic pulmonary artery disease and congestive heart failure, heighten the possibility of depression.

There is evidence of a relationship between depression and hopelessness (Butler and Lewis, 1982; Kasi and Rosenfield, 1980). Hopelessness is a negative expectation regarding oneself in the future. Hopelessness, as related to depression, is a serious concern of increasing numbers of older adults (Pfeiffer, 1980; Fry and Grover, 1982; Fry, 1983). Blazer (1982) suggested that the depressed elderly often express a sense of hopelessness. This is reflected in statements such as 'There is no sense in my doing anything, since I will be dead soon', and 'I have nothing to look forward to'.

Depression expresses itself in other ways, such as self-worthlessness, guilt and/or loss of interest in how one appears to others. Depression is more likely to occur in the physically ill, among the widowed and the retired than in the healthy, married and employed. The depressed person experiences physical aches and pains, fatigue, difficulty in remembering, eating problems, difficulty in early morning rising and futility in so doing.

Masked depression is difficult to identify in older people. As in younger people, withdrawal, somatic complaints, functional slowness and apathy are the principal symptoms, but in the case of older adults there is little self-report of depression. Hence it may be difficult to ascertain whether physical symptoms are psychological in nature, indicators of a physical problem, or both. Levy *et al.* (1980) pointed out that reluctance to respond to questions during an interview is frequently ascribed to 'just old age', whereas it could more appropriately be attributed to depression.

Two behavioural manifestations of depression among the ageing are alcoholism and suicide (Levy *et al.*, 1980). Schuckit and Miller (1975) concluded that between 2 and 10% of older adults have alcohol problems, with higher rates for widowers and the chronically ill. Apart from depression, other causes of alcoholism in old age include feelings of loss of status and poverty (Pascarelli and Fischer, 1974), feelings of uselessness and dependency (Bergman and Amir, 1973) and loneliness (Osgood, 1991).

Tolerance for alcohol is reduced with age. Perlmutter and Hall (1992) indicated that older adults appear to metabolize alcohol more slowly, while Zarit (1980) pointed out that it may cause greater changes in brain chemistry and be more toxic than when they were younger. Loftus (1980) spoke of its interference with the formation of new memories. However, the pattern of alcohol consumption may be significant. Parker and Noble (1977) found that, if men customarily drank heavily at a single sitting, cognitive processes and memory were impaired, whereas for those who consumed the same amount of alcohol but spread it over time, there was no sign of impairment.

Suicide is a real possibility in depressed older adults. In the US, approximately 25% of all suicide victims are over 60 (Richardson *et al.*, 1989). Zarit (1980) found that suicide reached a peak between the ages of 80 and 84, when the rate is 0.051%. Between the ages of 65 and 69, male suicides outnumber female suicides 4 to 1, but by age 85 the ratio increases to about 12 to 1 (Bromley, 1988). Tatai and Tatai (1991) confirmed this high rate of male suicide for Japan, where suicide among older male adults accounts for 24% of all suicides.

Problems such as depression, alcohol and suicide in old age are more likely to occur among males, according to Aiken (1982), since the assertive, achievement-oriented role of a typical middle-aged man is not as conducive to retirement as the more passive, nurturant role assumed by a typical middle-aged woman (Aiken, 1982). Butler (1975b) agreed when he suggested that loss of status for older white men was a cause of suicide. Other suicide-inducing factors included the desire to protect finances for a surviving wife, or a decision to avoid physical helplessness or pain. In attempted suicides, 16.7% of male cases and 5.7% of female cases were diagnosed as alcoholic (Hawton and Fagg, 1990). Loss of power and control was cited as the main reason by Osgood (1991), although she viewed depression as the main factor in suicide in older adults, a viewpoint supported by Venkoba Rao (1991). Other psychological causes identified by Osgood included loss of spouse, a dysfunctional family or a family history of suicide, increasing mental health problems in late life and relational problems.

Social isolation appears to be a factor in the suicide of older depressed people. In Arizona, men who committed suicide over a 5-year period had recently lost a confidant and had paid fewer social visits than men who died from natural causes (Miller, 1978). The same study found that three-quarters of suicides were committed within 1 month of a visit to a physician. Richardson *et al.* (1989) found that most suicidal older adults look to their doctor for help, although they may not express their suicidal intention. The visit more often took the form of seeking assistance for depression (Casey, 1994). Suggested approaches to resolve this problem will be outlined later.

PSYCHOSEXUAL DIFFICULTIES

The attitude of the older adult to sexual activity was summed up by Bowman and Engle (1963). Older people 'feel uncertain about their capacities and are very self-conscious about their power to please. They are afraid of having their pride hurt. They feel lonely, isolated, deprived, unwanted'.

The ability to have sexual intercourse is often associated with virility. Impotence can arise from lack of blood supply to the penis and from male hormone imbalance. Walsh (1992) stated that impotence 'can be summed up as the inability to obtain an erection which is hard enough to achieve penetration or to maintain an erection for long enough to satisfy his partner'. Impotence causes uncertainty regarding sexual capacity. Once it occurs, many males will eschew sexual activity voluntarily rather than risk losing face in repeated attempts (Masters and Johnson, 1966).

Impotence, according to Aiken (1989), is usually a temporary condition produced by emotional stress, medication, overdrinking or overeating, and lack of interest in one's sexual partner. It may also arise from physical or mental fatigue. Some degenerative conditions can cause impotence, as can the removal of the prostate gland. Retrograde or premature ejaculation may be related to diabetes (Weg, 1983a). Felstein (1983) held that the effects of drug treatment for hypertension can cause impotence. Possible consequences of damage to the autonomic nervous system as a result of stroke include partial erections, impaired ejaculation or total impotence in males, and decreased lubrication in females (Renshaw, 1981). Aiken (1989) pointed out that the problem of impotence may be further compounded by the resulting behaviour, which frequently leads to avoidance of sex or indulgence in alcohol.

Hersen and Bellak (1981) stated that a frequent belief reported in the literature is that 90% of erectile insufficiency is pathogenic. However, they point out that non-diagnosis of organic pathology due to lack of information on erectile dysfunction or insufficient examination by physicians has contributed to this high figure. Walsh (1992) claimed that, in 75% of cases, physiological or organic problems are at the root of impotence, although it is frequently aggravated by performance anxiety. However, treatment reported by Walsh, in the form of a combined vasodilator and muscle relaxant, has had promising results: 60% of all patients were able to perform normally after 6 months, 20% needed further time and the remaining 20% needed to stay on the treatment permanently. The report does not give precise statistics on the age categories used, apart from stating that they were 'as young as 22 and as old as 86'. A breakdown of these figures would be helpful in ascertaining the extent to which older men seek help for impotence and the extent to which treatment is effective. From the perspective of the counsellor it is important that medical referral be made in the first instance to eliminate possible physiological or pathological problems.

It is less likely that women will experience difficulty with respect to sexual intercourse in old age. However, some older women may suffer pain or irritation, which can occur due to reduced levels of lubrication, thinning of the vaginal walls, changes in vaginal tissue tone and shortening of vaginal length (Corby and Solnick, 1980).

Becoming impotent may be a fear of the male in old age, but women may become anxious about being less attractive to their partner. White (1975), in clinical interviews with eight female nursing-home residents, found that they all thought themselves to be unattractive to members of the opposite sex. Further support was obtained by Ludeman (1981), who found from interviews that 15 previously married women over the age of 60 considered themselves to be sexually unattractive. Victor (1987) stated that, as well as having lost physical attractiveness, older women are inhibited because they can no longer fulfil their reproductive role. Scrutton (1989) pointed out that women suffer from male-dominated ideas, being reared to the expectation that they should be sexually attractive. Since the numbers participating in the above studies were small, further investigations with larger samples are needed. Given recent advances on equality issues, physical and sexual attractiveness as a function of gender needs to be investigated.

To summarize, fear of impotence is probably the greatest difficulty for men while decreased physical attractiveness and its association with sex may be a major problem for women, although both areas need further empirical investigation. Males with impotence problems should seek aid in a clinic devoted to sexual counselling, while females may be helped by either gestalt or person-centred therapy (see Chapter 7).

ANTICIPATION OF DEATH

It comes to all to die sooner or later. Yet despite the universality of this fact, Wass (1977) found that nearly two-thirds of the books on ageing gave less than 1% of their space to the subject of death.

For many individuals anticipation of death may not be confined to their later years. Events in life, such as the deaths of parents, siblings and friends, may initiate awareness of one's own death. When I commiserated with a friend recently on the death of her 50-year-old brother, she replied, 'Mary [his wife] was not ready for it. The rest of us will be now'.

In a study of black Americans, Japanese Americans, Mexican Americans and white Americans, Kalish and Reynolds (1976) found that over one-third felt that the death of someone close had influenced their attitude towards death. Variation between the four groups was as follows: Japanese Americans 41%, Hispanics 39%, white Americans 35% and black Americans 26%. Shneidman (1970, 1973), in a study of 30 000 readers of *Psychology Today*, found that the death of someone else was the second most frequently mentioned (19%) influence on attitude towards death, while introspection and meditation was the most influential factor. Shneidman's sample was biased, in that 65% were female, 79% under 35, 53% single, 66% had high incomes, 19% were college educated and 72% were self-declared liberals. Future studies need to include the influence of introspection and meditation on attitude towards death.

Reflecting on death may trigger various fears in older adults: the fear of dying on one's own; annihilation and abandonment; what comes after death; and the moment of death itself. Ward (1979) held that fear of death is greater among older people who have less education, live alone, have greater feelings of rejection and depression, and have less belief in the afterlife, while Aiken (1989) mentioned that old people who are in poor physical or mental health or have a disabled spouse, dependent children or important goals yet to be attained were more afraid of death. Yet

Peterson (1980), in a study of older adults, found that religious faith comforted 35% when they thought of death, while 40% rely on their achievements and 25% depend on love from family and friends.

Death is viewed differently by older and younger adults. Binstock and Chanas (1985) stated that several studies show that older adults are more willing to talk about death than other age groups. Kalish and Reynolds (1976) found that older individuals were less likely either to alter lifestyle or attempt to complete projects. They were, however, more likely to adopt a more contemplative approach to impending death than younger adults. Cultural differences also exist. Fear of death was greatest in the Mexican (33%) and Japanese Americans (31%) and least in the white (22%) and black (19%) Americans. However, over half were unafraid; each of the four groups was in the 50–54% range.

Erikson (1976) held that acceptance of death was dependent on how one identified with the human race rather than on religious belief. The research of Kalish (1976) is interesting in this regard. He found that the greatest fear of death was experienced by people who were undecided about religion or had inconsistent beliefs. The strongly religious and confirmed atheists reported the fewest death fears. In a sample of 100 dying people, Kellehear and Lewin (1988–89) found that most took leave of their families and friends, although the manner in which they did so varied. While some preferred to do so early, others liked to leave it as near to the end as possible.

In a study of adults between the ages of 64 and 96, Marshall (1980) found that five circumstances could result in people losing all fear of death or wanting to die. These were: being totally inactive; being completely useless; becoming a burden to one's family; losing one's mental competence; and deteriorating in health. Kastenbaum (1981) found that over 25% of a group of terminally ill patients wanted to die soon. From a counselling perspective, both fear and lack of fear of death are important dimensions.

Kastenbaum (1992) found that denial, anger and depression appear and reappear during the dying process. In addition, dying people may fluctuate greatly between their need to know or not to know. Their personalities and coping capacities will determine, to a large extent, the manner in which they will deal with news of their impending death. Furthermore, Kastenbaum (1975) found that the concerns of the dying are dependent on gender. Men were more aware of pain and dependency, whereas women were more conscious of the effect of the illness on others. Yet many aspects remain unanswered, such as the effect of environmental influences, family and friends, and the amount of personal internal and external control.

It certainly seems that older individuals think more about death, are more accepting of it than younger people and are less likely to reorganize their lives because of impending death. Counselling the dying person will be discussed in the next chapter.

INSOMNIA

Another perceived problem for older adults is insomnia. As individuals age, changes occur in their sleep behaviour. In a US national survey, Mellinger et al. (1985) reported that serious insomnia was found in 25% of the 65–79-year-old age group, while less severe insomnia was discovered in a further 20%. They defined insomnia as considerable difficulty in falling asleep and/or staying asleep within the previous 12 months. Approximately 90% of 60–90-year-olds complain of insomnia at some time (Miles and Dement, 1980).

Dunkell (1977) outlined three kinds of insomnia: sleep-onset insomnia, where an individual cannot get to sleep because they may replay what happened that day or is likely to happen the following day; sleep maintenance insomnia, which Birren and Sloane (1980) estimated affects 50% of insomniacs; and terminal insomnia, where the sleeper wakes at an early hour and is unable to go back to sleep.

Older adults may experience more difficulty in falling asleep, early-morning awakening and daytime naps. Birren and Schaie (1977) claim that fragmentation of night-time sleep, with wakefulness and decreased slow-wave sleep, seems to reflect normal sleep in old age, since these characteristics were observed in healthy older adults who were screened for absence of sleep disorders. The amount of REM (rapid eye movement, i.e. dreaming) sleep remains unchanged until extreme old age, but non-REM sleep, which is deeper and restorative, decreases significantly (Berger, 1994). The sleep of older adults is shallow and numerous transient arousals (3–15 seconds) occur. Frequent awakenings during the second half of the night were reported by Webb (1982) and Hayashi and Endo (1982), who found that they averaged 21 times. This supports Zepelin et al.'s (1984) finding that older adults are more easily aroused from night-time sleep by auditory stimuli. Carskadon and Dement (1982) found that the extent of night-time arousals predicts the degree of daytime sleepiness. These arousals lead to problems in daytime functioning and alertness (Carskadon and Dement, 1982; Carskadon et al., 1982). If older adults nap during the day less sleep may be needed at night, but this is dependent on the length of naps. Kimmel (1990) stated that naps under 50 minutes do not affect falling asleep, and add to the total amount obtained.

Changes in sleep patterns in old age may develop into insomnia if people have the same sleep expectations they had when younger. Edinger et al. (1992) and Morin and Azrin (1988) found that if older adults understood that different sleeping patterns were normal, then they coped better and controlled both wakefulness and tiredness. However, certain practices affect the sleep–wake cycle: waking up at the same time each day is more beneficial than retiring at the same time each night: the person should not go to bed until they are sleepy, and engaging in some activity is best when they are unable to return to sleep.

There are gender differences with respect to sleep behaviour. Older women are more likely to complain of sleep disturbance and to be given sleeping pills (Miles and Dement, 1980). This may be due to the fact that older women find sleep deprivation to be more mood-disturbing than do older men (Reynolds *et al.*, 1986). Yet Reynolds *et al.* (1986) found that older women had better recovery sleep after 36 hours' sleep deprivation than older men, since they had longer uninterrupted sleep and more slow-wave sleep. Sleep-disordered breathing increases with age, but is more common in men than in women (Busse and Blazer, 1989).

Insomnia is often attributed to differing causes: daytime naps; depression; anxiety; illness; pain; drugs; change of environment; fear of death; uncomfortable sleeping arrangements; noisy environments (Birren and Sloane, 1980). In a study which compared 42 older insomniacs with 30 older adults without insomnia, Morin and Gramling (1989) found that insomniacs had more symptoms of depression and anxiety than those without insomnia. In addition, they showed greater discrepancies between their current sleep patterns and sleep requirement expectations. However, both groups engaged in daytime napping to the same extent, and did not differ in the amount of pain experienced or drug usage (excluding sleeping tablets).

Sleep disturbance is closely associated with bereavement, particularly on the death of a spouse. Sadavoy *et al.* (1991) point out that persistent sleep loss in bereavement may lead not only to depression but also to self-medication with alcohol and sleeping tablets. Sleeping tablets may increase the problem of insomnia (Davies *et al.*, 1986; Woodruff, 1985; Aber and Webb, 1986). Mulling over relationship difficulties can also prevent sleep. Butler and Lewis (1977) pointed out that it can also occur as a consequence of sexual deprivation, while Cartensen and Edelstein (1987) mentioned habitual heavy drinking, caffeine and nicotine, stress and inactivity. Bladder pressure can also lead to arousal from sleep.

In general the causes and consequences of insomnia are poorly understood. However, sleep-related behaviour often precipitates a family's decision to institutionalize an older adult (Rabins, 1982), hence there is an urgent need for further research in the area. Counselling can help older adults to understand that a different sleeping pattern is normal in old age. It can identify possible causes of insomnia and enable them to choose behaviours that will reduce the possibility of sleep reduction.

SUCCESSFUL AGEING: PERSONAL GROWTH

Discussion in this chapter has centred around manifest problems of old age. Individuals come to counselling to seek solutions to such problems; however, counselling not only provides solutions but can also enhance personal growth. Counselling for personal development is based on a model of the person which views emotional, social and spiritual growth as areas which may be enhanced until the end of life. The focus is on achieving maximum life satisfaction. Such an approach is, by its very nature, optimistic and refutes Stuart-Hamilton's (1994) assertion that 'The best therapies can do is help the elderly cope with their problems'.

Most of the 256 older adults in O'Leary and Kelly's (1990) sample were content with their lives. A research study by Flanagan (1978) obtained similar findings. In a US nationwide survey he investigated the relationship between age and quality of life in three groups aged 30, 50 and 70 respectively. Only slight differences were found between the 50-year-old and the 70-year-old group: 85% of the total reported that their lives were 'good, very good or excellent'. They considered three factors necessary for quality of life: the first included health, work and material aspects; the second related to having both close friends and a possibility to socialize; and the third emphasized the need for cognitive ability and creative expression.

Personal growth groups offer opportunities for the development of a network of friendships and social support. Friendship support is significantly related to psychological wellbeing (Israel et al., 1983) and is one of the most important factors associated with positive changes in health status among both married and widowed older respondents (Ferraro et al., 1984). Social support is inversely related to mortality in older adults (Blazer, 1982), but is positively related to life satisfaction, morale and wellbeing (Mancini, 1980; Hoyt et al., 1980; Tesch et al., 1981). From a review of the literature on social support Antonucci and Jackson (1987) concluded that social support can be beneficial to effective functioning and health in older people. Kimmel (1990) stated: 'Considerable research has explored the importance of social support for the elderly (Kahn et al., 1987) and, in general, the data affirm that social support is an important determinant of wellbeing'.

Medley (1976) suggested that five factors contributed to effective personal growth in older adults in a wide variety of situations: a sense of accomplishment; a sense of independence; satisfaction in interpersonal relations; interest in activity; and flexibility or willingness to change. Personal growth work allows older adults the opportunity to explore the presence or absence of these factors in their lives. It focuses on increasing awareness within individuals that they can be self-supporting in many areas. Lowenthal et al. (1975) found that the sense of inner control was the most important factor in whether a person dealt successfully with a major life transition. A sense of mastery develops as older people become aware of their emotions and what elicits them. They come to realize that these are not fixed factors to be accepted, but rather dynamic and changing possibilities. The perception of freedom enhances their responsibility for new meanings and directions (Polster and Polster, 1973). Attention to personal growth enables older adults to deal with the different transitions occurring in their lives, so that they can profit from the greater freedom in relation to time and responsibility. They become aware that new directions are possible, establish new goals for themselves and begin to implement them in their lives.

The main goals of personal growth are increased awareness of oneself and an enhancement of the quality of contact with others. This gives people the opportunity to recognize their needs and to act upon them. They focus on their present experience. Polster and Polster (1973) stated that 'awareness is a continuous means for keeping up with one's self'. Older adults are able to perceive their lives as they are right now, and this awareness allows the possibility of choice: the choice to keep the more enhancing aspects and to rid themselves of elements which are not satisfying. In awareness the person's uniqueness is discovered and expressed.

In personal growth work older adults allow more of their experience into their awareness. They recognize their thoughts, feelings and sensations and integrate them with their behaviour. As a result they can, if they wish, change their way of experiencing themselves and their lives. Page and Berkow (1994) stated that to grow in awareness individuals need to believe that there is more to be gained by acknowledging experience than by denying it. People learn that by integrating their feelings, thoughts, actions and sensations, they will come to be at peace with themselves. Personal growth allows older individuals to be aware of their experience and to enjoy a whole range of emotions. They notice how they interrupt the experiencing of emotion at the level of expression. Egan (1973) stated: 'Emotional expression is still undoubtedly a far greater problem than emotional overcontrol'.

Personal growth considers how one communicates with others and how to increase the quality of that communication. Deeper contact with others occurs through the elimination of cliché talk. Cliché talk was defined by Egan (1973) as the use of 'anemic language, talk for the sake of talk, conversation without depth, language that neither makes contact with the other nor reveals the identity of the speaker ... it fosters ritualistic, rather than fully human, contact ... it fills interactional space and time without adding meaning for it is superficial and comes without reflection'. Cliché talk is usually shallow and consists of token contacts, such as 'Good morning. How are you? It is raining again today'. Of course the culture in which an interaction takes place is of significance.

Working in a personal growth context allows older individuals to explore their contact functions. Seven such functions were identified by Polster and Polster (1973): seeing, hearing, touching, tasting, smelling, talking and movement. Each of these can be used in a way which increases or lessens communication with others. Communication can be interrupted or hindered by looking away from others; not listening to them; speaking in a low voice so that one is not heard; maintaining a rigid posture in interaction; not shaking hands or hugging friends when meeting them after an interval apart; not smelling the flowers given as a gift; leaving presents unopened.

Special difficulties with respect to contact functions may occur for older adults. Although one-third of all elderly people find that inadequate hearing hampers them in their daily lives (Whitbourne, 1985), only 10% use hearing aids (Olsho *et al.*, 1985). A valuable dimension of personal growth work for older adults who are beginning to experience hearing difficulties includes the exploration of the possibility of acquiring a hearing aid in order to increase communication. Some may find that they do not need to speak as loudly as others may need to speak to them.

In personal growth work older adults can explore their need for others to speak loudly and the necessity of asking them to do so in order to improve contact. In this way, impaired hearing need not result in impaired social communication and possible isolation. Learning to lipread at the first noticeable decrease in hearing ability may prevent long-term disruption in communication. The participation of a hearing-impaired older person can raise the awareness of the other group participants of the necessity of speaking more clearly. For older adults with reduced mobility, exploration of what is or is not appropriate movement is important. Decreased vision may be compensated for somewhat by an increase in the use of touch.

Personal growth counselling has developed within the humanistic–existential tradition of counselling, an approach which will be considered in more detail in Chapter 7. Chapter 6 outlines counselling approaches appropriate to older adults.

6 | Counselling approaches appropriate to older adults

The pioneer of counselling with older adults, Lillian Martin, developed the Martin method in San Francisco in the 1930s. Counselling was problem focused and lasted approximately five sessions. It included a comprehensive assessment of the life pattern of individuals. Counsellors emphasized the strengths of clients and encouraged and inspired them. Positive affirmations were used and homework assignments included daily activities (Karpf, 1992). Since then a few approaches have dealt specifically with the elderly: Sherman's (1981) integrative approach, Butler's (1963) life review therapy and Fry's (1984) counselling of depression.

COUNSELLING APPROACHES DEALING SPECIFICALLY WITH THE OLDER ADULT

The integrative approach

The central objective of Sherman's (1981) integrative approach is to identify, use and enhance the natural resources of the person. The underlying theme is that certain capacities and strengths are normally developed in the course of ageing which enable older people to overcome the demoralization that accompanies the losses and problems of growing old. When these capacities have not been used because of circumstances or events, they should be uncovered, strengthened and developed in the counselling process.

Sherman (1981) proposed a treatment continuum which takes into account every aspect of the older person's life. He outlined four stages which can be worked through in the counselling process, although not every older person needs to go through all the stages: one begins where one finds the client. In stage one, the importance of material needs in the lives of many older people is recognized, e.g. health, housing, physical and financial security. Sherman holds that critical and stressful material needs have first to be met before individuals can turn to their emotional needs. At this stage of intervention counsellors provide emotional support and encouragement, as well as practical guidance in using the services available. Their role is largely supportive and directive, yet they avoid the development of undue dependence on the part of the client.

The counselling objectives of stage two are more psychological or personal than material or situational. The counsellor is called on to provide support and coping strategies in order to stabilize the self-esteem and sustain the morale and coping efforts of the client. In the following example, Joseph, a 92-year-old, tells the group of a past experience:

Joseph: I walked the white line always.
Therapist: Really?
Joseph: Always the white line. I am afraid that I fell off of it often (Laughing). (Turns towards therapist). Did you climb Croagh Patrick?
Therapist: No Joseph, did you?
Joseph: Twenty-nine times.
Therapist: You climbed it twenty-nine times? My goodness!
Joseph: Yes, Yes (Rubbing his hands gleefully). I organized pilgrimages to it from the parish of Curraroe.
Therapist: From the parish of Curraroe? And how was it to climb Croagh Patrick?
Joseph: Oh! It was lovely, a beautiful view of Clew bay.
Therapist: Clew bay is beautiful.
Joseph: Twenty-nine times I did it.
Therapist: You are a good organizer then?
Joseph: Oh yes.
Therapist: A good organizer.
Joseph: Thank God.

Through reminiscence Joseph was able to recall pleasant times and achievements in the past and to acknowledge his organizational abilities.

At the third stage the two main elements are coping skills and cognitive mastery, reflecting Sherman's (1981) adoption of the techniques of cognitive psychotherapy. The naturally occurring use of a cognitive strategy for coping is reflected from the following disclosure by Sarah, an 89-year-old resident of a nursing home:

Sarah: Every night I pray and I go off to sleep. As I told you before I have to keep Grandad out of my head because he is alone at home and we were 59 years married last week.

Stage four deals with changes in basic attitudes towards self and towards one's life. The techniques in stages three and four are more cognitive and insight oriented than the techniques of stages one and two.

In Sherman's (1981) approach the centrality of the relationship with the counsellor is emphasized. Accurate empathy, warmth and genuineness on the part of the counsellor are seen as essential factors in effectiveness. Sherman uses natural helping networks such as family, friends, neighbours and peers in both support and therapeutic groups.

The approach is optimistic and positive in orientation: while acknowledging the negative and painful aspects of growing old, the main focus is on the strengths and capacities of individuals. This approach is based on a developmental model of ageing, with its emphasis on older individuals' ability both to adjust to life's stresses and to continue to grow and to be in control of their life.

Life review therapy

Although the concept of reminiscence in old age received attention in the 1930s from developmental psychologist Charlotte Buehler (Coleman, 1986), it was Butler who revived interest in its value in 1963 (Butler, 1982). He viewed reminiscence as a normal part of old age. Formerly it was viewed negatively as 'living in the past', with overtones of pathology, denial, dependence and regression. As Coleman asserted, ' it has changed in connotation from negative to positive – from being generally perceived as a symptom of mental deterioration to being valued as a normal if not essential component in successful ageing'.

Five reasons were outlined by Norris (1986) for the importance of reminiscence for older adults:

- it highlights their assets rather than their disabilities;
- it enhances their feelings of self-worth and esteem;
- it helps them to recognize their individuality and identity;
- it aids the process of life review;
- it is an enjoyable and stimulating experience.

Recognition of the importance of reminiscence in ageing and adjustment has grown remarkably in recent years (Coleman, 1986). Reminiscence serves both a communicative and an expressive function

(Butler, 1988). It communicates to other people the ideas and beliefs that form the content of the older adult's experience, and it also allows the ageing person to express feelings and share previous life experiences with other group members. In the following example, Hannah, an 87-year-old woman, shares with the group her relationship with her niece:

Hannah: I had a very happy married life but my niece was the most important person in my life.

Therapist: Your niece?

Hannah: She lived with me in Galway from 5 years of age. But I had to go back to England and she had to return to her father since he would not allow her to come to England with her sister and myself. She stayed with him 7 or 8 years. Unfortunately she got multiple sclerosis.

Therapist: How was that for you?

Hannah: She was not invalided for a long time. We went everywhere together. We went to France and to Fatima.

Therapist: Mmhmm.

Hannah: We went to Sweden. We went every place together except public houses because she did not like them. (Laughs).

Therapist: She did not like public houses and you did?

Hannah: Exactly. She had a very happy time and it was a very very sad moment 12 months last February when I lost her - a very sad moment because we lived so happily together. When I found that she was becoming more invalided, I came back to Ireland so that she would have her sisters to look after her.

Therapist: So it was very sad for you when you lost your niece?

Hannah: Yes I had thought that I would die first. I could not keep her standing on the Tuesday so I called in the doctor to her. Even though she had MS we were very happy together.

Therapist: So you liked being together a lot?

Hannah: Every night we would sit by the fire telling stories to each other and watching television, laughing and joking all the time.

Therapist: So you had many happy times with her?

Hannah: Yes. I went with her into hospital on the Wednesday in the ambulance. She was a week in there and I was getting worried that she was not coming home. They rang me from the hospital on Friday to tell me that she had passed away.

Therapist: It must have been very difficult for you?

Hannah: The heart.

Therapist: She died from a heart condition?

Hannah: Yes. I missed her so much. I could not do anything without her. I stayed there for 12 months but it was not home anymore.

Therapist: When she was not around.

Hannah: Yes when she was not there.

Therapist: Mmhmm.

Hannah: So I came in here. And we are very happy here the lot of us together.

Rose: We get on so well together.

Hannah: Yes great.

Therapist: So you are happy to be here.

Hannah: Yes indeed. She was very happy up to the day she died.

Therapist: She was probably very pleased to have you with her all the time.

Hannah: Yes she was. She was more like a daughter to me than a niece.

Therapist: How would you describe her Hannah?

Hannah: She was very like her mother, very fair and very slim but when she got into the wheelchair she put on weight.

Therapist: And how did you feel when she got MS?

Hannah: Fine. She had it since she was 25 and she did not die until she was 67.

Therapist: So she had a long life?

Hannah: She was very happy. She lived with it and she would say to me ' I have got it, I will live with it and no more about it'.

Therapist: She was very optimistic?

Hannah: She had a great sense of humour and a great religion.

Therapist: And how was it for you?

Hannah: I was happy as the days are long helping her because I was the only help she had.

Therapist: She depended on you?

Hannah: She had sisters but they were all married and they had their own children while I had no children. She filled in the gap as she always said. (Laughs).

Therapist: For you?

Hannah: Yes since I had no family. I filled in the gap for her too.

Hannah went on to speak of her husband and another niece, and concluded by saying ' That is my life. I have a good life to look back on'. Through reminiscing in this way Hannah was able to recall the many happy times she shared with her niece as well as re-experiencing the sadness she experienced around her death. Other group participants were able to get to know her at a deeper level through this disclosure of a very important dimension of her life to date. She was also able to acknowledge how happy they all were together in the nursing home, a fact that was very evident to the author on her visits to the group.

Lidz (1983) holds that reminiscence permits individuals to bring closure to their lives, and to evaluate how earlier events fit together in their overall life pattern. Coleman (1986) holds that reminiscence pays attention to the very real problems of adjustment that face older people. McMahon and Rhudick (1964) see a positive use for reminiscence, which is the role traditionally ascribed to older people in primitive societies as bearers and transmitters of their culture's stories and traditions. While this storytelling function has been devalued in modern society, there are signs of a renewed interest among psychologists and researchers in oral history and the memories of ordinary people, as a means to understanding older people and their needs. These positive aspects of reminiscence highlight its value in counselling the older adult.

Not all would agree that reminiscence in old age is an unmixed blessing. Butler (1988) himself stressed that the individual may remain obsessed with events and actions, obtain no solution, and develop chronic feelings of guilt and depression. Reminiscence may be unhealthy if it prevents people considering their lives in the present and focuses exclusively on the past. In a review of research on this topic, Coleman (1986) found that, taken altogether, no evidence exists for the positive value of reminiscence.

The life review is not synonymous with but includes reminiscence. Westcott (1983) equated the two terms and claimed that Butler used them interchangeably to remove the general negativism associated with the term reminiscence. This contradicts Butler and Lewis (1982) themselves, who distinguished between simple reminiscence and life review therapy, which they saw as a more structured and purposeful concept. The confusion which has surrounded the use of reminiscence is illustrated by Haight (1988), who found that 97 articles on the topic defined it differently.

Reminiscence therapy may proceed in an unstructured manner and may use a method similar to the free association of psychoanalysis. Life review therapy, on the other hand, has a definite structure and is characterized by the progressive return to consciousness of past experience, and in particular the resurgence of unresolved conflicts (Butler, 1982). It helps to reorganize and reintegrate these conflicts. Life review therapy involves the taking of an extensive autobiography from the older person, and other family members if appropriate. Items such as family albums, scrapbooks and searching out of genealogies may be helpful to fill the complete picture. If the older person has married children, feelings about being a grandparent are important. Butler and Lewis see this process as a re-examination of one's life that should result in the expiation of guilt, the resolution of intrapsychic conflicts, the reconciliation of family relationships, and the renewal of responsibility for creating a meaningful life. Life review therapy focuses older individuals on a specific event, topic or phase of life in order to evaluate its psychological relevance. If any of these events trigger negative emotions, attention is given to them to ensure their resolution.

The life review is a process that people may have to undergo if they are to come to terms with their lives to date. Storandt (1983) points out that the idea of the life review is congruent with Erikson's (1950) final stage of personality development. It is a process whereby acceptance of a person's life to date is achieved or not. Butler (1963) initially viewed the life review as providing the opportunity to set things right before life's end. Lewis and Butler (1974) point out that all the truly important emotional options remain available to people throughout life. In reviewing the past an opportunity is provided to choose how one wishes to spend the future.

Butler (1963) spoke of various manifestations of the life review. Initially it may be observed in brief stray thoughts about oneself. Other indications of a life review process may include dreams, imagery of past events and mirror-gazing. Regarding the latter, Butler noted a common phenomenon among older adults, namely to look in a mirror and speak to the reflection. All of these can be beneficial if integrated into the process of life review therapy. However, Butler believed that the life review process was a universal occurrence among older adults, but that where it proceeds in isolation it may result in severe depression, panic, guilt or obsessional ruminations. Negative consequences were also likely in people whose concern had always been with the future, and who now found this future diminishing. Those who recollect consciously injuring others in the past, and who cannot now rectify any damage done, can have similar negative reactions.

Waters (1984) agreed that life reviews are positive, but with the caveat that they may be painful for those who view themselves as failures, or who may have put great emphasis on the future throughout their lives, and for those who may have attached great significance to their now deteriorating physical appearance. A life review process structured to highlight wins and losses helps the counsellor to understand the aetiology of low self-esteem problems and the specific accomplishments of the individual client's life. When family relationships are not satisfying for older individuals, a life review will allow hurts to surface, to be dealt with and reinterpreted. However, hurts are only dealt with in life review therapy from a cognitive perspective. Their affective components are not dealt with sufficiently.

Life review therapy can be carried out individually or in a group, with counsellors using various techniques to encourage those in therapy to reminisce. Scrutton (1989) found that it can be adapted when counselling older people with problems relating to retirement, dependence, depression, ill-health, bereavement and death. Since life review therapy does not focus on current problems in the lives of older adults, it may initially present a difficulty to counsellors who concentrate on the here and now in their work with clients. It could be useful for these counsellors to keep the value of the life review approach in mind, and to find ways of integrating it with their usual way of working.

While noting the benefits of life review therapy in some instances, O'Brien *et al.* (1979) advocated the use of a teaching model by counsellors to assist older clients replace lost functioning. They outline nine structural techniques: family albums and scrapbooks; poetry; quotations and prayers; music; arts; crafts and recipes; TV and films; cartoons and field trips.

Photographs allow unfinished feeling regarding significant people to emerge as well as highlighting former pleasant experiences. Quotations and prayers may be sources of consolation if people reflect and meditate on them. Music, like photographs, can allow special joys to be re-experienced and repressed feelings to be examined. The following excerpt from a group therapy session illustrates this.

Therapist: What I would like you to concentrate on today is how do you have fun now in your life. (There is a few minutes' silence as the group does this task.)

Ruth: Every night I pull down the curtain and I think of some street and the people who lived in it. I ask myself what song used that person sing. I love music.

Therapist: So that way it comes alive to you again?

Ruth: Yes. By concentrating on the song I remember many of my happy times.

Esther: I love listening to music or singing. I love both of them.

Therapist: So you love listening to music as well.

Esther: Oh God I do! I love it.

Therapist: So have you a tape recorder you can listen to?

Esther: No. Nothing.

Ruth: Let us sing ' Galway Bay'. (Sings the song while others join in.)

Therapist: How was that for you Joseph?

Joseph: I cannot sing but I loved it.

Therapist: Did you know the song?

Joseph: I did.

In this passage, Ruth's love of song enables her to recreate happy times. At the same time Esther's love of music and singing was identified through her sharing. Later in the group, the therapist explored with Esther how she might obtain a tape recorder.

The creativity of individuals is often expressed through arts, crafts and recipes. Recalling these to mind can often initiate fresh creativity. With the increased amount of time available to them, watching TV and films can be a frequent activity of older adults. Storylines can often recall past experience. Cartoons often portray older adults, and the counsellor can use these to enable older people to confront their feelings about being old. Anger, resentment and laughter are possible emotions that can emerge. Finally, field trips to places associated with older adults in the past can be catalysts in the counselling process. All of these techniques help strengthen the gains of the past and deal with the losses, in order that the person may be free to view old age as an exciting period of life.

Life enhancement counselling is an expansion of life review which takes account of ecological assessment and intervention. Ecological assessment identifies environmental sources of stress and the resources available to older people which can enhance current life experiences. The assessment attempts to identify transactions that currently affect their lives, and also tries to identify which resources could facilitate improved personal and social relationships. There are three phases in ecological intervention: testing the validity of the identified resources, developing an ecological treatment plan and restructuring. The flexibility or rigidity of existing transactional patterns between older people and environmental resources is considered, and a plan is developed to restructure maladaptive person–environment transactions. Life enhancement counselling matches treatment to the client rather than the client to the treatment. Validational evidence for the model was first produced by Szapocznik *et al.* (1982).

Life enhancement counselling offers a creative alternative to pharmacotherapeutic treatment alone, using the older person's past strengths and competence in the context of the present. As such it represents an existential orientation to treatment that combines some of the methodology of reality therapy in its use of a treatment plan and of gestalt therapy in its living in the present. However, it requires much further elaboration, especially in the development of an ecological treatment plan.

Counselling depression in the elderly

Fry's (1984) approach to counselling depression in older adults emerged from a two-phase study of older adults themselves (see also Chapter 8). Several recurrent themes emerged from his interviews. The older adults expressed a need to strengthen their spiritual faith; to know their own worth; to be useful and worthwhile to others; to restore their declining energy; and to feel that they would be remembered and cherished after death. Fry proposed the unravelling of hopelessness themes in older adults as the first step in the treatment of depression.

Fry's (1984) suggested method of counselling the depressed older adult includes a relationship characterized by counsellor warmth and responsiveness, and an atmosphere free from all authoritative coercion and pressure. This is of particular importance in a nursing home setting, where residents and staff interact very closely together. The beginning of group therapy in such a setting is illustrated in the following transcript. The use of the tape recorder had already been discussed at this point.

Therapist: I want to assure you all that everything we discuss in the group is confidential. Nothing goes outside the group unless you give permission. Everything arising in the group is private.
Shirley: We do not tell anybody.
Therapist: That is right. Otherwise people may not feel free to speak.
Susan: That is a good idea.

Fry's approach is centred on the acceptance of the fundamental hypotheses of person-centred therapy, requiring counsellors to get behind clients' words of pessimism and into their feeling world. Older adults, more than any other group, need to experience unconditional positive regard to deal with their hopelessness and to verbalize their formerly inadmissible feelings of pessimism and despair. He also advocates Butler's (1963) life review therapy, which he sees as a process that can help older adults to conceptualize their lives over time and to cope with their sense of hopelessness regarding the future. If the older client is religious, Fry suggests that religion be enlisted as a powerful source for enhancing hope and faith for the future. With a client-oriented approach and a focus on the phenomenological world of the individual, depressed older individuals may receive the encouragement and affirmation that they need.

Sherman's (1981) integrative approach, Butler's (1963) life review therapy and Fry's (1984) counselling of depressed older adults are approaches which deal specifically with the elderly. Other approaches, although not especially designed for this group, have relevance insofar as they deal with issues that many older people encounter. Among these are Worden's (1983) grief counselling, Kubler-Ross's (1969) counselling of the dying and Natale's (1986) counselling for loneliness.

DEALING WITH PARTICULAR PROBLEMS IN OLD AGE

Grief counselling

Loss (see also Chapter 5) is one of the main issues with which adults who live to old age have to contend. The deaths of spouse and friends bring with them a period of mourning. Bowlby (1969a,b) and Parkes (1972) were among the first to deal with this topic. Bowlby found evidence for five stages in the process: concentration on the deceased; unresolved anger; appeals for help; despair and withdrawal; and reorganization and direction of love towards a new object.

Mourning was also perceived by Parkes (1972) as a process which develops in stages. The first stage is shock, followed by numbness, during which there is a lack of overt emotional responses. The next stage is characterized by pining and searching, as the individual becomes preoccupied with thoughts of the deceased. There is frequent recollection of the actual death and a feeling that an important aspect of one's own life is gone. The world now appears meaningless. When the permanence of the loss is recognized, this awareness may be accompanied by depression and apathy. Finally, recovery is heralded by a gradual reorganization of one's life. In the case of the loss of a spouse, the extent of the necessary reorganization will depend largely on how much individuals have relied upon their partners. The more self-sufficient they have been, the less reorganization is necessary.

If mourning is complete, the individual can recall the departed loved one without grief. In the following excerpt, John recalls his wife, Mary, without upset:

John: When I would bring visitors to the house, Mary would say as soon as they came in ' I wonder if they would like a cup of tea?'
Therapist: So she was a very kind person?
John: She would give you the nail off her finger.
Therapist: How long is she dead?
John: Nearly 17 years.
Therapist: So you were a long time without her before you came to the nursing home?
John: Oh I was.
Therapist: That must have been difficult for you?
John: Yes but I am never without her.
Therapist: She is with you always.
John: Absolutely. I still talk to her.

Whereas Bowlby (1969a,b) and Parkes (1972) dealt with the stages of normal mourning, it was Worden (1983) who outlined the procedures that help make grief counselling effective. He advocated counselling when the grief is prolonged or excessive and there are marked bodily or behavioural symptoms. The counsellor should set up the contract and establish an alliance with the client. Bereaved individuals need to realize that the person is dead or gone from their lives. Once this awareness has been achieved, feelings stimulated by these memories need to be identified and expressed. Worden pays particular attention to anger, sadness and anxiety, and suggests that anger should be effectively targeted while guilt needs to be evaluated and resolved. Sadness needs to be highlighted in that it is important that individuals know the reasons for their sadness. Bereaved individuals often feel that they cannot survive without the deceased. This is an anxiety that emerges from feelings of helplessness. The counsellor should help them to recognize the ways in which they managed on their own before the loss. This will help them to live independently again. Many find it difficult to enter new relationships because they think that this would be disloyal to the deceased. The emotional investment they had in the departed loved one has to be relocated in some new activities or relationships. The counsellor helps the bereaved person in this transition by acknowledging the finality of the loss and imagining the end of grieving.

Two critical times have been identified by Worden (1983) as important in the grieving process: 3 months after the event and the first anniversary. The counsellor should allow adequate time (at least 18 months) to counsel the bereaved. Sessions should be staggered at irregular intervals over the period. The counsellor needs to be able to interpret normal grieving behaviour for clients, since some bereaved people feel that they are becoming mentally unbalanced. As in all problems individual differences in clients will influence the form grieving will take. There is a need for continuing support over time by the counsellor of the bereaved, especially during the first year. Since bereavement accentuates coping styles and defences, the counsellor helps clients to examine these.

The ability to diagnose a complicated grief reaction is essential for the counsellor of older adults. Lazare (1979) identified 12 clues in this regard:

1. the inability of the person to speak of the deceased without intense grief;
2. some relatively minor event triggers off an intense grief reaction;
3. themes of loss emerge frequently in conversation;
4. the person is moved by the material possessions of the deceased;
5. the bereaved develops physical symptoms similar to those experienced by the deceased before death;
6. the individual makes radical changes in lifestyle, or excludes people or events associated with the deceased;
7. the person presents a long history of depression or experiences false euphoria;
8. the bereaved imitates the deceased;
9. the person exhibits a tendency to self-destructive impulses;
10. the individual experiences unaccountable sadness each year at anniversaries and holidays;

11. the bereaved develops a phobia concerning the illness from which the person died;
12. the client avoids visiting the graveyard or engaging in death-related rituals or activities.

Another approach to working through grief is described by Kelliher (1991). It is designed to assist those who have lost a spouse through death, separation or divorce. The emphasis is on sharing feelings in a person-centred framework. Possible problem areas are dealt with, including readjusting to single status; being alone or lonely; discovering and trusting oneself; being a single-parent family; relating to God and church; dealing with the deceased or ex-spouse; and accepting changes in relationships and social activities. The structure includes sharing by two facilitators who have undergone the experience, private reflection, and sharing feelings in a small group. The approach is one of the few that attends to the grief of individuals who lose a spouse through divorce. It also provides a relatively safe structure for those who are unused to dealing with feelings in a group. However, it fails to distinguish the process of grief from dying. It would seem more appropriate to use a staged approach to grief which has attended specifically to this experience.

Counselling of the dying

Insight into counselling the dying has mostly occurred through the work of Elisabeth Kubler-Ross (1969). From a study of more than 200 dying patients, she outlined five stages which characterize a person's reaction to dying. These are: denial, anger, bargaining, depression and acceptance. These can aid counsellors in understanding older dying people.

Denial serves the function of coping with the shock that death is imminent. When this information registers, the person can become angry and ask ' Why me?'. Realizing the anger is to no avail, the dying person then bargains with God or with the doctors. Both anger and bargaining are attempts to evade death. Once awareness of its inevitability emerges, depression may result. Kubler-Ross distinguished between reactive and preparatory depression. Reactive depression emerges when the impending loss of one's life reactivates unresolved losses in one's past. Emotions relating to these losses re-emerge since they form part of the unfinished business of the individual's life (cf. O'Leary, 1992). Having worked through these conflicts the person comes to accept the inevitability of death.

It is unlikely that every person moves through the five stages in sequence, and indeed in 1974 Kubler-Ross modified her original position. Dying people may fluctuate greatly between their need to know or not to know. Their personalities and coping capacities will, to a large extent, determine the manner in which they will deal with news of their impending death.

An alternative perception of the process of dying was presented by Pattison (1977). He identified three phases in the process of dying: the acute, the chronic living–dying, and the terminal. The acute period begins when an individual becomes aware that death is imminent. This results in anxiety and may include resentment and anger. In the chronic living–dying phase, the person may experience fear of the unknown, fear of suffering and pain, loneliness and sorrow. There may be a sense of losing one's body if the illness brings changes in it. Self-control may become less possible as either physical or mental capabilities become affected. There is a consequent loss of identity as contact with the body and mind diminishes. During the terminal phase the individual withdraws from people and events. The use of the word terminal is confusing: the word final may be more appropriate.

The work of both Kubler-Ross (1969) and Pattison (1977) highlights the process of dying rather than the actual moment of death itself. Kubler-Ross concentrated on the psychological processes while Pattison, in addition, attended to the physical changes. However, neither pays much attention to the presence or absence of pain. Shneidman (1973) pointed out that there was fluctuation in the emotions experienced, involving a constant interplay of hope and disbelief together with other moments which included terror, rage, surrender, disinterest, anguish and yearning.

Both Kubler-Ross (1969) and Pattison (1977) provided an initial framework for counsellors dealing with dying older people. Although Kubler-Ross originally conceived of them as stages, she later clarified her views when she stated: 'most of my patients have exhibited two or three stages simultaneously and these do not always occur in the same order' (Kubler-Ross, 1975). Yet many aspects of dying remain unexplored, such as the effect of environmental influences, family and friends, and the amount of personal external and internal control.

Counselling for loneliness

Counselling for loneliness received special attention from Natale (1986). He suggested that it is important to determine whether the loneliness is situational due to loss of spouse, friends, employment or declining physical abilities, or whether it is chronic and is the result of a lifelong lack of social skills. The following example illustrates an example of situational loneliness. Hilary was an 85-year-old who participated in a group in a home for old people in which she resided.

Hilary: One morning they gave me the tea with a teapot and I misjudged where the cup was when I was pouring the tea and I scalded my right leg.

Therapist: You scalded your right leg?

Hilary: Yes and it was very painful. But the worst part was that I was up there so long in the bedroom by myself that I got lonely. I had the radio but it was not the same as being with people.

Therapist: So you missed the other residents?

Hilary: Yes, especially being in the sitting room with them after lunch. I was really bored sitting in the corner of my room.

Therapist: Mmhmm. So you were really bored?

Hilary: Yes. I used to say to myself ' I hate this bed. I wish I could join the others in the sitting room'. But everyone of them used to come into my bedroom and ask me how I was.

Therapist: Mmhmm. How did that feel?

Hilary: It made me feel better. I realized that they cared about me.

In the above example Hilary's loneliness was related to being confined to her bedroom. Returning to the sitting room eliminated this feeling.

If loneliness is chronic and emerges from a dearth of social skills, Natale (1986) recommends the involvement of the counsellor at a number of levels simultaneously: they can assist the development of insight by the client on how such behaviour has occurred; they can encourage further exploration of the problem; and they can aid clients in cognitive–behavioural changes, particularly through the use of social skills training. If the loneliness is situational, Natale suggests that the counsellor may be the transitional link as the person reconnects to other people. However, it is desirable that counsellors also explore with clients the dynamics at work which resulted in the loneliness. Listening to clients reduces the sense of isolation and loneliness and enables them to frame their lives in terms of past achievements as well as facing the inevitability of death.

Some of the counselling approaches outlined in this section present a stage approach to counselling. However, it is likely that the stages outlined for each issue blend with one another and that they may not occur in the order outlined. In recent years one of the most frequently used approaches has been life review therapy. The approaches of Parkes (1972) and Worden (1983) to grief counselling, of Kubler-Ross (1969) and Pattison (1977) to the dying, and of Natale (1986) to loneliness offer the counsellor useful maps with which to approach a particular problem. The following chapter deals with the adaptation of general counselling approaches to suit the needs of older adults.

Adaptation of general counselling approaches to the needs of older adults

7

Counselling theories and approaches that apply to other age groups are also applicable to older adults. The present purpose is to concentrate on those that have been found to be particularly helpful to older adults. In this chapter, psychodynamic, humanistic, cognitive–behavioural, family and group therapies are outlined.

PSYCHODYNAMIC THERAPIES

The relevance of psychoanalysis, analytical therapy and Adlerian therapy will be discussed here.

Psychoanalysis

Freud's theory of personality was based primarily on childhood and adolescence, with little consideration of the middle and later years. Psychoanalysis used a retrospective view of older adults by explaining current behaviour in terms of childhood experiences. By 1949, however, an alternative possibility was introduced by Abraham, who stated: 'In my psychoanalytic practice I have treated a number of chronic neuroses in people over 40 and even 50 years of age ... To my surprise a considerable number of them reacted very favourably to the treatment' (in Strachey, 1978). He held that the age of the neurosis, rather than the age of the patient, should be the crucial issue in deciding on the usefulness of treatment. Several psychoanalysts (Martin and DeGrunchy, 1930; Grotjahn, 1940, 1955; Martin, 1944; Weinberg, 1951; Goldfarb, 1953; Meerloo, 1955a, 1961) modified traditional psychoanalytic technique in working with older adults by using a warm, supportive and active approach. Grotjahn (1951) was the first analyst to state that the weakening of the ego defences in older individuals may actually facilitate therapy. Older patients, he held, may have less difficulty in integrating interpretations than younger people.

However, although some psychoanalysts did work with the elderly, they expected little success. Storandt (1983) pointed to the unspoken value system of many dynamically oriented therapists, who placed emphasis on assisting young adults with many years of productivity ahead. These therapists did not deem it worthwhile to spend time and effort on restructuring the personality of people with only a few years of life left. In 1904, Freud had stated that the amount of material to be dealt with was not manageable and the time required for the treatment of older adults would be inordinately long.

The transference element in psychoanalysis has already been discussed in Chapter 4. Originally Freud viewed it as hindering treatment, but eventually he came to consider it as making a cure possible. By transferring feelings on to the therapist, clients are able to re-experience the difficulties of their earlier relationships and obtain insight. In this manner older adults may discover the causes of their present difficulties.

Two other techniques used in psychoanalysis are free association and dream interpretation. Free association is the spontaneous expression of everything that comes into the client's mind. There is no conscious or deliberate control of thoughts or feelings. By decreasing rational control, the associations reveal patterns which indicate significant underlying problems. Dreams, in psychoanalysis, are viewed as the royal road to the unconscious since they are means whereby people fulfil repressed wishes. A distinction is made between the manifest and the latent content of dreams: manifest content refers to the dream as it actually presents itself, whereas latent content is the material brought to consciousness in a disguised manner, and expressed in words and symbols which have meaning for both the therapist and the client. These words and symbols are interpreted so that the associated emotional tension disappears.

Within psychoanalysis, older adults, through analysing material brought to awareness through free association and dreams, may relive old emotions and frustrations in such a manner that they lose their harmful impact. Through analysis, they become part of older adults' conscious experience, the emotional tensions are discharged and the events become integrated into their lives. Consequently psychoanalysis has much to offer the older adult.

Despite this, Brink (1979) asserted that although some psychoanalytically oriented therapists have had success working with older people, the majority have not been encouraged to apply Freudian insights to their clients. Psychoanalysis, in its traditional form, is inaccessible to all but a small minority of people, whatever their age, owing to the considerable amount of time needed for a comprehensive analysis and the cost involved. Oberleder (1966) stated that, in most instances, therapy with the ageing has two main goals, namely the alleviation of anxiety and the maintenance or restoration of adequate psychological functioning. These goals require briefer forms of therapy which are more practicable and accessible to older adults. There is a lack of empirical validation of psychoanalysis, since the only research tools used were case studies, which give limited results. The work that has been done with the elderly in the psychodynamic tradition has had a Jungian emphasis.

Analytical therapy

The therapeutic techniques of free association, analysis of transference and interpretation of dreams are also used in Jung's analytical therapy, which assists clients to get in touch with their own private world and to accept that within this world lies the guiding force which can direct them to a fuller, integrated, more meaningful life. Jung believed that individuals must accept all parts of themselves in moving toward wholeness. The therapist assists them to become aware of the sources and meanings of their behaviour, feelings and values. Within analytical groups efforts to gain insight and control over behaviour are heightened by exploration of the participants' behaviour (Hartford, 1980). Jung (1965) spoke of four stages of treatment: catharsis, elucidation, education and transformation. Catharsis involves the outpouring of feeling; elucidation is the clarification of early memories; education aims to train clients in normal adaptation; transformation is the actual improvement that takes place. Counselling older adults in analytical therapy frequently involves assisting them to come to terms with their own life. This involves appreciating the growthful aspects of their lives to date, while grieving for ungrowthful aspects which cannot be remedied and living as fully as possible in the present.

Analytical therapy is useful when helping people for whom spirituality and the experience of God is an important part of their lives. Jung was one of the few psychologists who openly acknowledged the psychological value of religion. He considered that it was vital for clergy and psychotherapists to join forces. Two-thirds of Jung's patients were in the second half of life, and he believed that they were suffering from mental disturbance because they had lost contact with their religious traditions, and that the solution was to reintegrate them into their religious practice.

Adlerian therapy

Adlerian therapy helps counsellors of older people to understand, and clients themselves to confront, the issues of power, wholeness, perfection and intimacy (Brammer, 1984). Older people suffer compounded losses which may generate feelings of inferiority, powerlessness, helplessness and isolation. Adlerian counselling involves four stages. The first stage, establishing the counselling relationship, focuses on strengths and the ability of clients to use all their resources. Establishing a sense of the client's lifestyle is the work of the second stage, and seeing how this lifestyle affects the client's current functioning. Early recollections, dreams, information on family constellation and the priorities of the client all contribute to an assessment of lifestyle. The third stage involves developing insight into behaviour, which includes the recognition by the client of their own part in the creation of a problem. In the final stage actions occur as a consequence of insight.

Understanding the lifestyle of the client, especially in relation to feelings of inferiority, is central to Adlerian counselling. One of the latest developments in the field is the lifestyle report of Watkins (1992). Four steps are involved: gathering data; processing data; generating hypotheses; and integrating the data. Gathering data includes consideration of the presenting problem and its history, family history/description, work, social and emotional relationships, assessment data and conclusions. From the data gathered the counsellor discerns patterns and meanings, formulates hypotheses and develops a picture of the client's lifestyle. This report can be incorporated into the counselling process and given to clients to enable them to have a fuller understanding of their lifestyle. One of the disadvantages in its use with older adults is that it is a lengthy procedure. However, Watkins points out that the report itself can be eliminated as the counsellor is enabled to incorporate it into the process through familiarity with its use.

Brammer (1984) found that literature on coping capacity amply supports Adlerian emphasis on family-style support networks for older people. Analysis of family networks involving multiple generations is a growing counselling procedure. Brink (1979) saw the development of social interests, the cultivation of independent behaviour and the procurement of a sense of achievement as guidelines from Adler's work which counsellors could use to lessen inferiority feelings and neurotic lifestyles. He also stated that an Adlerian perspective can reinterpret the disengagement issues: 'The question is not how much social activity a person has, but to what degree his activities are guided by social interest'. While Adler's approach has possibilities in its application to older adults, there does not seem to be any research on its particular value in a therapeutic context.

HUMANISTIC THERAPIES

The underlying assumption of the humanistic approach is that older individuals have the capacity to develop psychologically right up to death, provided that there is no mental deterioration. The older individuals get, the more self-actualized they can become. Life is a dynamic, ever-changing and richly expanding experience. There are four main approaches within the humanistic field: person-centred, gestalt and reality therapies and transactional analysis.

The person-centred approach

The person-centred approach attempts to enter the world of experience of older people to obtain a clear perception of what is going on in their lives. Being listened to, understood and responded to is very supportive and affirming for older individuals who are lonely and isolated. It restores their sense of dignity and feelings of self-worth. This empathy can counteract many of the negative perceptions of old age and the ageing process.

Person-centred counsellors offer unconditional positive regard: their clients are assured that they are cared for unequivocally. This respect enables counsellors to become significant people in their clients' lives. Because unconditional positive regard is opposed to labelling, it provides a welcome antidote for older adults who may be suffering from stereotyped views regarding old age. Person-centred counsellors provide the opportunity for older adults to unburden themselves in the presence of another individual. Person-centred counselling emphasizes the immediate relationship between counsellor and client. Counsellors are congruent: they are as completely and fully themselves as possible. Consequently, clients view them as dependable and trustworthy. Thorne (1984) stated that counsellors cannot expect their clients to travel further than they themselves have journeyed. This presents a particular dilemma in the counselling of older adults, who are often older and have more life experiences than the counsellor. However, the important point in the development of congruence relates not to the number of years but rather to the level of attention and openness with which individuals involve themselves in their own psychological growth.

When the three core conditions of person-centred counselling – empathy, congruence and unconditional positive regard – exist, older adults are assisted in the growth process by getting closer to their own self-experience. Rogers (1961) viewed the person-centred approach as providing clients with an increase in their openness to experience, in their trust of themselves and in their own internal source of evaluation. Clients usually experience a discrepancy between their perception of themselves and their experience in reality when therapy is initiated. Denis, a 66-year-old man, was recently retired when he first entered counselling. He saw himself as a kind and generous father, who had lived all his life for his children, and could not understand why his family did not spend more time with him. Through counselling he realized that his perception of himself was indeed accurate, but that he had not given sufficient attention to his frequent outbursts of anger, which his offspring found terrifying.

In person-centred counselling older adults become aware that counselling is a process where they can find their own solutions to their problems. Uninhibited expression of feeling is encouraged. The recognition and expression of negative feelings frees clients both to explore their positive feelings and to work through their negative feelings. Counsellors pay attention to these expressions and appreciate their relevance for the client. Unconditional positive regard for clients' feelings, be they positive or negative, gives them the opportunity to understand themselves as they are. Self-understanding brings an awareness of a whole range of choices. Appropriate action can then ensue.

Person-centred counselling is likely to be effective with older adults who are self-motivated and possess high initiative, but it is less likely to be successful with those who are not in the habit of being responsible for their lives. A basic assumption of the approach is that individuals change by themselves without the direction of the counsellor. Rogers (1961) appeared to place some limitations on the freedom experienced by individuals, whom he described as 'defensively organized'. These people choose to follow a given course of action but find that they cannot behave in the fashion they choose because they are determined by factors in the existential situation, which include their defensiveness, denial and distortion of the relevant data. Although the solution lies in clients coming closer to their own self-experience, there is a possibility that in the present reality of their lives they may engage in behaviours that block constructive self-experience. Although person-centred counselling has given great attention to the desirable attitudes on the part of counsellors, less attention has been given to the minute changes which occur in the self-experience of clients.

Gestalt therapy

The main contribution of gestalt therapy to understanding older people is the principle that their behaviour is primarily a function of their perceptual field at that moment. Self-understanding is emphasized through asking clients to focus their awareness on the 'here and now', rather than on the past or future. The feelings, experiences, thoughts and present awareness of the person are explored. This implies a thorough knowledge on the part of the therapist of the ageing processes: biological, intellectual, psychological, social and spiritual.

Responsibility for oneself is central to gestalt therapy. It enables older adults to realize those aspects of their lives over which they have control, and to retain their freedom of choice for as long as is possible and/or desirable. Through gestalt therapy older adults are enabled to be responsible for major change at times of transition, such as retirement and/or the death of a spouse. They can decide for themselves whether to change their circumstances or to allow them to remain unaltered. It is suggested that the goal of gestalt therapy is one of self-support without reliance on the environment. This has led to the criticism that 'at a time when older people may frequently need more security and environmental supports, it can be very threatening to suggest that these be relinquished' (Brammer, 1984). This is a misunderstanding, because the importance of inter-dependence and cooperation exists in tandem with self-support. Self-support implies an ability to ask for appropriate support from the environment rather than a refusal to seek the help which may be available and necessary. Gestalt therapy assists older adults in self-empowerment by encouraging them not to depend prematurely on the environment. It is likely that older adults working from this perspective may ask themselves questions such as 'What can I do for myself? How can I obtain the assistance that I need?' Such requests for support are likely to be free from any element of manipulation.

One of the main concerns of gestalt therapy, namely unfinished business, is of particular relevance to older adults. Unfinished business refers to incomplete experiences and feelings that remain with individuals. It can sap them of the energy required to engage in other activities. Individuals do not wish to feel the pain involved in dealing with unfinished business, as to do so would necessitate a change in perception and thinking. The sudden death of a spouse can result in unfinished business for the surviving partner, who may avoid looking at it in order to postpone a final goodbye. Perls (1969) felt that most people avoid painful emotions rather than do what is necessary to change.

Various indices of unfinished business exist, such as frequent repetition of a story, tears when speaking of a long-dead relative, and resentments. Unfinished business is accompanied by emotional arousal without appropriate expression. Resentment is unexpressed anger aroused by the object of the resentment which, although unexpressed, may be hinted at indirectly. The emotion relating to issues in the past is re-experienced in the present in unfinished business. The therapist needs to focus on the age of the client at the time when the event was experienced. Older adults can be encouraged to re-enact these events by relating them in the present tense. In re-experiencing the emotion and the experience, older adults can gain an understanding which closes the disturbing past event. David, a 68-year-old man, was a member of a gestalt group. As the group facilitator, the author noticed that his eyes filled with tears whenever he mentioned his mother. Having witnessed this a number of times, the facilitator invited David to pay attention to his tears. She then asked him what he was recalling. He described a time when he was 23 years old, when he returned from England and found his mother baking in the kitchen in anticipation of his return. His mother's baking was, he explained, a very special part of his life. The facilitator invited him to remember the incident using the present tense. When he did so, David wept as he recalled her death 6 months later.

The 'empty chair' technique of the gestalt approach is one method of dealing with unfinished business. The older person can switch back and forth from their own place to the empty chair, engaging in a dialogue which expresses the unvoiced grief, resentment or anger together with the imagined response of the other person. The most important part of the work is the voicing by each party of the hitherto unexpressed feelings. For example, the author used the empty chair with a 79-year-old woman, Mary, to enable her to come to terms with the death of her invalid husband, Jim. Mary had not told Jim verbally for many years that she had loved him, and was overcome with remorse on his death. By imagining Jim in the empty chair she realized that he did know that she loved him through her years of care for him as an invalid.

Another valuable contribution of gestalt therapy is the awareness of introjection and projection. Introjection is the unquestioning acceptance of the attitudes and ideas of significant others. A frequent introject is 'Work hard'. Achievement is cherished to such an extent that individuals may become work addicted, and on retirement they may find it difficult to relax or to maintain self-esteem. Through gestalt therapy they can discover the undue importance they attached to work. By working through the introject they can be rid of it and find the freedom within themselves to enjoy old age.

Projection causes older people to attribute to others in their environment feelings and attributes that belong to themselves, and to blame others for their own deficiencies. Blamers are usually lonely individuals, since few people will listen sympathetically. They can assume the role of victims, since they do not realize that the behaviours are their own. Gestalt therapy offers these people release from their loneliness by helping them to recognize their projections. The energy which had been bound up in introjection and projection is freed for other experiences in the present.

Gestalt therapy provides older adults with an opportunity to finish the incomplete experiences of the past, thereby allowing them to live as fully from a psychological perspective as they did in previous phases of their lives.

Reality therapy

Reality therapy attempts to teach older people better ways of fulfilling their current needs. The first goal of the therapist is to establish a warm, supportive relationship with the client. The focus is on the present and there is little talk about the past, although a person's past is respected. Facing reality involves the acceptance that the past cannot be rewritten. If the past has been difficult, concentrating on it only gives clients excuses for their unhappy present. No matter what happened in the past, clients are responsible for their own present. The therapist concentrates on behaviour and the clarification of goals. Clients are helped to see how particular behaviours may be hampering progress, and to see other alternatives for attaining the desired goals.

Reality therapy outlines eight basic techniques for working with clients. These are: becoming friends; focusing on clients' daily activity and asking them what they are doing now; evaluating if what they are doing is helpful; assisting clients to make a plan to resolve the problems presented; obtaining commitment to the plan; accepting no excuses from the client; not punishing; and never giving up. The emphasis throughout is on the client's responsibility: unhappiness is the result of present irresponsibility.

Reality therapy is a very promising approach for work with older adults. Many old people do not feel loved and cherished, and may have a poor self-image, feel unrecognized and ignored. In order to feel worthwhile, older individuals need at least one other person to whom they are important and who regards them as a worthwhile human being. They must also regard this person as important to them. The reality therapist can offer this affirmation to clients by becoming a friend to them. Glasser (1990) recounted that he himself went jogging with a client when that appeared to him to be the best course of action to adopt. In 1980 he stated; 'Unless this kind of friendship is woven deeply into the fabric of therapy from beginning to end, the helping process will rarely be effective'. Reality therapy offers a therapeutic relationship to clients that is the opposite of the traditional psychodynamic approach, where the relationship is considered in terms of transference and countertransference. If reality therapy can help older adults find new ways of meeting needs, it is fulfilling a vital function in their lives. Storandt (1983) said that the focus on achieving a success identity rather than a failure identity might be helpful to older adults facing role changes in old age. Retiring workers may experience a sense of failure on leaving a lifelong occupation if their success identity has been defined in terms of their work role. Bart, a 68-year-old former train driver, had become depressed. Since his retirement at 65, his wife felt that he was under her feet in the house. Although he had engaged in some gardening at first, failing physical strength combined with deteriorating eyesight had forced him to discontinue this hobby. His mornings were spent in bed in order to give his wife space, while in the afternoons he usually sat by the fire, retiring to bed around 8.30 each evening. When asked what he wanted, he replied 'A sense of meaning'. With the help of the therapist he drew up an alternative plan for his day, rising earlier, listening to the radio in the morning, going for a short walk in the afternoon and inviting friends to the house three evenings a week. He also began to collect used stamps to buy guide dogs for the blind. In this manner a largely inactive day became quite active, and Bart attained a new sense of meaning.

Reality therapy in a group format may be helpful to older people working through similar life crises. Storandt (1983) gave an example of group reality therapy with war widows, where the focus of the therapy was on assisting each woman to gain an increased understanding of her individual potential. It has also been found useful in support groups for family members of older people suffering from Alzheimer's disease. A limitation of reality therapy is the concentration on the present, with little reference to the past. Hence it does not allow individuals to deal with unfinished situations and the feelings involved. The past is a vital link in the old person's sense of self-worth, and failure to integrate this reality into the therapy process is to neglect a valuable asset.

Transactional analysis

Transactional analysis considers ways in which people act or interact. It holds that people need recognition, and outlines ways in which they can hinder or assist this recognition. It takes clients through progressive stages: structural analysis, transactional analysis, game analysis and script analysis. Structural analysis involves the awareness of three ego states: parent, adult and child. Ego states are consistent patterns of behaviours, thoughts and feelings. The child ego state refers to the little boy or girl all individuals carry within themselves. This is spontaneous and uses behaviours and feelings which were first used from birth to 8 years of age. The parental ego state is a set of feelings, thoughts and behaviours that resemble those of one's parents, and which were introjected from them into the personality. When operating from the parental ego state, individuals behave in a manner similar to their own parents. The adult ego state objectively appraises reality and makes judgements. It develops as individuals learn to use reason. It is objective and unemotional.

Transactions are of three kinds: complementary, crossed and ulterior. Complementary transactions occur when an individual's communication gets an appropriate and expected response; crossed transactions occur when the response is inappropriate and unexpected, while an ulterior transaction happens when a hidden message is disguised under a socially acceptable transaction. A game is a set of ulterior transactions that individuals repeat during their lifetime, since they bring a desired pay-off. They may be played from the parent ego state if parents' games are imitated, from the adult ego state if they are consciously calculated, or from the child ego state if they are based on early life experiences. Scripts are preconscious plans which are the product of parental programming and which determine how individuals spend their lives.

Transactional analysts emphasize awareness and understanding of ego states, transactions, games and scripts as the route to behaviour change. Berne (1966) outlined eight techniques: interrogation, specification, confrontation, explanation, illustration, confirmation, interpretation and crystallization. In addition, Berne speaks of life position, which is a mental attitude people adopt between the first or second and seventh years of life. The four basic life positions are: I am OK you are OK; I am OK you are not OK; I am not OK you are OK; I am not OK you are not OK.

Transactional analysis can encourage older adults to re-examine their present communications. Often on retirement individuals who have placed an extremely high value on productivity can resort to the game of 'Yes but … '. The use of this game was apparent in a client named Frank, a recently retired 66-year-old. He came to counselling with the feeling that his life was over. Listening to his story, it became clear that Frank was financially secure and had a good relationship with his wife and family. However, equally apparent was the greater value he had always attached to paid employment, to the exclusion of these other resources. The counsellor sought to heighten his awareness of these, as can be seen from the following extract:

Frank: It is so demoralizing not to have a salary cheque coming into the house any longer.

Counsellor: You do have a substantial pension, a house which is your own and a loving wife and family.

Frank: Yes but I only see my daughter once a month, and my son once a year.

Counsellor: Now that you are retired you could consider changing those patterns.

Frank: Yes but I hate flying so going to the US to see Peter is impossible.

Change for Frank came gradually as the counsellor helped him to recognize his 'Yes but … ' game. Removing the game allowed several previously rejected options to emerge and gave his life a new sense of meaning.

Transactional analysis helps these individuals to be aware of and free themselves from game-playing behaviour. The concepts of transactional analysis are easily understood by older individuals, but one of the dangers is that insight can remain as an intellectual experience and not translate into actual behaviour. Concepts such as ego states remain at a hypothetical level and no methods have been devised for their empirical validation. Transactional analysis is useful in assisting clients decide which life position they hold. Through transactional analysis, older adults who are self-deprecating, depressed, suicidal, arrogant or lacking in trust can be helped to adopt a more healthy life position.

BEHAVIOURAL AND COGNITIVE APPROACHES

Behavioural and cognitive–behavioural approaches to counselling possess a number of similarities. They represent a more active and structural approach to therapy than either the humanistic or the psychodynamic approaches. Both entail describing the presenting problem in detail, designing specific operations based on these problems, and outlining definite goals. Both therapies assume that clients have acquired maladaptive patterns which can be unlearned. The therapies differ in that behaviour therapy deals with behaviour while cognitive therapy focuses on how people think.

Behaviour therapy

Behaviour therapy is based on the theoretical behavioural model of Skinner (1983), and its goal is to eliminate maladaptive behaviour. It is a systematic approach which involves designing a programme to deal with problem behaviour, concentrating on actual behaviour rather than possible underlying causes. Four main phases are involved: systematic assessment and measurement of the problem; selection of clearly defined goals of treatment; changing behaviour through specific intervention; and overall evaluation. Therapist and client together identify the problem, the goals of the therapy and the methods to be employed. A detailed behavioural description of the problem is obtained. The therapist pinpoints events in the environment which are maintaining undesirable behaviour or are preventing the client learning new models of adjustment, e.g. aspects of their social behaviour. A commonly used method is systematic desensitization, where the therapist combines relaxation with imaginary recreation of anxiety-provoking situations. Clients are progressively presented with stimuli known to produce anxiety until the most intense stimulus elicits no reaction. Two other methods used in behaviour therapy include flooding and implosive therapy. In flooding, the therapist encourages the client to confront the feared object in real life, or in imagination in a supportive atmosphere. Implosive therapy is a development of flooding, in that the confronting of the feared object in imagination occurs in an exaggerated form (cf. O'Leary, 1986). By looking at the worst possible consequence the unrealistic aspect is identified. Systematic desensitization can be profitably used with older adults who suffer from fear, while flooding is particularly useful for the treatment of anxiety.

Cognitive therapies

Two of the main cognitive approaches to counselling are rational–emotive therapy (RET) and cognitive–behavioural therapy.

Rational–emotive therapy

A development of behaviour therapy occurred with the incorporation of images, symbols and thought, which led to the cognitive approach. Two cognitive–behavioural therapies which are worthy of special attention are Ellis's rational–emotive therapy and Beck's cognitive therapy. The rational–emotive view of personality is dominated by the principle that emotion and reason are intricately and inextricably entwined in the psyche. Ellis (1962) contended that frequently the thought comes first, and the emotion results from it. In their thinking, people often distort and generalize owing to preconceptions and misguided ideas. Hence dysfunctional emotions or behaviours are the consequence of interpretations or beliefs held by clients. The role of the counsellor is to teach clients healthier perspectives. By its nature, RET is a directive approach where counsellors assume an active teaching role to re-educate clients. They demonstrate to clients that many of their thoughts are irrational, and teach them to question the beliefs and the interpretations on which they rest. Homework is given to clients to enable them to take risks, to gain new experiences and to change their irrational beliefs. Rational–emotive imagery is used to enable clients to change dysfunctional emotions to functional ones. In this context it is useful for older adults to imagine the negative event and distinguish between rational and irrational beliefs surrounding it.

Belkin (1984) cited studies which suggest that because the greatest strength of RET resides in its emphasis on learning, it can be applied quite flexibly to many settings. Its application to older adults would seem to be appropriate, given the losses and stresses in old age which often produce feelings of self-defeat, depression and despair. RET may be particularly helpful to older adults with minimal psychopathology but with substantial problems that result from subscription to societal myths or irrational thinking (Storandt, 1983). Storandt also feels it may be helpful in a preventive way at times of transition, such as retirement or widowhood.

One of the problems of RET in relation to older adults is the directive teaching role taken by the therapist. At a time when older people are striving to keep their independence in other areas of their lives, it would not be helpful if they became dependent on their counsellor. Patterson (1986) stated that though Ellis claims to provide unconditional positive regard for his clients, he clearly does not have confidence in their ability to change or correct their perceptions and beliefs without an active, direct confrontation on the part of the therapist. This attitude could further erode the confidence of older clients in themselves and their capabilities.

Cognitive–behavioural therapy

Beck's (1976) cognitive therapy is similar to Ellis's RET in that it attempts to alleviate emotional disorders by correcting faulty interpretations of reality and faulty reasoning. It can be used for the treatment of depression and anxiety by assisting older people to confront the irrational thoughts and assumptions that underlie their depressive behaviour.

Unlike RET, cognitive therapy does not challenge the older individual's thoughts but rather asks questions to assist them to examine their beliefs and develop alternatives. A dysfunctional thought such as 'I am too old to change' may be questioned by the therapist and recent small changes in behaviour identified. Part of cognitive therapy includes the client keeping a record of dysfunctional thoughts. By doing this the dysfunctional thoughts surrounding events that trigger emotion can be identified. The therapist's role in identifying thoughts may follow the sequence: identifying in general terms the nature of the problem; finding a recent example; conducting a mental action replay which includes exactly what happened; when the emotion was first experienced and the thoughts surrounding it; weighing the intensity of the feeling (1–10); identifying the thoughts that accompanied the feeling. An important element of the therapy is the format of the interview, which consists of an agenda, feedback and homework. Therapist and client together identify the problem and the best method to resolve it. Throughout the session the therapist seeks feedback. Homework involves the assignment of specific tasks to be completed between therapy sessions.

Beck (1976) held that his approach was particularly suitable to the treatment of depression, providing an alternative approach to that of Fry (1984) (outlined in Chapter 6) for counselling older adults. According to the cognitive–behavioural approach, depressed people think in a negative way. They have negative self-concepts and view the present and the future unfavourably. The greater the depression, the greater the number of negative thoughts. For older individuals the means to combat depression consists of learning to recognize when they are thinking negatively and of seeking positive ways of viewing their experience and testing them out in action. Sheila, a 74-year-old grandmother, suffered from depression for 6 months. She had a sense of feeling down without being aware of any specific cause. The first step involved noticing each day when she began to feel bad and what was running through her mind beforehand. These thoughts were then recorded. Questioning and altering of negative thoughts consisted of asking Sheila what evidence existed for her negative thoughts, could she have interpreted the experience otherwise, and what were the effects of thinking the way she did? Typical thinking errors in which she engaged were identified, such as jumping to conclusions, over-generalizing from specific experiences, and taking responsibility for what was not her fault. Storandt (1983) claimed that the majority of people experiencing depression in later life do so as a result of a significant environmental event (e.g. loss of spouse, retirement) and she states that Beck's therapy was designed for this type of reactive depression.

Sherman (1981) stated that cognitive theory is very precise in outlining the endogenous factors in depression: self-hate, irrational feelings of incompetence, and worthlessness. Beck and Clark (1988) stated that the treatment of anxiety lasts from 5 to 20 sessions, while Salkovskis and Clark (1991) found remarkable decreases in panic attacks over 12 sessions. The short-term nature of the therapy is a particularly appealing aspect for older adults. The research and professional literature contains little information about the use of cognitive–behavioural therapies with older people. However, Storandt (1983) stated that this approach would seem to be the most promising with respect to the treatment of distresses that accompany physical, psychological and social ageing. Sherman (1981) found that some of the cognitive techniques are particularly well suited to the problem of anxiety in older people, whereas others are especially good for depressed moods or actual depression.

FAMILY THERAPY

Family therapy was originally used as a treatment in child guidance referrals and in the treatment of schizophrenics, particularly adolescents and young adults. In the late 1960s some authors (Shanas and Streib, 1965; Brody, 1966; Brody and Spark, 1966) stressed the possible origins of the problems of older adults in family interactions and the relevance of family therapy. Its underlying assumptions are that the family is the main source of social support; that its members influence and are influenced by one another; that difficulties emerge within the family context; and that resolution occurs within that framework. Problems experienced by older adults are considered to have less to do with the stresses of ageing than with difficulties in other areas of family life. These difficulties may arise from problems encountered by the family in adjusting and realigning itself as the members grow older.

In family therapy the family is viewed as a unit or system, organizing and directing itself and maintaining a balance in its own characteristic fashion. It is also a subsystem of the extended family and community. Adjustment to changing life stages requires change in all members, including adapting to new views, acquiring new skills and relinquishing responsibility and control. If a family has difficulty in negotiating these changes, a problem or symptom develops. Although this problem reflects the difficulties of the entire family system, the family may view it as the concern of one member. In this case the counsellor needs to address the context of the problem, including the family life stage and the views of other members (McHale, 1995, personal communication).

In keeping with developmental psychology theory, the family therapist will also explore whether the family has negotiated previous lifecycle stages. The transition of parent–child to adult–adult relationships is considered appropriate by the midlife stage of the second generation (Carter and McGoldrick, 1980). The interplay between family relationships and changing values within the culture and social structure are also included in family therapy. These dimensions are viewed as particularly relevant to family estrangement, where parents and their adult children have lost contact with one another (Jerrome, 1994).

Belkin (1984) outlined four goals of family therapy: to assist family members to communicate openly with each other; to help them to learn constructive new ways of solving their own problems; to preserve the socioemotional intactness of the family even where physical and legal separation is necessary; and to be able to individuate themselves from the family as a total unit.

Interaction among family members can sometimes hinder effective functioning. Sterns et al. (1984) identified four such possibilities: older adults may be used as a scapegoat; older adults may find it difficult to allow their children to function independently; dyadic alliances may be present – for example, a mother–son alliance may have emerged over the years and the father may be overwhelmed by its power; and older adults may insist on an overdependent attitude on their children. These four patterns can in time become rigid. They give a certain comfort and security, but their rigidity can lock people into unhealthy situations, which frequently can only be changed by outside intervention.

Family therapy may be helpful in a variety of situations with older adults. Retirement may bring stress to the family system, requiring therapeutic intervention. Marital counselling is sought when conflict surfaces which may be either long-standing or recent in origin, or when illness occurs leading to changes in the physical and emotional dimensions of the relationship. The sexual components of the marital relationship are often ignored because of negative attitudes about the role of sexuality in later life. According to Murphy et al. (1980), approximately 20% of couples over 40 have clinically significant sexual problems. Older adults may have emotionally disturbed, substance-abusing or mentally handicapped children. When chronic illness occurs lifelong established patterns begin to crumble and necessitate intervention. The family may undergo considerable stress if they experience bereavement, or have to move house, or when failing health in older members requires them to be placed in institutional care. Conflict can occur with respect to the nature of the institution, or alternatively the distribution of care among the children. Consequently, any old age-related problem or rites of passage should be seen in the context of the entire family, rather than as solely coneening the particular individual.

Obstacles arise when the family is not ready to accept outside assistance: a false loyalty to the family may hinder them from obtaining the help they require. The ability to seek family therapy may also be hindered by cultural taboo. O'Leary (1990) found that Irish people ignore problems and/or keep them to themselves. Often the family views the problem as belonging to the older adult. In this situation the cooperation of the entire family may be obtained by arranging a meeting with all members to gain a clearer perspective.

The passage of time brings changed roles within the family. The dependent child becomes an adult, and is frequently the carer of the older person. This transition can be difficult. Counsellors should determine the nature and quality of intergenerational relationships, which will indicate to them whether the needs and expectations of the different generations are being met. Patterns of dependence and independence need to be examined and their acceptance or rejection by other members considered. Unresolved stress and conflict need to be confronted. The nature of former parental relationships with the children and the impact of these on current relationships, both in the case of children still living at home and of those who have left, can be a source of conflict.

Within family therapy there are five main theoretical approaches: structural, strategic, transgenerational, experiential and behavioural family therapy. Minuchin (1974), the main advocate of structural family therapy, stated that its immediate goal was to alter the family's organization and alliances. Structural family therapists focus on the interactions of family members to understand how, when and to whom they relate in order to change the structure of the family with a view to resolving the client's problem. In strategic (brief) family therapy, the therapist's goal is to change interactional patterns which are stuck. The therapy concentrates on the sequence of interactions among family members which maintain the problem. A fundamental principle of the approach is that solution requires one or more family members doing the opposite to what they normally do. The method employed consists of reframing the beliefs of the individuals and setting small but significantly different ways of responding to others. Herr and Weakland (1979) gave case examples which illustrate the application of this form of therapy to older adults suffering from hypochondriasis, loneliness, grave disability, death and grief, intergenerational conflicts and confusion.

Transgenerational family therapy focuses on family dynamics across three or more generations. Therapists are particularly interested in how current family interactions have emerged through the generations. A useful tool is the genogram, which depicts the family tree of older individuals. Completing a genogram allows them to view their lives in context and to deepen their sense of identity: it assists the counsellor in obtaining a visual representation of the family structure, together with the feelings, attitudes, values and experiences of older individuals connected with it; it highlights sibling position, size of the family in three to four generations, and decades in which major events of the family occurred, and it provides an opportunity for unfinished business relating to the family to emerge. The therapist seeks to lessen the effect of the past on the present and emphasizes the need for rational rather than affective behaviour throughout the family. The genogram can play a significant role in the achievement of ego integrity.

Whitaker (Whitaker and Keith, 1981) and Satir (1967), the leaders in experiential family therapy, stressed the personal growth of each family member rather than unhealthy interaction patterns. Growth involves experiencing the present moment and sharing that moment with other members. Members are expected to share their personal problems, to help clarify what the difficulties are, and to be involved in achieving a resolution. In behavioural family therapy, problems are viewed as arising from ineffective patterns of reinforcement within the family. Therapists focus on dyadic interactions between parent and child, or between the marital partners. The goal is to provide a new understanding of the problem by all members, as well as an agreed method of dealing with situations and of interacting in the future.

Less common techniques in family therapy are concomitant therapy, in which the same therapist treats the family members individually; collaborative therapy, in which different therapists treat different family members and consult about their progress; and the family psychoeducational approach. This last reflects the view that the family members who provide the care play a very important role in contributing to the wellbeing of older adults. The main initiatives in this area have been in designing programmes to increase carers' knowledge, skills and use of community support services (Schellenberg et al., 1989; Myers, 1988) and in helping caregivers to identify the source of stress in the family situation (Sheehan and Nuttall, 1988). Psychoeducational groups therefore provide support, information, skill training and increased self-awareness primarily for carers (Richardson et al., 1994). Garrison and Howe (1976) described an approach which they called network building for the older adult, using network sessions involving all significant others in the person's life. The aim of the sessions is to rebuild interpersonal relationships for older people. However, according to Levy et al. (1980), no empirical support is provided for this mode of intervention.

In general there are no controlled outcome studies of the application of family therapy to older adults, but it does seem a useful approach to use when the presenting problem indicates a possible family origin.

GROUP COUNSELLING

Models of group counselling have their origin in the intergroup relations workshop organized by Kurt Lewin in Connecticut in 1946, and in the subsequent workshops held in Bethel, Maine, in the summers of 1947, 1948 and 1949. These groups consisted of discussion groups which considered the problems presented by the members. Subsequently other psychologists began working with groups. Carl Rogers experimented with the intensive group experience as part of the training of personal counsellors, and presented an intensive full-time 1-week workshop for the American Psychological Association in 1950.

Group approaches are more appropriate than individual counselling with older adults because of the nature of their problems, such as social isolation, loneliness, role loss and widowhood. Involvement in a group provides support during loss and an opportunity for developing new relationships. Group counselling gives older participants the opportunity to develop an awareness of some of the social, psychological, physical and environmental aspects of their lives. The group can provide support, increase self-awareness, develop alternative solutions to personal problems and provide an opportunity to learn new social roles. Levy *et al.* (1980) hold that it makes great sense to treat older clients within a group framework. Group counselling 'would seem particularly appropriate for older people whose social identity may be greatly undermined by role loss, as employment and even spouse and friends become unavailable for support and self-confirmation'. Sharing experiences and interacting with others helps to provide a sense of emotional security and a positive self-image as coping abilities decrease.

The focus of group counselling will vary according to the nature of the problems presented. Brink (1979) identified four features arising from the group approach with older adults:

1. Older adults can benefit by just being in each other's presence and trying to communicate: interaction is a significant benefit, especially for the socially withdrawn.
2. Group counselling with older people should focus on reality: present life situations and the strengths and limitations of individuals.
3. Group work can assist the life review process: group exposure gives individuals the chance to hear how others have lived their lives. It also gives them an opportunity to talk about their own life and have others react to it.
4. Group counselling should include some form of remotivation.

Corey and Corey (1987) dealt with the importance of the initial stage in group counselling with older adults. In group counselling with institutionalized older people, members were encouraged to speak directly to one another rather than directing their statements to the leader. When a participant voiced a particular experience, other members were encouraged to share similar experiences which they may have had. Both of these activities were aimed at ensuring that the older adults did not remain isolated in their own world. Other aspects which Corey and Corey consider important in group counselling with older adults include listening to group members and then working with immediate problems and sharing reminiscences.

Butler and Lewis (1982) advocated age-integrated group counselling, which helps to minimize the sense of isolation in the older person. They describe four age-integrated groups which they conducted and studied from 1970 to 1975. Ages in the group ranged from 15 to 80. They found that the composition of the group provided an opportunity for a rich exchange of feelings, experiences and support among the generations.

Within group counselling some of the most frequently used approaches with older adults include psychodynamic, life review, gestalt, cognitive group counselling and remotivation group counselling. The psychodynamic group setting provides members with many opportunities for transference feelings towards other members. By paying attention to them, older adults can increase their self-understanding. The use of these groups with older adults has mostly occurred with outpatients. Feil (1967) used psychodynamic group therapy in her work with nursing home residents. She saw the group as achieving two goals: an increase in interaction among group members, and the development of self-worth in each participant. This latter goal was enhanced by individual participation in activities of the nursing home. However, before group interaction could be achieved, she had to develop a relationship with each individual member. In one group this took 3 years.

The use of paintings in analytic group therapy was outlined by Kymissis (1976). These provide an additional tool of expression which allows the discharge of emotions. Repressed affect may be released in paintings. A non-verbal channel of communication makes the initial stages less threatening. Kymissis pointed out that at the beginning participants may paint inanimate objects relating to each other, while subsequently they draw people, including members of the group or the therapist. They then begin to interact and express positive or negative feelings.

Life review therapy (see Chapter 6) is frequently conducted in a group context. Edinberg (1985) enumerated four triggers which may be used in stimulating life reviews: music, including old records or a sing-along; scents, comprising perfumes, spices or flowers; images embracing emotional events in the past; memorabilia, comprising old photographs, newspapers, cards or favourite possessions. Sherman (1991) studied cherished objects as inducers of reminiscence in 100 older adults from four urban senior service centres: 96 people possessed at least one object which encouraged reminiscence. Photographs were identified by more than two-fifths of the sample. Sherman found that when cherished objects served as stimuli for reminiscence, they triggered memories that would reconstruct a whole era in the person's life.

In using life review in a group context it is important that all participants tell their story during the life of the group. The group leader can identify themes in the life review and highlight strengths and positive coping techniques. As each life review is recounted, members can discover a number of similarities. A variation of this process is to use a guided life review. The group counsellor invites participants to close their eyes and to reconstruct a scene in their childhood. A number of questions are asked, such as: Where are you? What are you doing? Who is with you? When this episode is completed, participants may be invited to consider another scene at a later stage in their childhood. The amount of material explored will depend on the length of time available for the group.

Gestalt therapy groups may take different forms depending on the particular approach used. If they are modelled on the traditional orientation of Perls, the leader and an older adult will consider a problem together while other participants watch the work. In the model used by Polster and Polster (1973), participants use a 'floating hot seat', a technique which encourages older adults to become involved in the work of another member spontaneously. In this approach the work of another member may be the method whereby participants become involved in their own work.

Cognitive group therapy uses a problem-oriented approach, which deals mainly with depression and anxiety problems in older adults. It is usually short-term. Effective collaboration is maximized through the setting of agendas between the group therapist and members. Relevant information relating to the concerns of older adults may be presented. Participants can use role play to experiment with new behaviours and to obtain feedback from participants.

Freeman et al. (1993) identified three types of cognitive groups: open-ended, rotating theme and programmed groups. In open-ended groups, participants are usually screened beforehand. They are requested to come to the group with two or three issues. From this variety of agendas the group usually focuses on what is of general interest. Bowers (1989) developed rotating theme groups for use in hospital settings. The therapist focuses each of the groups on a specific theme and an effort is made to match the topics to the particular problems of the group. In programmed groups, the main focus is on the educational dimension of problem solution. The recognition and modification of automatic thoughts and cognitive errors, the stepwise approach to the attainment of goals and the use of homework are outlined. In this manner participants' knowledge of the use of cognitive therapy develops.

Remotivation therapy ties in well with the focus on reality and the life review (Brink, 1979). The former defines older adults' tasks and the means at their disposal; the latter demonstrates where they have coped successfully in the past. The purpose of the group is to motivate older adults to use their present resources to cope with their problems. Guilt, anxiety, loneliness, grief, anger and resentment can all be expressed in safety in the group. The energy previously invested in these negative emotions can then be invested in more positive endeavours.

Group counselling is not always appropriate for older people. Waters (1984) has found that groups are inappropriate for those who are so preoccupied with and overwhelmed by their own problems that they are unable to listen or respond to other people. Individual counselling is indicated in such cases. Some people, both young and old, are very concerned with privacy, which would preclude their discussing personal issues in a group situation.

Research in counselling older adults

8

The approaches outlined in Chapters 6 and 7 provide a range of options with which to counsel older adults. But how effective are they? Studies that have sought to provide some answers are reported in this chapter. They may be categorized as psychodynamic therapy, humanistic therapy and cognitive and behavioural therapy.

PSYCHODYNAMIC THERAPY

Shulman (1985) presented a 6-year case study of psychodynamic group therapy with women aged 55–75 who were outpatients at a community health centre. The aim of the group was to help socialize participants who had somatic complaints with no medical basis. The initial screening of subjects covered diagnostic assessment, appraisal of the client's motivation for affiliation and socialization, and the expectation of a minimal ability to relate to others. Their psychiatric diagnoses included chronic paranoid schizophrenia, masochistic character disorder and borderline personality organization. The group began with six members. Over the years many new members joined and others left. One member stayed for the 6 years, while two of the original group stayed 2 years. There were five to eight core members at any one time, with an average of five in attendance weekly. Members left because they had achieved their goals, or their medical condition had worsened, or they resisted the group. Joining the group was described as an opportunity for the patient to learn about herself, her feelings and her relationships with others. Members agreed to attend regularly, to be on time, to keep group business in the group, to share feelings, to give the group a fair chance before leaving, and to talk about termination in the group.

Shulman addressed the group process in terms of object-relations theory. The first and primary task of the group was to create a safe environment, one with secure boundaries that would 'hold' its members. She parallels this task with the 'schizoid' stance of object-relations theory. Just as in early infant development, in the early stages of a group members are needy and dependent – concerned about their own safety. During the initial stages members found it difficult to own their feelings on these issues and used denial and projection as coping mechanisms. The issue of safety predominated throughout the lifespan of the group, a factor which Shulman attributed to the ego deficits of the group. The process was monitored in order to establish a sense of security and stability, of object constancy. This was difficult owing to frequent absences, and some departures from the group. Later responses around the threat to boundaries saw members beginning to own their feelings. It was during this stage that anger towards the group leader for not making it safe enough started to emerge. The frequent changes may have affected safety in the group. Yet surprisingly Shulman does not offer this as a possible explanation for members' preoccupation with the safety issue. The departure of the clinician highlighted the patients' perception of personal loss and gave them a chance to come to terms with those losses. By the end of the group, cohesion and support were apparent.

The initial behaviour of the group was self-absorbed, but as it evolved members became more supportive and altruistic. Functioning outside the group improved or was stabilized. One member was helped to stay within the community during a serious illness rather than be admitted to a nursing home; another's physical symptoms abated, and on the whole there was a reduction in the frequency of visits to medical personnel. A developing awareness was expressed by participants of the relationship between symptoms and emotional stress.

The study is interesting in that it applies group therapy to a group with varying psychiatric diagnoses. However, it would be preferable from a research viewpoint to work with a group comprising individuals with only one of these disorders. It is difficult to come to any conclusion regarding the effectiveness of the group, since it takes the form of an anecdotal account and the group itself was composed of such changing membership. The study illustrates many of the difficulties encountered in researching psychodynamic group therapy (apart from reminiscence therapy), namely, the absence of controlled measurements. Simple outcome measures using a rating scale would greatly improve such studies.

In a study of supportive psychotherapy with the physically ill, Godbole and Verinis (1974) assigned inpatients to three separate groups: supportive psychotherapy, psychotherapy with confrontation or a non-treatment group. Those in therapy received 6–12 15-minute sessions three times a week. Pre- and post measures included nurses' and therapists' ratings of functioning, doctors' ratings of anticipated rehabilitation and self-report measures of self-concept and depression. Patients in the confrontation group were judged as improved by nurses (6/14) and therapists (18/22 scales). The supportive psychotherapy group was judged as improved by nurses (5/14) and therapists (7/22 scales). The control group was not considered improved by the majority (1/14 nurses and 2/22 scales for therapists). Only in the confrontation group did a significant proportion show improvement on the depression and self-concept scales. A significantly greater proportion of both psychotherapy groups was considered by the doctor as fit to go home than in the no-treatment control group. The results, however, have to be interpreted with caution since all raters had preconceived views of the status of patients. In addition, the amount of therapy the treatment groups received was quite low (18–36 minutes a week).

The psychodynamic approach has included the use of reminiscence as a therapeutic technique since Butler's (1963) introduction of the concept. Perrotta and Meacham (1981) investigated the effect of a reminiscing intervention on depression and self-esteem. Twenty-one community residents attending a senior centre were randomly assigned to one of three groups: a treatment reminiscing group, a current life events group, and a non-treatment control group. The average age was 77 years. The distribution of participants by sex was similar in each of the three groups. An unspecified number were regarded by staff as depressed.

A pretest–post-test control group design was employed. Participants were measured on a modified version of the Zung Depression Scale (1965) and the Rosenberg (1965) Self-Esteem Scale. The groups had similar scores on both scales prior to the intervention. The treatment group met five times and was encouraged to reminisce. The current life events group spoke of their current life situation, problems and enjoyable activities. The no-treatment control group did not engage in the intervention. For participants in the reminiscing group there was an average of 21 episodes of reminiscing per session, while an average of two reminiscing episodes per session crept into the current life events group.

Results indicated that there were no significant differences between the three groups in their post-intervention scores. The study did not support the hypothesis that a structured reminiscing intervention would reduce depression and increase self-esteem in older adults. The apparent lack of control over reminiscence in the current life events group diminishes the value of the study.

Hedgepeth and Hale (1983) assessed the effect of brief reminiscing on affect, expectancy and performance among a group of older women.

It was hypothesized that subjects who reminisced about positive experiences would report less depression and anxiety, and that they would express greater confidence in their abilities and would then perform better on a psychomotor test. Sixty white females aged 6–98 years were recruited from various community settings and from church and community organizations. The anxiety and depression scales of the Multiple Adjective Checklist (Zuckerman and Lubin, 1965) and a digital symbol test similar to the one used in the Wechsler Adult Intelligence Test were administered to all subjects. In addition, each subject was asked to predict how well she would perform on a subsequent test compared to 100 other individuals her age. They rated themselves on a 19-point ladder from 'better than 5%' to 'better than 95%'. Subjects were randomly assigned to one of three groups, two treatment and one non-treatment. All groups received one hour-long interview. In the first group subjects were asked to reminisce about past successes, while the second group was encouraged to discuss positive present experiences. Both groups were administered the dependent measures. Subjects in the control group were given the dependent measures and then invited to talk about past or present experiences. No significant differences between the groups were found on any measure. The results are not surprising, in that it is unlikely that significant change can occur in one session.

Berghorn and Schafer (1987) considered ways of predicting who from a group of nursing home residents would benefit from reminiscence-group interventions. A total of 277 individuals from 30 nursing homes who were considered to be mentally and physically capable of participating in discussions over a 3-month period were selected to participate in the study. They were randomly assigned to one of three treatment conditions or a non-treatment condition, to assess the efficacy of literary materials prepared by the US National Council on the Aging (NCOA) in a nursing home setting. The NCOA materials used in the first treatment condition were originally designed for use in senior citizen centres as a springboard for personal reflection and reminiscing (1977–1982). The materials consisted of excerpts from fiction and non-fiction grouped in printed anthologies and audiotaped cassettes to reflect previous experiences of older adults. Nursing homes in the second condition did not use NCOA materials, but old photographs and newspapers were used to evoke memories. The third treatment condition used NCOA materials, but this condition employed a closed-circuit radio broadcast of the excerpts with on-the-air discussions and call-in opportunities. Leaders in all the treatment conditions were given training in their particular condition and in eliciting reminiscences.

Eight variables were used to provide an index of change (pre- and post-test) evidenced by each participant: whether or not one had a confidant;

whether or not one knew any of the participants in the discussion group; the quality of one's interpersonal activity; the number of people in a discussion group known to the participant; short-term memory (measured by recall of a 19-word list); life satisfaction (Life Satisfaction Index; Neugarten *et al.*, 1966); perceived friendliness of other residents in the home; and self-rated health, both of the latter being measured by a Cantril ladder (Cantril, 1965). The number of references by time orientation (past, present or future) were recorded by observers in ten nursing homes.

One hundred and eighty-five participants completed the programme. The majority of recorded time references (90%) were to the past, indicating that participants did engage in reminiscence. Participants in the first two treatment conditions experienced more significant change from pre- to post-test than did the controls. Further analyses revealed that those who are not adaptive and who hold to values not supported by the social structure of the nursing home are most likely to be affected positively by a reminiscence-group intervention, whereas those who are adaptive and adjust their values to the nursing home environment are least likely to be affected positively by such an intervention. Reminiscence afforded residents whose values were not adapted to the nursing home the opportunity to vicariously experience highly valued situations, which resulted in a modified attitude toward some aspects of the nursing home and their sense of wellbeing. The results were predictable to the extent that the maladjusted group had more room for change and were more likely to experience improvement.

The study was a large-scale one in group counselling terms. Considerable detail is given at times, with the result that it is difficult to extract the essentials of the study. At other times essential detail is omitted. For example, no details of the training and experience of the counsellors are given, except that they were trained in the specific condition and in the elicitation of reminiscences.

An investigation of life review therapy was carried out by Haight (1988). She regards life review as very different from ordinary reminiscences in that it guides the older person through personal memories. She randomly assigned 51 recipients of a meals-on-wheels programme to one of three groups: a life review, friendly visiting or no treatment. In the first two groups a student visited for 1 hour a week for 6 weeks. In the first group a structured life review was conducted, while in the second there were informal conversations. Life satisfaction, psychological wellbeing, depression and activities of daily living were measured by a researcher who did not know to which group the individual belonged. These were administered 1 week after participants agreed to participate and again 7 weeks later. Life satisfaction and psychological wellbeing were significantly improved in the life review group, while level of depression was not. The study was well designed and thus provides strong support for the efficacy of life review for increased life satisfaction and psychological wellbeing. Replication studies need to be carried out.

The life review concept was the basis for a guided autobiography approach with older adults by Malde (1988). This was an attempt to standardize the life review process. The study aimed at evaluating the effect of guided autobiography on self-concept, time competence and purpose in life. A pilot study was carried out 2 months before the main study, with four female participants whose mean age was 70. Participants were recruited for the main study by means of flyers, bulletin and newspaper notices, telephone calls and announcements at meetings. Individuals 60 years and older were sought to participate in an educational, personal development course with a focus on autobiographical writing. A total of 39 volunteered and were randomly assigned to one of three groups of 13. The average age was 70, with a range of 60–82.

The treatment lasted 5 weeks, with two 90-minute meetings per week. The first treatment group received a guided autobiography approach consisting of four components: lectures on writing and psychological development; sensitizing exercises that highlight specific issues related to the writing assignments; a written autobiography focused on selected life themes; and a small-group discussion of the written autobiography sections. The second treatment group consisted of guided autobiography with the first three components and a large, literary discussion group replacing the small sharing groups. Waiting-list candidates served as the control group.

After the course was completed, participants in the three groups were administered the Tennessee Self-Concept Scale (Fitts, 1965), the Time Competence Scale of the Personal Orientation Inventory (Shostrom, 1974), and the Purpose in Life Tests (Crumbaugh, 1968). A post-test-only design was employed to avoid confounds due to a pretest. No significant differences between groups on the three dependent measures were obtained. Hence guided autobiography did not produce positive changes in the older person's self-concept, time competence and sense of purpose in life.

A follow-up study was carried out to see if changes might be more apparent over time. A questionnaire designed to tap the same general areas as the original instruments was mailed to all participants 1 year after the course. Thirty-three of the original 39 participants responded, and in general the feedback received was positive. With regard to their view of self, a significantly greater number reported either no change or positive change rather than negative change. A significantly greater number of participants reported positive change rather than negative change or no change with respect to their view of their present life, their past and their future. In the follow-up results no comparisons were made between the two treatment groups. Hence the lasting effects of the group sharing of the autobiography cannot be assessed.

Guided autobiography holds promise in that it may permit older adults to identify unfinished situations in their lives. A better design for future studies would be to use two comparison groups, one in which discussion of the autobiography takes place, while in the second the group could have a trained counsellor. The relative values of the two approaches could then be compared.

Sherman (1987) used two types of reminiscence groups to enhance the development of social support and a sense of wellbeing among the elderly: a life review–reminiscence group and an experiential group that focused on feelings and thoughts. He also hoped to determine whether participation in these groups led to an increase in the frequency and enjoyment of reminiscing in their everyday lives, to a change in the quality of the reminiscence and to the resolution and integration of issues from the past.

Volunteer participants from four community centres were randomly assigned to either a non-treatment condition in which the members did not formally meet in groups, or to one of two treatment groups. In each centre three samples were generated for a total of 12 groups.

Initially there were 104 participants, with a mean age of 73.8 years. They were randomly assigned into four non-treatment samples and four samples of each of the two types of treatment group. The total number of participants was 35 for each of the two treatment groups and 34 for the non-treatment group. The groups were conducted on ten occasions of 90 minutes each. Pre- and post-tests were carried out and a follow-up test was conducted 3 months later.

The measures used were participant reports of numbers of new friends made and maintained; numbers of new confidants; frequency and degree of enjoyment of reminiscence; the Life Satisfaction Index Form Z (LSI-Z) (Wood *et al.*, 1969); and the Monge (1975) Self-Concept Measure. Two other measures, engagement in reminiscence and experiential level of reminiscence (based on Klein *et al.*'s 1970 Experiencing Scale), were used to assess 3–5-minute audiotaped time samples of reminiscence of each individual in each group, including the control group, for each of the three testing periods. These latter were then rated by trained judges.

A social worker practitioner conducted all the reminiscence groups. The life review group was based on Lewis and Butler (1974). The other approach to group reminiscence was experiential, based on the method of Gendlin (1981), which consisted of six steps for teaching a person how to focus on the bodily-felt inner meaning of an experience.

Over 90% of the participants had confidant relationships in the pretest, so there was no significant increase in the number of confidants at the end of the project. However, participants indicated that they had made new friendships and these were maintained at the follow-up period. The control group and the treatment groups showed positive, though not significant, changes in life satisfaction and in self-concept. Because the control participants had come together for testing, by the third testing they considered themselves 'a group' and claimed to be heavily engaged in reminiscing. Consequently, the results showed no significant difference between non-treatment and treatment groups on life satisfaction, self-concept and frequency and enjoyment of reminiscence. When all three groups were combined, however, the total sample showed statistically significant positive changes on all these outcome variables from pre-testing to follow-up.

A difference in the type of reminiscence of both treatment and non-treatment groups emerged at follow-up. The non-treatment participants tended to be more selective in their reminiscences, whereas the treatment groups were more inclusive and more fully engaged. Furthermore, the treatment groups showed significantly higher Experiencing Scale scores than the non-treatment groups, and the experiential group demonstrated significantly higher Experiencing Scale scores than the conventional reminiscence group. Members of the experiential group reported that the present was enlivened by their memories and they appeared to have a newer, more open and more accepting attitude toward the past. The author also reports that this group incorporated the greatest measure of feelings and thoughts in reconstruction of the past.

The study highlights the importance of the manner in which reminiscence groups are conducted, in that the experiential approach appears to be more beneficial. In three of the four settings treatment members and some of the control group participants met independently and formed an ongoing peer mutual support group. It appears that reminiscence groups have the potential for the development of peer support groups for older adults. The very act of socializing in a group has a notable therapeutic effect. The low financial outlay in such a process suggests the merits of further investigation. The initial design of the study was confounded by the appearance of peer support groups and provides a good example of the difficulties encountered by the researcher in the applied field. A replication study is desirable where agreement is obtained from the control participants not to engage in a group experience until the conclusion of the research.

Harp Scates *et al.* (1986) investigated the contribution of reminiscence, cognitive–behavioural and activity treatments to life satisfaction and reduction of anxiety in the elderly. Participants included 60 volunteers from a rural Retired Senior Volunteer Programme (RSVP) who met the following criteria: aged 65 or over; ability to hear in a group setting; freedom from psychotropic medications; and a written willingness to participate. Of the 60 volunteers, 50 met the criteria and their average age was 75 years. Every subject reported having a confidant.

Level of life satisfaction was measured by the Adams (1969) modified version of the Life Satisfaction Index A (Neugarten et al., 1966) and anxiety by the State-Trait Anxiety Inventory (Spielberger et al., 1983). These questionnaires were administered at initial contact, pregroup, postgroup and follow-up.

Participants were randomly assigned to the cognitive–behavioural, reminiscence or activity condition. Each group met for 1 hour-long session twice a week for 3 consecutive weeks. Two Master's-level therapists, who were unaware of the purpose of the investigation, served as co-facilitators for each of the group conditions.

The cognitive–behavioural group participated in didactic lecture, discussion, role play, modelling and homework, which emphasized changing self-statements from negative to positive where they existed. For the reminiscence group there was didactic lecture, discussion and homework, which stressed the integration of the past with the present. In the activity group participants were free to choose the group's activities, except in those instances where the leader specifically guided discussion away from the content that might be expected to arise in the other group conditions. The activity group was videotaped and a content analysis was conducted to verify that the activities did not overlap with those of the other treatment group conditions.

Results indicated no significant differences on the life satisfaction scores of the three groups at any stage. On the state anxiety scale, no significant differences were obtained at initial contact, pretest and post-test, but at follow-up the reminiscence group decreased their state anxiety levels significantly. On the trait anxiety scale, no significant differences were obtained at initial contact, pretest, post-test and follow-up. The study offers no support for the effectiveness of the three interventions in their contribution to life satisfaction or the reduction of anxiety. The method of reminiscence used was based on Wolpe (1969). As such it offers a different means of working with reminiscence from that usually based on Butler and Lewis (1977). This difference is not dealt with in any depth by the authors, either in their description of treatment or in the discussion. Since the study does not provide evidence of its effectiveness, the method of reminiscence based on Butler and Lewis is preferable. The use of a videotape and content analysis in the activity group is to be recommended, and could have been extended to the cognitive–behavioural and reminiscence groups.

Leszcz et al. (1985) conducted a psychotherapy group for older men which was based on Yalom's (1975) interactive and interpersonal approach and incorporated reminiscence and life review. The men had resigned themselves to disengagement and depression despite reasonable physical and mental health. Because of their similarities and their persistent resistance to engagement in ongoing home programmes and activities, they were invited to join a psychotherapy group. The seven men selected to take part in the initial group averaged 85 years and were residents of the same floor in a nursing home. All received an invitation to participate. They were told that the group would consist of men like themselves who were depressed and who spent a lot of time alone. It was suggested to them that the group would provide an opportunity for confidential discussion of what their life was like, a chance to get to know each other and a chance to share their mutual problems to see what could be done about them.

The group met weekly for 75 minutes and was led by a male psychiatrist and a female social worker. The latter was known to all the men and this was considered important to limit initial resistance to the process. The group was encouraged to respond to each person's reminiscences and to explore their own personal reactions to the material presented at the level of the here-and-now. The number of weeks the group continued is not reported. The only information in this respect is a single reference in the text referring to 'Several months after the group's beginning'.

The authors reported that during the first meetings the men were very passive, discouraged and hopeless. They entered the group expecting the therapists to solve problems regarding feelings of neglect, poor food and other institutional complaints. They approached it with much scepticism and were cynical about the therapists' interest in them. They asked what would younger people want with them. They owned society's projections of ageism and lack of worth, as well as regarding depression as their normal state. Thus the first issue in the group became one of addressing the negative identification which was subsequently projected on to their own peers, whom they would then devalue and avoid.

Psychotherapeutic approaches that counteracted this initial negative orientation included empathizing with this sense of discouragement as a way of reducing the men's sense of being trivialized and ignored, and at the same time fostering within the group an active interpersonal approach to discussing these issues. Group members were encouraged to give feedback, as a way of staying engaged in the present. Rounds were used during which members were asked to recount a time in their lives when they felt more satisfied, more powerful or more proud. This was a form of life review, which helped to minimize their sense of unique isolation and despair.

The authors reported that the group went through many states of disengagement and depression, which were not fixed but in fact fluid, reversible and responsive to environmental influences. Members were able to bolster their sense of self-worth and value to the group. At its conclusion the men had a greater sense of involvement with each other, were more available both to each other and to staff, and continued to meet regularly on their own initiative. They were also found to be more amenable to participating in other activities and programmes offered by the institution. They showed increased affect, a willingness to renegotiate rather than to give up, and a preference for engagement rather than disengagement. Unfortunately, all the noted changes are based only on the observations of the author.

The reporting of the study takes the form of an uncontrolled case study of a group. It is regrettable that simple outcome measures were not incorporated in the design, such as the use of a Likert scale to measure the degree of involvement before and after the study. A simple frequency count could also have been used to measure pre- and postinvolvement in social activities and programmes offered by the institution. A major weakness of the study is the absence of a control group.

Rattenberg and Stones (1989) conducted a controlled evaluation of reminiscence and current topics discussion groups in a nursing home context. They investigated the effect of both of these interventions on psychological wellbeing, activity level and the rated level of functioning in the home. The subjects were 24 volunteer geriatric residents who met the criteria for participation in the study: good visual and auditory capabilities and freedom from any obvious impairment. The participants were randomly assigned to one of three conditions: the reminiscence discussion group, the current topics discussion group and a control group. The average age of the participants was 85. The group leaders were a clinical psychology graduate student specializing in gerontology and a registered nurse who had experience of working with older adults.

Measures used included: psychological wellbeing (Memorial University of Newfoundland Scale of Happiness (MUNSH), Kozma and Stones, 1980); activity (Memorial University of Newfoundland Activities Inventory (MUNAI), Stones and Kozma, 1986a); rated functioning level (Stockton Geriatric Rating Scale (SGRS), Meer and Baker, 1966); mood (Memorial University Mood Scale (MUMS), McNeil, 1986).

The three groups did not differ on any of these measures at the pretest stage. Analysis of pre–post changes showed a significant change on scores for the MUNSH but not on the other three measures. Both intervention groups showed significant improvement on the MUNSH relative to the no-treatment group, with no significant differences between the intervention groups. A talking score was calculated per subject per week. The mean talking score for both treatment groups increased as the weeks progressed. There were significant correlations between changes on the MUNSH and talking ($r = -0.62$) and change scores on the SGRS and talking ($r = 0.52$). These scores indicated that subjects who talked more gained the most in happiness and had greater rated functioning level.

The study provides support for the effectiveness of both reminiscence and current topics discussion groups on psychological wellbeing. The question arises as to why the reminiscence group was not more effective? A possible explanation lies in the use of the two group leaders. There is no suggestion that either of them had training in group counselling. If this was the case, the reminiscence group was no different from a discussion group, since it lacked a trained group counsellor. A novel feature of the study is the use of the talking score. The number of verbal interactions for a 30-minute session was counted by specifying the number of 15-second intervals when the participant spoke. These frequencies were averaged across the group sessions, yielding one talking score per subject per week. This procedure holds possibilities for measuring the amount of contact in the group through talking.

Garrell Hern and Weiss (1991) described a group counselling experience using a modified remotivation and structured reminiscence format with six elderly nursing home residents ranging in age from 85 to 99 years. They were referred on the basis of their tendency to isolate themselves in their rooms and avoid social contact with other residents. Remotivation therapy is usually aimed at the reconciliation of participants, and does not deal with personal problems and family relationships. However, in this group participants were encouraged to share issues from the past. The group process consisted of 12 weekly 75-minute sessions and was facilitated by a doctoral student in psychology. On occasion the groups lasted 50 minutes due to the energy level of the group.

As the group progressed the researchers found that the quality of the interaction improved. Participants discussed topics such as Christmas, Thanksgiving, faith, patience and trees. After sharing an experience other group members were encouraged to give feedback. Each member became increasingly attentive to and supportive of other members. The sharing and cohesion experienced in the group became an effective means of reducing feelings of alienation and isolation, and increased feelings of belonging among group members.

Group progress was often slowed down owing to the sensory impairments of some participants. The authors emphasize the need for the following characteristics in the group leader: an ability to express warmth, genuine caring and concern, to be patient and to use touch. Even more importantly they stress the effort often involved in conducting group counselling with the very old, where confinement to wheelchairs necessitates extra consideration in assembling the group. The study is refreshing in taking such practical difficulties into consideration. However, it needs more empirical support through the use of quasi-experimental or experimental design.

Stevens-Ratchford (1993) investigated the effect of life review reminiscence on depression and self-esteem in older adults. Twenty-four healthy older adults, with a mean age of 80 years, living in a retirement community were divided into male and female groups. They were then randomly assigned to treatment and non-treatment groups. A pretest–post-test control group design was employed. All subjects were administered Rosenberg's (1965) Self-Esteem Scale and the Beck Depression Inventory (BDI) during orientation sessions 1 week before the study began and at post-test. All subjects were free of depression as measured by the BDI. The non-treatment group was instructed to continue their normal routines and to return in 4 weeks for the administration of post measures. The treatment group participated in six 2-hour sessions of life review reminiscence activities during which slide presentations of the 1920s, 1930s and 1940s were shown, including both pleasant and unpleasant events.

No significant differences emerged between the treatment and non-treatment groups on the self-esteem and depression measures, or in the depression and self-esteem scores of the males and females in the two groups. However, a significant negative relationship was found between depression and self-esteem (the F statistic was 5.67, $P = 0.03$).

The study is flawed in that neither the treatment nor the non-treatment groups had scores which indicated depression as measured by the BDI at pretest, or had been classified as depressed. A further weakness of the study is that both treatment and non-treatment groups had high self-esteem scores at the pretest stage.

Studies of psychodynamic interventions with older adults reviewed in this section were characterized by the use of reminiscence and life review therapy. Group work was most frequently used. Of 13 studies, 10 dealt with the effect of reminiscing: reminiscence (6); life review (2); guided autobiography (1); reminiscence and life review (1). Three of these (Leszcz et al., 1985; Sherman, 1987; Garrell Hern and Weiss, 1991) were uncontrolled case studies and thus only offer anecdotal evidence for their effectiveness. Nine studies (Perrotta and Meacham, 1981; Hedgepeth and Hale, 1983; Haight, 1988; Harp Scates et al., 1986; Malde, 1988; Sherman, 1987; Berghorn and Schafer, 1987; Rattenberg and Stones, 1989; Stevens-Ratchford, 1993) used more controlled experimental groups, randomly assigning subjects to a reminiscence-type group as well as another intervention or control group. Five of these studies did not provide evidence for the effectiveness of a reminiscing intervention, while the study by Stevens-Ratchford (1993) was seriously flawed with respect to the dependent variables at the pretest. The remaining three studies provide some evidence for the effectiveness of a group reminiscing intervention in reducing anxiety and in the use of individual life review for improvement in life satisfaction (Haight, 1988; Rattenberg and Stones,

1989) and psychological wellbeing (Haight, 1988). The two other studies reported in this section were Berghorn and Schafer (1987) and Shulman (1985). Since Shulman used an anecdotal approach, no conclusions can be drawn from the investigation. The study by Berghorn and Schafer (1987) found that nursing home residents who were not adaptive to their current environment and held different values from it were most likely to benefit from a group reminiscencing intervention.

Future research in the area needs to consider carefully both the kind and length of training of the facilitator and relevant experience in using a group reminiscencing intervention. Only then will it be possible to consider the effect of more or less expert facilitators on outcomes. Without such data it is difficult to know what precisely a study is telling the reader, since non-significance may be due to lack of appropriate training and experience. Uncontrolled case studies such as that of Leszcz et al.(1985) should be eliminated, as they absorb valuable time and resources and lack the benefits of a controlled case study.

HUMANISTIC THERAPY

Lieberman and Gourash (1979) conducted a group programme entitled SAGE (Senior Actualization and Growth Encounter), which was based on humanistic principles and assessed its impact on the lives of older adults. Sixty people aged between 60 and 80 were recruited either by word of mouth or by publicity generated by the SAGE organization. They were screened by staff for psychological and physiological suitability. Participants had higher mean symptom level scores on the Hopkins Symptom Checklist (Derogatis et al., 1974) than those reported in a random sample of people over 60 living in the Greater Chicago Metropolitan Area (Pearlin and Schooler, 1978). In addition, 37% reported seeking professional help within the previous year for an emotional problem.

The first 30 people accepted into the programme were randomly divided into two groups of 15 participants and two or three leaders. They met for 3–4-hour sessions for 9 months. Group work consisted of structured exercises, dyad work and homework. The remaining 30 were asked to enter a delayed group, who would begin their SAGE experience approximately 10 months later and serve as a control group. Before the groupwork started a 3–4-hour interview was conducted with each participant, where they were asked to describe their major goals and objectives. At the end of the group programme individuals were asked to rate on a nine-point scale the degree to which they accomplished these target goals. This technique provided information on the issues that brought people to SAGE and allowed an assessment of the value of the group experience from the perspective of the individual.

The psychotherapeutic impact of SAGE was assessed by using the Hopkins Psychiatric Symptoms Scale, the Rosenberg (1965) Self-Esteem Scale, the Gottschalk–Gleser Anxiety and Depression Rating Scale of sentence completion (Tobin and Lieberman, 1976) and measures of various coping strategies (Pearlin and Schooler, 1978) to assess the amount of strain associated with the marital and parental roles as well as the mechanisms used to cope with these strains. Other measures included the Social Resources Scale developed by Tobin and Lieberman (1976) to determine both the size and breadth of the social network. The Life Satisfaction Index (Neugarten *et al.*, 1966) was used to provide a subjective appraisal of a person's life. In addition the Srole Anomie Scale (Srole, 1956) was used to determine the degree of detachment from the social world. The individual's orientation towards others was assessed using a checklist of phrases (LaForge, 1963; LaForge and Suczek, 1955). Finally the researchers investigated two intrapsychic processes that reflect important developmental themes: the maintenance of self-image and the use of one's personal past. Maintenance of self-image was measured by asking participants to give examples that supported their selection of phrases describing interpersonal orientation. A rating scale developed by Rosner (1968) was used to determine whether examples were rooted in the past, in the present, in a sense of conviction or were wishes based on sheer mythology.

Of the two groups, results indicated that the control group had significantly higher depression and anxiety scores, higher scores on anomie and parental strain, and lower scores on life situation at the initial interview. The evaluation of the target goals indicates that participants accomplished their desired goals to a greater extent than those in the waiting control group. Group members also described themselves as becoming more engaged in desired activities than the control group. Analysis of mental health variables yielded significant differences between participants and controls in symptoms and self-esteem. Psychiatric symptoms, particularly obsessive and depressive symptoms, diminished more among SAGE participants than among members of the control group. Self-esteem increased more for SAGE participants, although both groups showed an appreciable increase on this measure. A comparison of participants and controls on changes in anxiety about health showed that SAGE group members exhibited a reduction in anxiety regarding illness and physical deterioration, in contrast to the controls, who exhibited a slight increase in health anxiety over the 9-month waiting period.

Significant changes were found in social functioning in the way participants coped with marital strain. At the end of the SAGE experience group members were more likely to sit down and talk problems out and to express their feelings directly to their partner. They consistently decreased their involvement in reminiscence activity, in its case for problem solving, and the level of importance attached to reminiscence. They emphasized current interactions as a source of feedback in maintaining their self-image. In contrast, the control group tended to shift towards an emphasis on the past.

Within the developmental perspective the impact of SAGE could be seen in the mechanisms used to maintain a consistent self-image. Subsequent to the group experience participants emphasized current interactions as a source of feedback in maintaining their self-image. In contrast, the control group tended to shift towards an emphasis on the past. After the SAGE experience, group members also consistently decreased their involvement in reminiscence activity, in their use of reminiscence activity for problem solving, and the level of importance attached to reminiscence.

The study highlights the dimensions of a growth programme which could be desirable in a humanistic approach to the developmental needs of older adults. However it is not clear how individual goals and objectives and measuring instruments related to the SAGE programme. The study is further flawed due to differences between the two groups at the initial interview.

Johnson (1985) used a psychotherapy drama group based on role play and physical movement with nursing home residents. The group consisted of nine residents ranging in age from 64 to 96 years. The mental and physical condition of the subjects varied from mild confusion to complete alertness, and from severe physical impairment to physical integrity. The group met for 1 hour a week for 4 years. No control group was employed.

It was noteworthy that the death rate in the group was one-third that of the nursing home at large during the 4 years. A case study approach was used in describing the structure and process of the group. No instruments were used to evaluate the outcomes, and so the results are limited to the interpretations of Johnson (1985) on the basis of his experience facilitating the group. He believed that creative drama enabled them to concretize, symbolize and verbalize difficult feelings. He concentrated on physical limitations, the notion of the death of their parents and themselves, and transference to the therapist. He highlighted three aspects of the group which he regarded as enabling participants to confront and develop insight into anxiety-laden issues: the playful atmosphere, which allowed the expression of material relating to conflict; the role playing and physical movement, which concretized and simplified complex feeling states; and the group itself, which allowed the reinvestment in other people as vehicles for meaningful relationships.

The absence of a control group diminishes the value of the investigation. Nevertheless, the positive aspects emerging suggest that the study needs to be replicated in a scientific manner.

A more scientific approach was used by Berger (1983), who conducted expressive group therapy with residents of a transition unit attached to a general hospital. The patients had stabilized medical and/or psychiatric conditions, and had been evaluated by the treatment team of the unit as possessing sufficient potential for successful placement in a less restrictive environment outside the institution. From a total of 24 residents, 12 were randomly assigned to the treatment. By implication a control group existed, although from the data it is unclear whether any use was made of it.

Expressive group therapy consisted of sensory flooding activities – mainly poetry, but with some song and movement which heightened stimulation that evoked verbal expression. The treatment group met twice weekly for 6 weeks for 90 minutes per session. A participatory mode of research was used where the entire process was recorded by a participant observer. This participant observer was expected to record (1) the number of verbal statements of recognition from person to person; (2) the number of times each person spontaneously touched another person; (3) the kinds of facial expressions made during a session and the number of times; (4) the length of attention span for each patient in each session; (5) the number of self-initiated ideas, statements, writing or appropriate acts during each session; (6) the number of disruptive/interruptive behaviours during each session; (7) the number of obvious signs of pleasure or displeasure; and (8) elicited evaluative comments by participants.

Five staff members, including two therapists, one of whom was the researcher, rated the nine patients who remained at the end of treatment on a five-point scale from 1 (a lot worse) to 5 (a lot better). Seven of the nine participants obtained a mean score in the direction of the better or a lot better range, while only two mean scores were in the no change to worse range. The use of ratings by staff members is to be admired, although the rating instrument is poor. The use of a participant observer and a participatory mode of research is refreshing. It is unfortunate that no results for the eight listed process criteria are given, but this is not surprising given the amount of work assigned to the participant observer, which would appear to make it impractical to implement. Furthermore, the dual role of the researcher/therapist was unfortunate given the possibility of significant biases: by playing this dual role he had more difficulty in being objective.

Cooper (1984) investigated expressive group psychotherapy with older adults aimed at the resolution of issues concerning loss and death. Members of the group were chronic patients of a geriatric unit at a public psychiatric hospital. Their mean age is not given, but the group consisted of six women and two men ranging in age from 63 to 74 years. Length of hospitalization ranged from one and a half to 45 years. The group met twice weekly for 9 months. Patients were given the time and space to explore and express their their feelings of loss and death. Loss was a predominant theme. Cooper concluded that expressive group psychotherapy can lessen social isolation and provide participants with opportunities to share their fear and anxiety and gain control over it. The author felt that an important aspect of the group was the therapist's recognition of countertransference reactions, so that he was empathically available to group members to aid them in their therapy. Neither a control group nor instruments to evaluate the outcomes of the group psychotherapy were used. The study takes the form of a case study of a group.

Johnson and Wilborn (1991) investigated the effectiveness of group counselling for anger expression and depression in older female adults. Seventeen older women with a mean age of 76 years from senior citizen centres and retirement centres volunteered to participate in six 60-minute counselling sessions. A matched control group of 17 women with a mean age of 74 years was also employed. Both groups were matched on age, marital status, education, occupation, type of residence and perceived health. The BDI and the Anger Self Report Scale (ASR; Zelin et al., 1972) were administered to both groups directly after treatment and again 1 month later. No details are given on the training and experience of the group counsellors. The sessions were designed to increase the awareness and expression of anger.The study used a humanistic orientation while including cognitive–behavioural methods. At post-testing the treatment group scores were significantly higher than the control group's on the BDI. The higher depression scores of the treatment group were maintained at follow-up. No significant differences were found between the two groups on the ASR at post-testing.

Focusing on anger awareness and expression in the group did not result in a change in either of the two dimensions of anger in the women. However, this may be due to the lack of either training or experience of the leader. The intervention also used different counselling approaches, such as rational–emotive therapy and anger experience and expression, although sufficient detail is not given of the counselling approach used in the latter. It is also possible that six sessions are not sufficient to change anger awareness and expression in older adults. Possible explanations offerred by the authors for the higher BDI scores of the treatment group include (a) increased awareness that they have problems which had antecedents in childhood, and (b) normal depression which occurs at the termination of the group. The study is interesting in that it focuses on specific emotions in old age. However, the interventions to be used in future studies should be more firmly rooted in a specific counselling approach, and details of the training and experience of the group counsellor(s) given.

Humanistic therapy with older adults is greatly underinvestigated. Only two of the studies reported in this section used a control group (Lieberman and Gourash, 1979; Johnson and Wilborn, 1991). However, both were flawed: in the Lieberman and Gourash study the control group had higher depression, anxiety, anomie and parental strain scores at pretest, while the Johnson and Wilborn study gave no details of the training and experience of the facilitator. Hence humanistic therapy with older adults is virgin territory and any well-designed study would provide a welcome beginning.

COGNITIVE–BEHAVIOURAL THERAPY

Evans *et al.* (1986) developed a counselling programme for severe physically disabled older outpatients based on cognitive group therapy by telephone. The aim of the programme was to solve problems related to feelings of dissatisfaction, loneliness and inactivity. A sample of 50 outpatients was randomly selected. Clients had a mean age of 62 years and had been discharged from a 16-bed rehabilitation service within a 30-month period. Out of the original 50 subjects, 43 completed testing for the project. These were randomly assigned to a treatment group of 21 and a non-treatment group of 22. Three instruments were used to measure the emotional states of the participants before and after the group. These were: the Wakefield Self-Rating Depression Scale (Snaith *et al.*, 1971); the UCLA Loneliness Scale; and the Life Satisfaction Index. Goal attainment scaling was used to see whether clients attained their personal objectives. This procedure involved randomly selecting blocks of transcript of the therapy process for analysis. Behaviours were identified which the participants considered undesirable and would like minimized, as well as favourable behaviours which they would like strengthened. Level of achievement was rated as minimal, partial, satisfactory, substantial or complete. Groups met once a week for 1 hour for 8 weeks. At the time of the group meeting each participant was called on the telephone and placed on the same trunk line. The material discussed was determined by the participants without any form being imposed.

In the treatment group only three reported minimal goal achievement and two reported partial goal achievement (e.g. less anxiety, increased energy level). A close relative's opinion as to whether the described treatment would facilitate goal attainment was significantly correlated with the subject's report of outcome. Changes in loneliness and expectation of outcome were significantly related to meeting goals. Reduced loneliness was positively correlated with goal attainment scores. The treated group decreased significantly in its reporting of loneliness.

The study is very badly reported, with much deduction left to the reader. For example, mention is made of 43 older people completing the original testing and of 21 counselling participants. The non-treatment group of 22 is never explicitly mentioned and only arrived at by deduction. It is also difficult to separate the medium from the message.

Kemp *et al.* (1992) investigated the effects of cognitive–behavioural group psychotherapy on older depressed people with chronic disabling illness and other depressed individuals who were free of such illness. The illness group included rheumatoid arthritis, stroke, severe osteoporosis, severe heart disease and pulmonary disease. Fifty-one possible participants were recruited by means of notice boards at geriatric health and social service centres, and referrals from health or social service professionals or from families. Ten of these individuals were excluded for medical or neurological reasons. The average age of the 41 participants was 74 years: 18 had a chronic disabling illness while 23 did not. All were assessed as having major depression according to DSM-III-R.

Two measures were used: the Geriatric Depression Scale (GDS) (Yesavage *et al.*, 1983) and the Older Adult Health Mood Index (OAHMI) (Kemp, 1988). Two further questionnaires were developed by the authors: a knowledge of depression questionnaire and a questionnaire which assessed activities of daily living and leisure. The measures were administered before therapy, at 6 and 12 weeks (end of therapy), and at 6 and 12 months follow-up. The cognitive–behavioural therapy was conducted with both groups for 2-hour sessions for 12 weeks. Therapy was conducted by two licensed psychologists with 3 and 10 years' advanced training in geriatrics and extensive therapy experience.

Both groups improved significantly and to the same degree on depression as measured by the GDS. The improvement was continued for the group without a disabling illness up to 6 months after the therapy, while scores in the other group levelled off. Worsening of health problems, occurrence of family problems and changes in residence were more common among participants with a disabling illness, factors which could account for non-continued improvement once therapy ceased. For those without disabling illness depressive symptoms, including mood, cognitive–behavioural and physiological, as measured by the OAHMI, decreased while only mood symptoms decreased for those with disabling illness.

The study did not use either a control group or a comparison group. Hence it is akin to an uncontrolled case study in many respects. All change could have been due to other sources.

Deberry *et al.* (1989) compared cognitive–behavioural techniques and meditation–relaxation for reducing anxiety in a geriatric population. Fourteen male and 18 female volunteers with a mean age of 68.9 who complained of anxiety, nervousness, tension, fatigue, insomnia, sadness and somatic discomfort were selected from a senior citizen centre. A pretest–post-test follow-up control group design was employed. Following a prescreening interview all subjects were administered the Spielberger Self-Evaluation Questionnaire (SEQ, Spielberger *et al.*, 1983) as a measure of state trait anxiety, and the BDI. Participants were randomly assigned to one of three groups: relaxation–meditation; cognitive restructuring; pseudotreatment control. All groups met for 45-minute sessions twice a week for 10 weeks. In the first two sessions all groups received explanations of anxiety, stress and tension, as well as physical exercises which demonstrated the differences between relaxed and tense muscles. The cognitive restructuring group then received cognitive restructuring and assertiveness training. In these sessions participants were taught constructive positive thinking and rational coping strategies. The meditation–relaxation group received progressive muscle relaxation and meditation. The pseudorelaxation group received a combination of relaxation and assertiveness training but no formal training in these techniques.

Results indicated that meditation–relaxation significantly reduced state anxiety. Constant practice was necessary for maintaining a low level of state anxiety. Cognitive restructuring and assertiveness training did not significantly affect symptoms of anxiety or depression. The study points to the usefulness of meditation–relaxation in reducing anxiety in older adults. Further studies could profitably indicate the relative individual effects of meditation and relaxation. The study does not give any details of the training and experience of the facilitators.

Steuer *et al.* (1984) investigated the extent to which depressed geriatric patients would respond to group psychotherapy, and the differential effects of cognitive–behavioural and psychodynamic group psychotherapy. Thirty-five volunteer community residents (26 women and nine men) with a median age of 66 years participated in the study. All suffered from a major depressive disorder (DSM-III) and scored 16 or higher on the Hamilton Depression Scale (HAMD; Hamilton, 1967). One man died and one woman dropped out after the commencement of the groups.

Four groups, two cognitive–behavioural and two psychodynamic, were conducted. Each group had two female co-leaders, one who had at least 1 year of supervised clinical experience and 1 year of didactic training in the specific therapy. Patients were assigned to these groups on the basis of time entering the study. A pretest–post-test design was employed. Groups met twice a week for 10 weeks and once a week for the following 26 weeks, for a total of 46 sessions over a 9-month period. Each meeting lasted 90 minutes. Twenty individuals completed the 9-month treatment. Participants were rated by observers on the Hamilton Depression Scale and the Hamilton Anxiety Scale (HAMA; Hamilton, 1959) and rated themselves on the Zung Depression Scale (ZDS; Zung 1965) and the Beck Depression Inventory (1961) at pretreatment, 4, 8, 12, 26 and 36 weeks. Groups were combined for treatment type, resulting in two groups of ten each for data analysis.

Both groups showed significant reductions in observer ratings of depression and anxiety as well as on self-report measures of depression and anxiety. Forty per cent of those who completed treatment and 27% of those who started treatment went into remission, as measured by the HAMD. For those who completed treatment, the cognitive–behavioural group reduced their level of depression compared to the psychodynamic group. The authors make the case that the lack of use of a control group was due to ethical considerations in withholding treatment. However, the use of a within-group design would have been more appropriate and allowed more meaningful comparisons in the absence of a control group.

Two recent studies have considered the effectiveness of cognitive–behavioural therapies for insomnia in older adults. Engle-Friedman *et al.* (1992) evaluated behaviour therapy for insomnia in older adults. Fifty-three volunteer insomniacs were randomly assigned to one of four conditions: support and sleep hygiene information alone; support and sleep hygiene information plus progressive relaxation training; support and sleep hygiene information plus stimulus control instructions; measurement control group. The mean ages of subjects in the support and sleep hygiene, relaxation and stimulus control groups were 61, 60 and 57 years respectively. No figures are given for the other groups, although the authors do state that the age range was 47–76 years. Given this age range, the group can hardly be viewed under a strict chronological definition of older adult.

A pretest–post-test control group design was employed. Participants received 4 weeks of weekly individual treatment sessions. Follow-up was measured 3 weeks after the last therapy session, and at 2-year follow-up. Subjects were required to refrain from taking sleep medication for 2 weeks prior to and during the course of the study. Participants were measured on the Beck Depression Inventory, the Taylor Manifest Anxiety Scale (TMAS), the Eysenck Personality Inventory (EPI), Hazlewood's sleep self-efficacy measure, a general sleep questionnaire developed by the authors and an abridged form of the Northwestern University medical history questionnaire. There were no significant differences between the treatment groups on sleep questionnaire variables at the initial interview. While all of the behaviour therapies were effective in improving the sleep of the older adult insomniac, the differential effects of treatment revealed that the stimulus control instructions were most effective. This group felt most refreshed upon wakening and showed trends towards the greatest sleep time and the shortest onset of sleep. At the 3-week follow-up the support and sleep hygiene plus progressive relaxation group and the sleep hygiene and support group had the most restful sleep. At the 2-year follow-up, a higher proportion of stimulus control subjects were still using elements of the treatment and reported the most gains.

Morin *et al.* (1993) evaluated the efficacy of cognitive behaviour therapy for treating late-life insomnia. Subjects were recruited from the community through media advertisements and fulfilled the following criteria: 60 years of age or older; sleep maintenance insomnia defined as time awake after sleep onset greater than 30 minutes per night for a minimum of 3 nights per week during a 2-week baseline assessment; duration of insomnia of at least 6 months; complaint of at least one negative effect (e.g. fatigue, impaired functioning, mood disturbances) during waking hours attributed to poor sleep. The 40 subjects completed daily sleep diaries for a 2-week baseline period and underwent two consecutive nights of polysomographic evaluations. Fourteen were excluded because of sleep apnoea or periodic leg movement during sleep, or a combination of these two conditions. Two additional subjects were excluded because of their failure to refrain from using sedatives. The remaining 24 were randomly assigned to two groups of 12: a cognitive–behavioural therapy group or a non-treatment group.

The cognitive–behavioural group therapy sessions were of 90 minutes' duration and were held for 8 weeks. Measures included polysomography (PSG), sleep diaries, the ratings of significant others and psychological measures. The psychological measures included the Beck Depression Inventory; the State-Trait Anxiety Inventory; the Profile of Mood States (POMS: McNair *et al.*, 1971) and the Brief Symptom Inventory (BSI: Derogatis and Melisaratos, 1983).

After therapy the cognitive–behavioural group was significantly more improved than the non-treatment group on measures of wake after sleep onset, total wake time and sleep efficiency. They also improved significantly on all sleep parameters except for total sleep time, whereas the non-treatment group failed to show significant changes on any of these measures. Cognitive–behavioural subjects were significantly more improved than the non-treatment group subjects on total wake time. In addition, they also improved significantly from pre- to post-treatment on measures of wake after sleep onset, total wake time and sleep efficiency, whereas the non-treatment group showed no change for the same period except for an increased sleep time. On sleep stage variables the treatment group increased its percentage of REM sleep from pre- to post-treatment, whereas the non-treatment group decreased its time spent in stage 1 sleep.

Significant others' ratings indicated that cognitive–behavioural subjects were perceived to be significantly more improved on all variables, while the non-treatment subjects were not. The treatment subjects rated their sleep problem at post-treatment as less severe, less interfering and less noticeable than did the non-treatment subjects. They also indicated less distress and more satisfaction with their sleep patterns. While significant pre- to post-treatments on all ratings were obtained for the cognitive–behavioural group, none occurred for the non-treatment group. The treatment subjects rated the degree of change in their sleep patterns at post-treatment as significantly better than did the non-treatment group. There was a significant reduction in depression scores as measured by the BDI in the cognitive–behavioural group, but not in the non-treatment group. No difference was found on the POMS. It is interesting to note that an improvement in sleep pattern in the treatment group was accompanied by a reduction in depression.

A significant increase on total sleep time from post-treatment to 3-month follow-up was obtained, but no conclusion can be arrived at since no control group was used during the follow-up period. Thirteen of the 24 subjects (54%) had used sleep medication prior to enrolment in the study. At post-treatment, one subject in each group reported using a sleeping aid an average of 2 nights per week. The study indicates that late-life insomniacs can be treated effectively with cognitive–behavioural therapy.

All behavioural therapies are effective in the treatment of insomnia in older adults. However, stimulus control instructions may be the most effective. The goal of the stimulus control instructions is to help the insomniac gain a sleep rhythm, to strengthen the bed as a cue for sleep, and to weaken it as a cue for activities which may prevent sleep (Bootzin, 1977). This form of behavioural therapy appears promising for the treatment of insomnia. Replication studies which restrict the sample to subjects over 65 are desirable.

In a study of individual psychotherapy, Gallagher and Thompson (1982) investigated the effects of cognitive, behavioural or relational insight psychotherapy on older adults in a current major depressive episode. Participants were referred from regional health centres and private physicians, or were self-referred. The Schedule for Affective Disorders and Schizophrenia (SADS: Endicott and Spitzer, 1978) and the Research Diagnostic Criteria (RDC: Spitzer et al., 1978) were used to ascertain whether clients were in a major depressive episode while the Hamilton Rating Scale for Depression and the Beck Depression Inventory were administered to determine the level of depression at the time of the interview. Only individuals with scores greater than 17 on the BDI and greater than 14 on the HRSD were included in the study. The Mini Mental State Exam (Folstein et al., 1975) was given to screen out clients with gross cognitive impairment. A second interview was conducted by the project psychiatrist to evaluate health-related problems and to assess the risk of remaining off antidepressant medication during the course of psychotherapy. Thirty clients were considered suitable and were randomly assigned to one of three psychotherapy conditions (cognitive, behavioural or relational insight psychodynamic).

The treatment consisted of 16 individual sessions over 12 weeks. Clients were seen twice a week for the first 4 weeks and then once per week for the remaining 8 weeks. Each session lasted for 90 minutes. All therapy was conducted by people experienced in the particular modality they were utilizing. Participants were measured on the HRSD, the BDI and the Zung Depression Scale. Measures were obtained before and after therapy and at four follow-up times of 6 weeks, 3 months, 6 months and 1 year post-treatment. In addition, the SADS-Change (SADA-C; Spitzer and Endicott, 1977) interview schedule was used 1 year post-treatment to determine current diagnosis.

Comparable improvement in depressive symptoms occurred in all three treatment conditions from pre- to post-test. However, improvement during the 1-year follow-up was maintained more effectively by clients treated with behavioural or cognitive therapy than with relational/insight psychodynamic therapy. Hence although all three individual psychotherapies can be effective in the treatment of older adults with depression, cognitive and behavioural therapies appear to be more suitable. Eight participants, five from behavioural therapy, two from relational/insight psychodynamic psychotherapy and one from cognitive therapy, dropped out during the course of treatment. Yet the findings up to 3 months post-testing are reported for ten participants per group, and at 1-year follow-up for nine participants. This is less than desirable. From a positive viewpoint such comprehensive reporting of descriptive statistics, together with the inferential statistics employed, is to be encouraged since it gives readers more information on which to examine the study.

In a further study of individual psychotherapy, Thompson et al. (1987) compared the effectiveness of cognitive therapy, behaviour therapy and psychodynamic therapy in the treatment of depression in older adults who suffered from a major depressive disorder. One hundred and twenty elderly subjects were randomly assigned to one of the three treatment conditions or to a delayed treatment condition of 6 weeks' duration; 20 patients were assigned to the latter. Subjects were assessed as having a major depressive disorder using the RDC and as depressed if they obtained a minimum score of 17 on the BDI and 14 on the HRSD. Patients received 16–20 sessions of individual therapy scheduled twice a week for the first 4 weeks and once a week thereafter. All therapists were doctoral-level psychologists with at least 1 year specialized training in the modality they used. All had experience working with the elderly and they were supervised weekly.

In addition to the initial screening patients were assessed immediately prior to treatment (time 1); 6 weeks into treatment, corresponding with the completion of the delayed treatment condition (time 2); and at the end of therapy (time 3). Results indicated that by the end of 6 weeks patients in the treatment conditions showed improvement, whereas those in the control group did not. Ninety-one subjects completed the study. Of these 70% were either no longer depressed or had improved substantially as assessed by the SADS-C. The remaining 30% were still diagnosed as having a major depressive disorder. On the HRDS, 75% of the patients overall showed a clinically significant change. There were no significant differences across the three treatment groups, suggesting that the three modes of therapy were equally effective. The study supports the use of cognitive, behavioural and psychodynamic therapy in individual psychotherapy with older adults suffering from depression.

On the evidence presented it seems that individual cognitive or behaviour therapy is more effective than psychodynamic therapy in the reduction of depression. The absence of follow-up measures in the Thompson *et al.* (1987) study hinders evaluation of the long-term effects of the three treatments.

A study by Campbell (1992) sought to determine whether nurses could identify maladaptive depression in healthy older adults, and whether cognitive therapy made a significant difference in the levels of depression of these adults. Nurses were given classes on the use of the DSM-III-R (American Psychiatric Association, 1980) and on interventions to be used. Eighty women and 23 men ranging in age from 64 to 82 with a diagnosis of maladaptive depression that was non-suicidal and non-psychotic based on the criteria of the DSM-III-R were randomly selected from two city-owned housing units and two privately owned high-rise apartments for low-income elderly.

Subjects were divided into three groups. Group 1 received planned nursing intervention based on cognitive therapy techniques, including a daily diary to record their thought patterns. This included tasks such as assisting in the expression of anger, identifying incidents leading to depression, assisting in the acceptance of the realistic effects of loss, supporting feelings of hopelessness, commenting on performance and problem solving. The nurses focused on positive aspects of the life stages of participants and reinforced these positive patterns and behavioural activity. Group 2 served as a non-treatment group and received no nursing intervention. Group 3 received group classes and practice on crafts, but no specific treatment from nurses in order to rule out the Hawthorne effect, whereby behaviour can be altered due to awareness of observation. Treatment consisted of two 1-hour sessions per week for 8 weeks.

The Mental Status Questionnaire (Pfeiffer, 1975) and the Face–Hand Test (Fink *et al.*, 1952) were used to rule out organic brain syndrome. The Holmes–Rahe Social Readjustment Scale (1967) determined losses experienced during the past year that might have contributed to the subjects' depression. Finally, depression was measured by the ZSRDS.

Use of the ZSRDS confirmed the nurses' ability to identify depressed people with a 92% accuracy. In contrast with the original scores for depression (69 or higher), the treatment group scored below 60 after the cognitive therapy intervention, suggesting mild or no depression. This change was statistically significant. The control group showed no change from the initial scoring of greater than 69. Following nursing intervention there was a significant difference between the medians of the crafts group and the treatment group with the treatment group having lower depression scores.

The study holds promise in the use of community-based nurses in the diagnosis of depression. These front-line workers could possibly make referrals for depression if working under the appropriate supervision of a psychologist. No details are given with respect to the length of the training they received on using diaries and enhancing self-esteem in cognitive therapy, but given the significant change that occurred in the treatment group, the study raises interesting questions in this area.

Deutsch and Kramer (1977) investigated the value of group psychotherapy for older outpatients, most of whom were depressed about physical, mental or social losses. A total of five brief therapy groups was established. Each group had a maximum of 12 members and met in the hospital for one and a half hours a week for 12 consecutive weeks. The option was available to continue in subsequent sessions if they desired. Over a 2-year period the researchers had approximately 90 referrals from doctors, nurses and social workers within the hospital. In the early groups there were more women than men, but in the later sessions the researchers were more successful in recruiting men. As a result of participation in the groups many members became involved in volunteer or part-time work, renewed contact with friends and family, and were more able to cope with life's stresses. The study is limited in that no quantitative methods were used, the composition of the groups varied and results were based on two in-depth case studies and self-report by participants.

It is difficult to come to any conclusion regarding the effectiveness of the group since it comprised such changing membership. The study illustrates much of the difficulty encountered in researching group therapy with outpatients, namely the lack of a constant sample and reliable and valid measuring instruments.

Depression was the most frequently investigated problem in studies involving the use of cognitive–behavioural, cognitive or behavioural therapy. Five of these studies (Kemp *et al.*, 1992; Steuer *et al.*, 1984; Gallagher and Thompson, 1982; Thompson *et al.*, 1987; Campbell, 1992) provided evidence for the effectiveness of these interventions in treating major depression. The first two considered their effectiveness in a group situation while the two studies involving Thompson considered their relevance in an individual therapy context. The Campbell study found that nurses could identify depressed people and that cognitive therapy reduced depression. The length of treatment varied from 16 hours (Campbell) to 69 hours over 9 months (Steuer *et al.*)

Insomnia was investigated by two studies (Engle-Friedman *et al.*, 1992; Morin *et al.*, 1993) which provide evidence for the effectiveness of behaviour and cognitive behaviour therapy in its treatment. The remaining two studies dealt with loneliness and anxiety. The Evans *et al.* (1986) study found that cognitive group therapy by telephone reduced loneliness, while the Deberry *et al.* (1989) study found that group meditation–relaxation rather than cognitive–behavioural group therapy was effective in decreasing anxiety.

CONCLUSION

Investigations which involved the three main approaches to group counselling, namely psychodynamic, humanistic and cognitive–behavioural therapy, are reviewed in this chapter. What is immediately apparent from the studies is that these approaches are at different stages of development in relation to their application to older adults. Most attention to date in the psychodynamic field has been devoted to a particular type of intervention, namely reminiscence. In the cognitive–behavioural field endeavours have included investigations into both one-to-one and group counselling, into one of three different types of interventions, namely cognitive, behavioural or cognitive–behavioural, and into four main problem areas: depression, insomnia, loneliness and anxiety.

In the humanistic field the non-use of a control group, differences between treatment and control groups at pretest and lack of detail on the training and experience of the facilitator limit any conclusions being made on the research undertaken to date. The psychodynamic school appears to be in what Thoresen (1992) refers to as a 'context of discovery'. In this context, he holds, conjectures are constructed, concepts altered and theory revised. One conjecture which has emerged in the psychodynamic approach is that reminiscence is helpful to old age. This has led to an exploration of the concept which has resulted in further developments such as life review and guided autobiography. As yet the theory has not been revised as a consequence.

The other context of research, the confirmatory (Thoresen, 1992), was engaged in by the cognitive–behavioural approach. The reasearch to date has found that it is effective in the treatment of depression and insomnia. In the latter area, strong support was obtained for stimulus control treatment (support, sleep hygiene information and stimulus control instructions), since the older adults were still using elements of it 2 years after treatment.

It is not surprising that the cognitive–behavioural interventions that investigated depression were more effective than the psychodynamic with older adults, since there was a difference in the length of treatment. The cognitive–behavioural studies varied from a minimum of 16 hours (Campbell, 1992) to a maximum of 69 hours (Steuer *et al.*, 1984). The range for the psychodynamic studies was one session (Hedgepeth and Hale, 1983) to 15 hours (Malde, 1988). Four of these studies used an experimental design with a reminiscencing intervention (Perrotta and Meacham, 1981; Hedgepeth and Hale, 1983; Haight, 1988; Stevens-Ratchford, 1993). It is impossible to assess the effectiveness of the Leszcz *et al.* (1985) study since it is reported as an uncontrolled case study. The lack of effectiveness of reminiscence with respect to depression may be due to insufficient length of treatment rather than to the unsuitability of its application to depression. However, initial indications are that reminiscence, when used in its life review form, can improve life satisfaction and psychological wellbeing. Finally, there is an urgent need for well-designed studies with older adults in the humanistic field.

| 9 | **Issues: research and ethical** |

RESEARCH ISSUES

There are few well-controlled and well-designed studies dealing with counselling older adults. A number of issues need to be taken into consideration in future research developments to ensure that this deficiency is rectified. Since counselling and psychotherapy involve change, the measurement of such change is a primary focus. Age differences derived from cross-sectional data do not necessarily measure age changes. The latter require a longitudinal rather than a cross-sectional design. Campbell and Stanley (1963) outlined three appropriate designs which may be employed. These include the pretest–post-test control group design; the post-test only control group design; and Solomon's four-group design. The first and second are self-explanatory. In the latter a pretest is not essential since participants are randomly assigned to the two conditions. Solomon's four-group design uses two treatment and two control groups. One treatment and one control group are pretested and post-tested while the remaining two groups are post-tested only. This enables the separation of the main effects of testing, and the interaction of testing and treatment and multiple analyses of the treatment effects are obtained.

A second issue relates to the type of intervention used. Within the psychodynamic approach the use of reminiscence takes many different forms. In its conventional use, reminscence groups share memories from childhood through adulthood to old age. In life review therapy, clients are guided through these personal memories. Attempts by Malde (1988) to standardize the life review have been referred to as guided autobiography. These have included lectures, sensitizing exercises, written autobiography and either small-group discussions or large literary discussion groups. Lectures are not usually associated with counselling interventions and their contribution needs to be assessed through the use of between-subjects designs.

The use of reminiscence experientially based on the focusing method of Gendlin (1981) appears promising. In this method, reported by Sherman (1987), the first two sessions are conducted according to standard reminiscence procedure. In the third session members are introduced to guided relaxation, invited to think about pleasant situations and to focus on bodily sensations. It is necessary when using the term reminiscence therapy to describe what precisely is meant.

A defect in most intervention research with older adults is the acceptance of what Kiesler (1966) called the uniformity myth, which holds that all older adults are essentially the same. The use of statistical techniques based on group means and standard deviations further encourages this perception. This can be avoided by an analysis using standard statistical techniques supplemented by individual profiles which deal with more in-depth analyses of participants with regard to particular behaviours. This could include the behaviours, their frequency and intensity, the types of situations that elicit them and the manner in which they are expressed.

The contextual myth holds that all older adults operate similarly in similar situations. To date, research on group counselling with older adults has focused mainly on intrapersonal variables, while the environment has been relatively neglected. Although there are practical problems in observing a person closely in the situational context, modern observation technology in the form of the video recorder would obviate this difficulty.

The treatment myth holds that all older adults need the same amount and type of treatment. The duration of studies has varied enormously. A rationale needs to be included in investigations for the varying types of treatment. For example, an active and directive group intervention may be more effective with more externally determined people, while a more person-centred approach may suit a more internally directed person.

Outcome research in counselling older adults must be based on a clearly testable hypothesis. Without such a hypothesis success or failure cannot be clearly evaluated. The hypothesis should be based upon the theoretical assumption that underpins the particular counselling approach. Without such clarity, the intervention process cannot proceed under optimum conditions. Frequently not enough attention is directed to this aspect, which results in underreporting of the interventions used. In such instances the possibility of replicability necessary for good scientific practice is absent.

Outcome research studies rarely report with sufficient clarity the qualifications of the counsellors and therapists used in the investigations. Such details should include both the type of professional training and the length of professional experience. Lack of improvement in therapy may be due to the lack of counsellor/therapist skill, rather than the particular approach used. This information should be clearly specified in the case of psychiatrists, social workers and psychologists. These titles do not of themselves guarantee adequate counselling preparation. The wide variety of training experience introduces wide variability in skill. The effectiveness of intervention can only be assessed if the counsellors/therapists are competent and able to provide the interventions appropriately.

Well-designed studies can be enhanced by the use of appropriate comparison groups. From those studies discussed in Chapter 8, Thompson *et al.* (1983) used a treatment group (behavioural), two comparison groups (brief psychodynamic and cognitive) and a waiting control. The results indicated that all three treatment groups improved while the waiting group did not. Through the use of the comparison groups it was possible to show that all treatments were equally effective. Without them a much more limited conclusion would have been obtained, namely that behaviour therapy led to improvement. Much of the research used only one treatment group, and hence limited the findings considerably. A further development would be the evaluation of what combination of treatments in what order is most effective.

Outcome studies with older adults which examine improvement in a particular problem area must take into account the type of intervention to be used. This involves a thorough review of outcome studies dealing with the particular problem in old age and the identification of the most suitable psychometric measures. When evaluating the effectiveness of a particular therapeutic approach it is much more difficult to identify suitable psychometric measures. The semantic differential holds potential in this regard.

Outcome is not a single variable but encompasses the professional report of the therapist; reports by observers who are close to clients while in their homes, at work or at leisure; and the self-reports of clients (O'Leary, 1992). These measures should be included in all outcome studies with older adults. In addition, the reliability and validity of the measures used should be provided. In the case of observational measures it is important to obtain an estimate of interjudge reliability.

A number of outcomes need to be distinguished to obtain optimum results. These include session outcomes, which are apparent at the end of a particular session; transfer effect outcomes, which are outcomes relating to behaviours, feelings and attitudes which occur outside sessions; final outcomes, which are apparent at the conclusion of treatment; and follow-up outcomes, which remain once treatment has concluded and a time interval has elapsed. As in most intervention research this last type of outcome data is sorely lacking in treatment outcomes with older adults.

ETHICAL ISSUES

Counselling, unlike psychotherapy, which is frequently based on a medical orientation to human beings, is rooted in the humanistic tradition. The autonomy of individuals is central to this approach: the right of people to make choices affecting their lives. Principle 6 of the American Psychological Association Ethical Principles (1981) stressed informed consent and freedom of choice throughout the treatment process. The focus of law is also based on free will, in contrast to medicine, where people are viewed principally in biological terms.

Older people in counselling differ from other age groups in many ways. Most people have at least one chronic illness by the age of 75 (Rowe, 1985). However, chronic illness does not of itself deprive people of the right and ability to make decisions concerning their own lifestyle. As counsellors we must seek to work in a collaborative relationship based upon both mutual respect and the informed consent of the client. It is important that we do not override our obligations to older adults more often than with other adult groups. There is no ethical justification for doing this. In the case of chronic illness, it is important to inform them of any risks which may arise from their illness so that this can be taken into consideration in their choices.

Gurian (1975) suggested the use of three questions when there is a report of symptoms of mental illness in an older adult: Who is asking for help? Who has established that the behaviour is a symptom? What are the intrapersonal versus the interpersonal issues? Clients who are mentally ill do not fall within the brief of the counsellor and appropriate referral should be made. It is unethical and paternalistic to take away the decision-making capacity of older adults under the guise of doing good if there is no clear danger. Only when it is quite clear that the client suffers from impairment should intervention occur. This position is in accord with John Stuart Mill's view that one could interfere in the life plans and actions of others if, and only if, they either could not properly determine the consequences of their actions, or those actions could harm others. This principle of autonomy involves freedom from constraints.

Older adults should not be coerced into participation in any group counselling programmes. This is particularly relevant in an institutional setting. On the other hand, professionals should not prevent such participation. Thus the ability to choose is an important element of any counselling programme. The freedom to know one's choices involves access to information with respect to the purpose of counselling, be it individual or group. Older individuals may be physically handicapped in terms of movement, hearing or sight but still have the mental capacity to benefit from counselling.

Roth *et al.* (1977) outlined criteria for psychiatrists to use in the judgement of mental capacity: whether the patient evidences a choice; whether that choice is a reasonable one; whether the choice is based upon rational reasons; whether the patient has the ability to understand the information vital to the decision-making process; and whether the patient has an actual understanding of that information. However, in all of these criteria there is a difficulty in judging precisely what is rational behaviour. For example, giving away a major portion of one's economic security may be irrational for a middle-aged person while the same action in older adults may be a very rational one. The question of appropriateness is one criterion to be taken into consideration. Judgements of incompetence should be used with prudence since when such a label has been assigned it is very difficult to have it reversed. Its existence will influence other individuals with whom older adults come in contact.

An interesting case in Tennessee reported by Cassell (1984) illustrates the inconsistencies that exist in the area. Mary Northern, a 75-year-old single woman with mild cognitive impairment who lived alone, developed frostbite on both feet which resulted in gangrene with superinfection. In hospital the doctors wished to amputate from below the knee, since they considered her to have a less than 10% chance of survival. She refused, with the result that the surgeons took the case to court to have her declared incompetent on the basis of her 'irrational' decision. The interesting point in this case is that if she had consented it would be very unlikely that the issue of her mental competence to give informed consent would have been raised.

Another consideration is whether the behaviour of older adults is dangerous to themselves or others. Yet even here it is important not to proceed with undue haste. Side effects from medication may cause hallucinations in the morning, yet the same person may be completely lucid for the remainder of the day. Reported symptoms of incompetence by carers have to be carefully checked by counsellors to ensure that they are not permanently excluding from their service older clients who may be in most need of their services. Consequently, it is imperative that psychological tools are well developed which will enable more accurate assessment of cognitive capacity. However, if older adults are suffering from senile dementia it is important that they do not suffer from exploitation, abuse or neglect. A less obvious area where the autonomy of older adults needs to be taken into consideration is nursing home settings. Often in such environments, although physical independence may be valued, control over details of their lives may be withheld from residents. In the US the Omnibus Budget Reconciliation Act 1987 (cf. Ackerman, 1990) gave residents authority over choices and decisions. The counsellor needs to maximize opportunities for increased independence for older adults.

Hofland (1990) distinguished between three dimensions of personal autonomy: physical, psychological and spiritual. Physical autonomy is freedom of movement; psychological autonomy is the freedom available to choose between different options; and spiritual autonomy relates to long-term values and the life meaning of individuals. A complication for older adults is that the exercise of psychological autonomy may be limited by lack of physical autonomy. For example, the desire of wheelchair-bound older adults to attend group therapy in a community or institutional setting is dependent on the goodwill of others.

Another issue which may impinge on the work of the counsellor is that of diagnosis. It is important that older clients not accepted for counselling or therapy be referred to appropriate agencies. Counsellors should not allow themselves to add to society's lack of interest in an already neglected group.

Particular care is needed when either facilitating group therapy or counselling older adults individually. For example, it is important to arrange meetings at a time which is convenient for them. Access to toilet facilities is also essential. The use of a room at ground level can further assist those who suffer from some form of physical impairment. Counsellors need to communicate clearly and unambiguously. The tone and pitch of voice must be loud enough for the hard-of-hearing to understand: gentle reassurance may fall on deaf ears! Failing sight may make older adults dependent on carers for transport. Although this is a problem also faced by this segment of the population when visiting other professionals, such as doctors and dentists, the overtly helping role of counsellors demands that older adults not be kept waiting for appointments. Bernstein (1990) spoke of the necessity for flexibility in schedules and suggests that possible locations might be the client's home, a park bench or a coffee shop. However, the last two of these might present some difficulties relating to confidentiality. Glasser (1978) also included going for coffee as one of the possibilities for becoming involved with the client in reality therapy.

Counsellors must ensure that information regarding their services is available to older adults. This involves activities not often associated with counselling, such as informal networking or giving talks relating to the issues of older adults, and indicating where appropriate help may be sought. The difficulties may be well known but a certain helplessness exists in the absence of choice.

Counselling older adults should be undertaken by individuals who have a sound theoretical knowledge of the issues of old age, have acquired formal counsellor training and have dealt with their own attitudes towards old age. Older individuals deserve a counselling provision which is equal to that provided to everybody else.

Ethical issues which arise in the context of all group therapy need to be considered when working with older adults. Before participating in a group, participants should be fully aware of the number of sessions and their duration. They should also be informed of the training and qualifications of the group leader. During the initial session confidentiality should be discussed, the right of each person to leave the group be stated, and their choice to speak or remain silent be clarified. It should be understood that there is no moral compulsion to self-disclose. In studies where treatment and control groups are being used, it is essential that control group members should be allowed to participate in the experience subsequently and allowed to experience group work for themselves at a later stage if such participation has clearly shown benefits in past research. This does raise some difficulties with respect to follow-up studies. But as with all group interventions, the good of the person must take precedence.

Finally, it is important that all counsellors and psychotherapists who intend working with older adults are aware of the ethical issues mentioned above. In 1990, the American Association for Counselling and Development (now the American Counselling Association) proposed that professionals intending to work with this population have specialized training (Myers, 1989). It is desirable that ethics training be included to consider the various ethical issues that may be encountered in counselling work with older adults. Such a training enables counsellors to make explicit values which are implicit in the counselling situation.

Conclusion

Pioneering efforts in both counselling older adults and conducting research on counselling outcomes with this population are beginning to emerge. Developmental theory relating to older adults has a more long-standing tradition within psychology. For example, few students of the subject have not heard of Erikson's (1950) stages, including the ego integrity versus despair conflict of old age. Yet a theoretical model of itself is not sufficient. The operationalization of such concepts as ego integrity needs to take place. A scientific practitioner model could use-fully be adopted by the increasing number of counsellors working with older adults. Three possibilities emerge in this regard: optimally all counselling training courses could prepare the future practitioner with expertise in conducting research; in-service courses could be offered to provide competence in the field; a research team could be established which included both a researcher and a counselling practitioner. Such research would result in an increase in knowledge of the older adult with respect to their psychological issues and appropriate interventions. Theoretical models, counselling expertise and research confirmation are all needed to provide conceptually firm and empirically validated approaches to counselling older adults.

References

Aber, R. and Webb, W. (1986) Effects of a limited nap on night sleep on older subjects. *Psychology and Aging*, **1**, 300–6.

Ackerman, R.J. (1990) Career developments and transitions of middle-aged women. *Psychology of Women Quarterly*, **14**(4) (Special issue), 513–30.

Adams, D.L. (1969) Analysis of a life satisfaction index. *Journal of Gerontology*, **24**, 470–4.

Aiken, L.R. (1982) *Later Life*, New York: Holt, Rinehart and Winston.

Ainley, S.C. and Smith, D.R. (1984) Aging and religious participation. *Journal of Gerontology*, **39**, 357–63.

American Psychiatric Association (1980) *Diagnostic and Statistical Manual of Mental Disorders*, 3rd edn, Washington DC: American Psychiatric Association.

American Psychological Association (1981) Ethical principles for psychologists. *American Psychologist*, **36**, 633–8.

American Psychological Association (1994) *Vitality for Life: Psychological Research for Productive Aging*. Washington DC: American Psychological Association.

Anderson, M. (1972) Household structure and the industrial revolution. In *Household and Family in Past Time,* ed P. Laslett, Cambridge: Cambridge University Press, pp. 215–35.

Ansbacher, H. and Ansbacher, R.R. (eds) (1956) *The Individual Psychology of Alfred Adler*, New York: Basic Books.

Ansello, E.F. (1977) Age and ageism in children's first literature. *Educational Gerontology*, **2**, 255–74.

Antonucci, T. and Jackson, J. (1987) Social support, interpersonal efficacy and health: a life course perspective. In *Handbook of Clinical Gerontology*, eds L. Cartensen and B. Edelstein, New York: Pergamon Press.

Arie, T. (1981) *Health Care of the Elderly*, London: Croom Helm.

Atchley, R. (1976) *The Sociology of Retirement*, Chichester: Wiley.

Austin, D.R. (1985) Attitudes toward old age: a hierarchical study. *Gerontologist*, **25**, 4.

Baltes, P.B. and Schaie, K. W. (1982) Aging and IQ: the myth of the twilight years. In *Readings in Adult Psychology*, eds R.L. Allman and D.T. Jaffe, New York: Harper and Row.

Bassili, J.N. and Reil, J.E. (1981) On the dominance of the old age stereotype. *Journal of Gerontology*, **36**(6), 682–8.

Beck, A.T. (1967) *Depression: Clinical, Experimental and Theoretical Aspects*, New York: Harper and Row.

Beck, A.T. (1976) *Cognitive Therapy and the Emotional Disorders*, New York: International Universities Press.

Beck, A.T. and Clark, D.M. (1988) Anxiety and depression: An information processing perspective. *Anxiety Research*, **1**, 23–36.

Belkin, G.S. (1984) *Introduction to Counselling*, 2nd edn, Dubuque, Iowa: William C. Brown Publishers.

Bell, B.D. and Stanfield, G.G. (1973) Chronological age in relation to attitudinal judgements: an experimental analysis. *Journal of Gerontology*, **16**, 75–80.

Belsky, J. (1990) *The Psychology of Aging: Theory, Research and Interventions*, California: Brooks Cole.

Bengtson, U.L. and Haber, D.A. (1975) Sociological approaches to aging. In *Aging: Scientific Perspectives and Social Issues*, eds D.S. Woodruff and J.E. Birren, New York: Van Nostrand Company.

Bengtson, U.L. and Treas, J. (1980) The changing family context of mental health and aging. In *Handbook of Mental Health and Aging*, eds J.E. Birren and B. Sloane, Englewood Cliffs, NJ: Prentice-Hall.

Bengtson, U.L., Kasschau, P.L. and Ragan, P.K, (1977) The impact of social structure on aging individuals. In *Handbook of the Psychology of Aging,* eds J.E. Birren and K.W. Schaie, New York: Van Nostrand.

Berger, A. (1983) Unlearning 'learned helplessness' through expressive interactions of poetry and song. Unpublished Ed D dissertation, University of Boston.

Berger, K. (1994) *The Developing Person Through the Life Span*. New York: North.

Berger, P.S. (1983) The economic well-being of elderly Hispanics. *Journal of Minority Aging*, **8**, 36–46.

Berghorn, F.J. and Schafer, D.E. (1987) *The Urban Elderly*, New Jersey: Universe Books.

Berghorn, K. and Thompson, R. (1994) *The Developing Person through the Lifespan*. New York: Worth.

Bergin, A.E. (1980) Psychotherapy and religious values. *Journal of Consulting and Clinical Psychology*, **48**, 95–105.

Bergin, A.E. and Payne, I.R. (1991) Proposed agenda for a spiritual strategy in personality and psychotherapy. *Journal of Psychology and Christianity*, **10**(3), 197–210.

Bergman, S. and Amir, M. (1973) Crime and delinquency among the aged in Israel. *Geriatrics*, **28**, 149–57.

Bernardo, F. (1968) Survivorship and social alienation: the care of the aged widower. *Family Coordinator*, **19**, 58–61.

Berne, E. (1966) *Principles of Group Treatment*, New York: Oxford University Press.

Bernstein, L.O. (1990) A special service: Counselling the individual elderly client. *Generations*, **14**(1), 35–8.

Bibby, R. (1993) *Unknown Gods: The Ongoing Story of Religion in Canada*, Toronto: Irwin.

Binstock, R. and Shanas, E. (1985) *Handbook of Aging and the Social Sciences*, New York: Van Nostrand Reinhold.

Birkhill, W.R. and Schaie, K.W. (1975) The effect of differential reinforcement of cautiousness in the intellectual performance of the elderly. *Journal of Gerontology*, **30**, 373–83.

Birren, J.E. and Schaie, K.W. (1977) *Handbook of the Psychology of Aging*, San Diego: Academic Press.

Birren, J. and Sloane, B. (1980) *Handbook of Mental Health and Aging*,

Englewood Cliffs, NJ: Prentice-Hall.

Birren, J.E., Cunningham, W.R. and Yamamoto, K. (1983) Psychology of adult development and aging. *Annual Review of Psychology*, **34**.

Bjorksten, J. (1974) Crosslinkage and the ageing process. In *Theoretical Aspects of Aging*, eds M. Rockstein, M. Sussman and J. Chesky, New York: Academic Press.

Blackburn, J.A., Papalia-Finlay, D., Foye, B.F. and Serlin, R.C. (1988) Modifiability of figural relations performance among elderly adults. *Journal of Gerontology*, **43**, 87–9.

Blackwell, J., O'Shea, E., Moane, G. and Murray P. (1992) *Care Provision and Cost Measurement: Dependent Elderly People at Home and in Geriatric Hospitals,* Dublin: Economic and Social Research Institute.

Blau, Z.S. (1973) *Old Age in a Changing Society*, New York: New Viewpoints.

Blazer, G.G. (1982) *Depression in Later Life*, St. Louis, MO: C.V. Mosby.

Booth, C. (1980) *The Aged Poor in England and Wales*, New York: Garland Publishing.

Bootzin, R.R. (1977) Effects of self-control procedures for insomnia. In *Behavioural Self-Management: Strategies, Techniques and Outcomes*, ed R.B. Stuart, New York: Brunner/Mazel, pp. 176–95.

Botwinick, J. (1970) Learning in children and adults. In *Life Span Developmental Psychology: Research and Theory*, eds L.R. Goulet and P.B. Baltes, New York: Academic Press.

Botwinick, J. (1977) Individual abilities. In *Handbook of the Psychology of Aging*, eds J.E. Birren anbd K.W. Schaie, New York: Van Nostrand Reinhold.

Bowers, W.A. (1989) Cognitive therapy with inpatients. In *Comprehensive Handbook of Cognitive Therapy*, eds A. Freeman, K.M. Simon, L.E. Beutler and H. Arkowitz, New York: Plenum Press, pp. 583–96.

Bowlby, J. (1969a) *Attachment*, New York: Basic Books.

Bowlby, J. (1969b) Psychopathology of anxiety: The role of affectional bonds. In *Studies of Anxiety*, ed. M.H. Lader, London: Royal Medico-Psychological Association.

Bowman, K.M. and Engle, B. (1963) Geriatrics. *American Journal of Psychiatry*, **119**, 652–4.

✗ Brammer, L.M. (1984) Counseling theory and the older adult. *Counselling Psychologist*, **12**(2), 29–38.

Brearley, C.P. (1975) *Social Work, Ageing and Society*, London: Routledge and Kegan Paul.

Brearley, C.P. (1977) *Residential Work with the Elderly*, London: Routledge and Kegan Paul.

Brecher, E.M. (1984) Love, sex and aging counselling. *Journal of Sex Research*, **22**, 6.

Breckenridge, J., Gallagher, D., Thompson, L. and Peterson, J. (1986) Characteristic depressive symptoms of bereaved elders. *Journal of Gerontology*, **41**, 163–8.

Brink, T.L. (1979) *Geriatric Psychotherapy*, New York: Human Sciences Press.

Brody, E. (1966) The aging family. *Gerontologist*, **6**, 4.

Brody, E. (1982) Aging and family personality: A developmental view. In *Readings in Adult Psychology*, eds R.L. Allman and D.T. Jaffe, New York: Harper and Row.

Brody, E.M. and Spark, G.M. (1966) Institutionalisation of the aged: A family crisis. *Family Process*, **5**, 76–90.

Bromley, D.B. (1988) *Human Ageing,* 3rd edn, London: Penguin Books.

Brown, G.W. and Harris, T. (1978) *Social Origins of Depression*, London: Tavistock.

Brubaker, T.H. and Powers, E.A. (1976) The stereotype of 'old': A review and alternative approach. *Journal of Gerontology*, **31**, 441–7.

Bultena, G.L. and Powers, E.A. (1978) Denial of aging: Age identification and reference group orientations. *Journal of Gerontology*, **33**(5), 748–54.

Busse, E.W. and Blazer, D.G. (1989) *Handbook of Geriatric Psychiatry*, Washington DC: American Psychiatric Press.

Butler, R.N. (1963) The life review: An interpretation of reminiscence in the aged. *Psychiatry*, **26**, 65–76.

Butler, R.N. (1969) Ageism: Another form of bigotry. *Gerontologist*, **9**, 243–6.

Butler, R.N. (1975a) *Why Survive? Being Old in America*, New York: Harper and Row.

Butler, R.N. (1975b) Psychiatry and the elderly: An overview. *American Journal of Psychiatry*, **132**, 893–900.

Butler, R.N. (1980) Ageism: A foreword. *Journal of Social Issues*, **36**, 8–11.

Butler, R.N. (1982) The life review: An interpretation of reminiscence in the aged. In *Readings in Adult Psychology*, eds R.L. Allman and D.T. Jaffe, New York: Harper and Row.

Butler, R.N. (1984) Senile dementia: Reversible and irreversible. *Counselling Psychologist*, **12**(2), 75–9.

Butler, R.N. (1988) Ageism. In *Encyclopedia of Aging*, ed. G.L. Maddox, New York: Springer.

Calasanti, L. (1993) Bringing in diversity: Toward an inclusive theory of retirement. *Journal of Aging Studies*, **7**, 133–50.

Calderone, M.S. and Johnson, E.W. (1981) *The Family Book About Sexuality*. London: Harper and Row.

Campbell, D.T. (1992) Treating depression in well older adults: Use of diaries in cognitive therapy. *Issues in Mental Health Nursing*, **13**, 19–29.

Campbell, D.T. and Stanley, J.C. (1963) *Experimental and Quasi-Experimental Designs for Research*, Chicago: Rand McNally.

Canter, S. and Canter, D. (1983) Professional growth and psychological education. *Bulletin of the British Psychological Society*, **36**, 283–7.

Cantril, H. (1965) *The Pattern of Human Concerns*, New Brunswick, NJ: Rutgers University Press.

Carskadon, M.A. and Dement, W.C. (1982) Nocturnal determinants of daytime sleepiness. *Sleep*, **5**, 73–81.

Carskadon, M.A., Brown, E.D. and Dement, W.C. (1982) Sleep fragmentation in the elderly: relationship to daytime sleep tendency. *Neurobiology of Aging*, **3**, 321–7.

Cartensen, L. and Endelstein, B. (1987) *Handbook of Clinical Gerontology*, New York: Pergamon Press.

Carter, E.A. and McGoldrick, M. (1980) *The Family Life Cycle*, New York: Gardner.

Casey, D. (1994) Depression in the elderly. *Southern Medical Journal*, **87**, 559–63.

Cassell, C. (1984) Ethical issues in the mental health of the elderly. In *Geriatric Mental Health*, eds J. Abrahams and V. Crooks, New York: Grune and Stratton, pp. 228–35.

Cattell, R.B. (1971) *Abilities: Their Structure, Growth and Action*, Boston: Houghton Mifflin.

Cavanaugh, J.C. (1993) *Adult Development and Aging*, 2nd edn, Grove, Brooks Cole.

Charlesworth, A. Wilkin, D. and Durie, A. (1983) *Careers and Services: A Companion for Men and Women Caring for Dependent Elderly People*, Manchester: Equal Oppprtunities Commission.

Chudacoff, T. and Hareven, T. (1978) Family transitions in old age. In *Transitions, the Family and Life Course in Historical Perspective*, ed. T. Haraven, New York: Academic Press.

Clark, R.D. and Hatfield, E. (1989) Gender differences in receptivity to sexual offers. *Journal of Psychology and Human Sexuality*, **2**(1), 39–55.

Cohen, G. (1977) Approach to the geriatric patient. *Medical Clinics of North America*, **61**2, 855–66.

Coleman, P.G. (1986) *Ageing and Reminiscence Processes*, Chichester: Wiley.

Comfort, A. (1974) Sexuality in old age. *Journal of the American Geriatric Society*, **xxii**(10), 440–2.

Comfort, A. (1976) *A Good Age*, New York: Crown.

Comfort, A. (1978) A new operating milieu: The buyer's market. *Lifelong Learning: The Adult Years*, **1**(8), 12–13, 27.

Comfort, A. (1980) Sexuality in later life. In *Handbook of Mental Health and Aging,* eds J.E. Birren and B. Sloane, Englewood Cliffs, NJ: Prentice-Hall.

Conway, K. (1985–6) Coping with the stress of medical problems among black and white elderly. *International Journal of Aging and Human Development*, **21**, 39–48.

Cooper, D.E. (1984) Group psychotherapy with the elderly: Dealing with loss and death. *American Journal of Psychiatry*, **131**, 825–7.

Corby, N. and Solnick, R.L. (1980) Psychosocial and physiological influences on sexuality in the older adult. In *Handbook of Mental Health and Aging*, eds J.E. Birren and B. Sloane, Englewood Cliffs: Prentice-Hall, pp. 893–921.

Corey, M.S. and Corey, G. (1987) *Groups: Process and Practice*, Monterey, CA: Brooks Cole.

Corso, J.F. (1977) Auditory perception and communication. In *Handbook of the Psychology of Aging*, eds J.E. Birren and K.W. Schaie, New York: Van Nostrand Reinhold.

Courtney, B., Poon, L., Martin, P. *et al.* (1992) Religiosity and adaptation in the oldest old. *International Journal of Aging and Human Development*, **34**(2), 47–56.

Covey, H.C. (1988) Historical terminology used to represent older people. *Gerontologist*, **28**(3), 291–7.

Cox, R.H. (1973) *Religious Systems and Psychotherapy*, Springfield, Ill: Charles C.Thomas.

Cox, R.H. (1988) *Later Life: the Realities of Aging*, Englewood Cliffs, NJ: Prentice-Hall.

Creacy, R.F., Berg, W.E. and Wright, R. (1985) Loneliness among the elderly: a causal approach. *Journal of Gerontology*, **40**, 44–51.

Crockett, W.H., Press, A. and Ostenkamp, M. (1979) The effect of deviations from stereotyped expectations upon attitudes toward older persons. *Journal of Gerontology*, **34**, 368–74.

Crumbaugh, J.C. (1968) Crossvalidation of purpose in life test based on Frankl's concepts. *Journal of Individual Psychology*, **24**, 74–81.

Cumming, E. and Henry, W.E. (1961) *Growing Old: The Process of Disengagement*, New York: Basic Books.

Cumming, E., Dean, L.R., Newell, D.S. and McCaffrey, I. (1960) Disengagement: A tentative theory of aging. *Sociometry*, **22**, 23–35.

Curtin, S.R. (1972) *Nobody Ever Died of Old Age*, Boston: Little Brown.

Cutler, N.E. and Marootyan, R.E. (1975) Demography of the aged. In *Aging*, eds D. Woodruff and J.E. Birren, New York: Van Nostrand.

Cutler, S.J. (1977) Aging and voluntary association participation. *Journal of Gerontology*, **32**, 470–9.

Daly, M. and O'Connor, J. (1984) *The World of the Elderly: The Rural Experience*,

Dublin: National Council for the Aged.

Danish, S.J. (1981) Life-span human development and intervention: A necessary link. *Counselling Psychologist*, **9**, 40–3.

Datan, N., Rodeheaver, D. and Hughes, F. (1987) Adult development and aging. *Annual Review of Psychology*, **38**, 153–80.

Davies, L. (1977) Attitudes toward old age and ageing as shown by humour. *Gerontologist*, **17**, 220–6.

Davies, R., Lacks, P., Storundt, M. and Baartelson, A. (1986) Countercontrol treatment of sleep-maintenance insomnia in relation to age. *Psychology and Aging*, **1**, 233–8.

De Beauvoir, S. (1977) *Old Age*, London: Penguin.

Deberry, S., Davis, S. and Reinhard, K.E. (1989) A comparison of meditation–relaxation and cognitive/behavioural techniques for reducing anxiety and depression in a geriatric population. *Journal of Geriatric Psychiatry*, **22**, 231–47.

De Clue, G.S. (1984) Patterns of intellectual functioning: Ability, personality and problem solving style. *Dissertation Abstracts International*, **44**, 3928B.

Derogatis, L., Lipman, R.S., Rickels, K. *et al.* (1974) The Hopkins Symptom Checklist (HSCL): A measure of primary symptom dimensions. In *Psychological Measurements in Psychopharmacology: Modern Problems in Pharmacopsychiatry*, Vol. 7, ed P. Pickot, Basel: Karger.

Derogatis, L.R. and Melisaratos, N. (1983) The Brigg Symptom Inventory: An introductory report. *Psychological Medicine*, **13**, 595–605.

Deutsch, C.B. and Kramer, N. (1977) Outpatient group psychotherapy for the elderly: An alternative institutionalisation. *Hospital and Community Psychiatry*, **28**, 440–2.

Dixon, J. and Gregory, L. (1987) Ageism, *Action Baseline*, **Winter**, 21–3.

Dixon, W., Heppner, P.P. and Rudd, M.D. (1994) Problem solving, appraisal, hopelessness and suicidal ideation: Evidence for a mediational model. *Journal of Counselling Psychology*, **41**, 91–8.

Dowd, J. (1975) Aging as exchange: A preface to theory. *Journal of Gerontology*, **30**, 584–94.

Dunkell, S. (1977) *Sleep Positions: The Night Language of the Body*, New York: William Morrow.

D'Zurilla, T.J. (1986) *Problem-Solving Therapy: A Social Competence Approach to Clinical Intervention*, New York: Springer.

D'Zurilla, T.J. and Goldfried, M.R. (1971) Problem solving and behaviour modification. *Journal of Abnormal Psychology*, **78**, 107–26.

Edinberg, M.A. (1985) *Mental Health Practice with the Elderly*, Englewood Cliffs, NJ: Prentice-Hall.

Edinger, J., Moelscher, T., Marx, G. *et al.* (1992) A cognitive behavioural therapy for sleep-maintenance insomnia in older adults. *Psychology and Aging*, **7**, 282–9.

Egan, G. (1973) *Face to Face*, Monterey, CA: Brooks Cole.

Egan, G. (1975) *The Skilled Helper: A Model for Systematic Helping and Interpersonal Relating*, Belmont, CA: Brooks Cole.

Eisdorfer, C. and Wilkie, F. (1973) Intellectual changes with advancing age. In *Intellectual Functioning in Adults*, eds L.F. Jarvik, C. Eisdorfer and J.C. Blum, New York: Springer, pp. 21–9.

Ellis, A. (1962) *Reason and Emotion in Psychotherapy*, New York: Lyle Stuart.

Endicott, J. and Spitzer, R. (1978) A diagnostic interview for affective disorders and schizophrenia. *Archives of General Psychiatry*, **35**, 837–44.

Engle-Friedman, M., Bootzin, R.R., Hazelwood, L. and Tsao, C. (1992) An evaluation of behavioural treatments for insomnia in older adults. *Journal of*

Clinical Psychology, **48**, 77–90.

Erikson, E.H. (1950) *Childhood and Society*, New York: W.W. Norton.

Erikson, E.H. (1963) *Childhood and Society*, 2nd edn, New York: W.W. Norton.

Erikson, E.H. (1976) Reflection on Dr. Borg's life cycle. *Daedalus*, **105**(2), 1–28.

Erikson, E.H. (1980) On the generational life cycle: An address. *International Journal of Psychoanalysis*, **6**, 213–23.

Erikson, E.H. (1982) *The Life Cycle Completed*, New York: W.W. Norton.

Erikson, E., Erikson, J. and Kivnick, H. (1986) *Vital Involvement in Old Age*, New York: W.W. Norton.

Espenshade, T.J. and Brown, R.E. (1983) Economic aspects of an aging population and the material well-being of older persons. In *Aging in Society: Selected Reviews of Recent Research*, eds M.W. Riley, B.B. Hess and K. Bond, New Jersey: Lawrence Erlbaum.

Estes, C.L., Swan, J.S. and Gerard, L.E. (1982) Dominant and competing paradigms in gerontology. *Aging and Society*, **2**, 151–64.

Evandrou, M., Arber, S., Dale, A. and Gilbert, G.N. (1986) Who cares for the elderly? Family care provision and receipt of statutory services. In *Dependency and Interdependency in Old Age: Theoretical Perspectives and Policy Alternatives*, eds C. Phillipson, M. Bernard and P. Strong, London: Croom Helm.

Evans, R.L., Smith, K.M., Werkhoven, W.S. *et al.* (1986) Cognitive telephone therapy with physically disabled elderly persons. *Gerontologist*, **26**, 8–10.

Feil, N.W. (1967) Group therapy in a home for the aged. *Gerontologist*, **7**, 192–5.

Felstein, I. (1983) Dysfunction: Origins and therapeutic approaches. In *Sexuality in the Later Years*, ed. R. Weg, New York: Academic Press.

Ferraro, K.F., Murtan, E. and Barresi, C.M. (1984) Widowhood, health and friendship support in later life. *Journal of Health and Social Behaviour*, **25**, 245–59.

Fillmer, H. (1984) Children's descriptions of and attitudes toward the elderly. *Educational Gerontology*, **10**, 99–107.

Finch, C.E. (1977) Neuroendocrine and autonomic aspects of aging. In *Handbook of the Biology of Aging*, eds C.E. Finch and L. Hayflick, New York: Van Nostrand Reinhold, pp. 262–80.

Fink, M., Green, M. and Brender, M.B. (1952) The Face–Hand Test as a diagnostic sign of organic brain syndrome. *Neurology*, **2**, 46–59.

Finkel, S. (1978) Late life sexuality – clinical, psychological, social and aesthetic perspectives. Paper read to Society for the Life-Cycle, Chicago.

Fitts, W.H. (1965) *Manual: Tennessee Self-Concept Scale*, Nashville, TN: Counselling Recordings and Texts.

Flanagan, J. (1978) A research approach to improving our quality of life. *American Psychologist*, **33**, 138–47.

Fogarty, M., Ryan, L. and Lee, J. (1984) *Irish Values and Attitudes*, Dublin: Dominican Publications.

Folstein, M.F., Folstein, S.E. and McHugh, P.H. (1975) Mini-Mental state: A practical method for grading the cognitive state of patients for the clinician. *Journal of Psychiatric Research*, **12**, 189–98.

Ford, J. and Sinclair, R. (1987) *Sixty Years On*, London: Women's Press.

Fordham, F. (1966) *An Introduction to Jung's Psychology*, Harmondsworth: Penguin.

Freeman, A., Schrodt, G.R., Gilson, M. and Ludgate, J.W. (1993) Group cognitive therapy with inpatients. In *Cognitive Therapy with Inpatients: Developing a Cognitive Milieu*, eds J.H. Wright, M.E. Thase, A.T. Beck and J.W. Ludgate, New York: Guilford Press.

Freud, S. (1904) In *The Standard Editionof the Complete Psychological Works of Sigmund Freud,* Vol. VII. London: The Hogarth Press (1953).

Freud, S. (1917) *Mourning and Melancholia*. In Pelican Freud Library, Vol. 3: *On Metapsychology*, Harmondsworth: Pelican.

Fry, P.S. (1983) Structured and unstructured reminiscence training and depression in the elderly. *Clinical Gerontologist*, **1**, 15–37.

Fry, P.S. (1984) Development of a geriatric scale of hopelessness: implications for counseling and intervention with the depressed elderly. *Journal of Counseling Psychology*, **31**(3), 322–31.

Fry, P.S. and Grover, S.C. (1982) Cognitive appraisals of life stress and depression in the elderly: A cross-cultural comparison of Asians and Caucasians. *International Journal of Psychology*, **17**, 435–54.

Gallagher, D. and Thompson, L.W. (1982) Cognitive therapy for depression in the elderly: A promising model for treatment and research. In *Depression in the Elderly*, eds L. Breslau and M. Hang, New York: Springer.

Ganikos, M.L. and Blake, R. (1984) Introduction. *Counselling Psychologist*, **12**, 2.

Garfinkel, R. (1975) The reluctant therapist. *Gerontologist*, **15**(2), 136–7.

Garrellt-Hern, B. and Weiss, D.M. (1991) A group counselling experience with the very old. *Journal for Specialists in Group Work*, **16**, 143–51.

Garrison, J. and Howe, J. (1976) Community intervention with the elderly: A social network approach. *Journal of the American Geriatric Society*, **24**, 329–33.

Gendlin, E.T. (1981) *Focusing*, 2nd edn, New York: Bantam Books.

George, L.R. (1988) Psychiatric disorders and mental health service use in late life: evidence from the epidemiologic catchment area program. In *Epidemiology and Aging: an International Perspective*, eds J.A. Brody and G.L. Maddox, New York: Springer.

Ginn, J. and Arber, S. (1991) Gender, class and income inequalities in later life. *British Journal of Sociology,* **42**(3), 369–96.

Gitelson, M. (1948) The emotional problems of elderly people. *Geriatrics*, **3**, 135–50.

Gitelson, M. (1975) The emotional problems of elderly people. In *Human Life-Cycle,* ed C. William, New York: Jason Aronson.

Glasser, I. (1978) Prisoners of benevolence: power versus liberty in the welfare state. In *Doing Good*, eds W. Gaylin, I. Glasser, S. Marcus and D. Rothman, New York: Pantheon Books.

Glasser, W. (1987) Lecture: Reality-therapy. Cork: University College.

Godbole, A. and Verinis, J.S. (1974) Brief psychotherapy in the treatment of emotional disorders in physically ill geriatric patients. *Gerontologist*, **14**, 143–8.

Goldfarb, A.I. (1953) Recommendations for psychiatric care in a home for the aged. *Journal of Gerontology*, **8**, 343–7.

Graham, I.D. and Baker, P.M. (1989) Status, age and gender: Perceptions of old and young people. *Canadian Journal on Aging*, **8**(3), 255–67.

Green, S.K. (1981) Attitiudes and perceptions about the elderly: Current and future perspectives. *International Journal of Aging and Human Development*, **13**, 99–119.

Grotjahn, M. (1940) Psychoanalytic investigation of a seventy one year old man with senile dementia. *Psychoanalytic Quarterly*, **9**, 80–7.

Grotjahn, M. (1951) Some analytic observations about the process of growing old. *Psychoanalysis and the Social Sciences*, **3**, 301–12.

Grotjahn, M. (1955) Analytic psychotherapy with the elderly. *Psychoanalytic Review*, **42**, 419–27.

Gurian, B.S. (1975) Psychogeriatrics and family medicine. *Gerontologist*, **15**(4), 308–10.

Haber, C. (1983) *Beyond Sixty-Five: The Dilemma of Old Age in America's Past*, Cambridge: Cambridge University Press.

Haight, B.K. (1988) The therapeutic role of a structured life review process in homebound elderly subjects. *Journal of Gerontology*, **43**, 40–4.

Hall, G.S. (1922) *Senescence: The Last of Life*, New York: Appleton.

Hall, J. (1986) *The Jungian Experience*, Toronto: Inner City Books.

Hamilton, M. (1959) The measurement of anxiety states by rating. *British Journal of Medical Psychology*, **32**, 50–5.

Hamilton, M. (1967) Development of a rating scale for primary depressive illness. *British Journal of Social and Clinical Psychology*, **6**, 278–96.

Harman, D. (1968) Free radical theory of aging effect of free radical reaction. Inhibitors on the mortality rate of male LAF' mice. *Journal of Gerontology*, **23**, 476–82.

Harp Scates, J.K., Lee Randolph, D., Gutsch, K.U. and Knight, H.V. (1986) Effects of cognitive–behavioural, reminiscence and activity treatments on life satisfaction and anxiety in the elderly. *Aging and Human Development*, **22**, 141–6.

Harris, L. *et al.* (1975) *The Myth and Reality of Aging in America*, Washington DC: National Council on the Aging.

Hartford, M.E. (1980) The use of group methods for work with the aged. In *Handbook of Mental Health and Aging*, eds J.E. Birren and B. Sloane, New Jersey: Prentice-Hall.

Hasegawa, K. (1985) The epidemiology of depression in later life. *Journal of Affective Disorders*, **1**, Suppl, 3–6.

Havighurst, R.J. (1972) *Developmental Tasks and Education*. New York: David McKay.

Havighurst, R.J., Neugarten, B.L. and Tobin, S.S. (1968) Disengagement and patterns of aging. In *Middle Age and Aging*, ed. B.L. Neugarten, Chicago: University of Chicago Press.

Hawton, K. and Fagg, J. (1990) Deliberate self-poisoning and self-injury in older people. *International Journal of Geriatric Psychiatry*, **5**, 367–73.

Hayashi, Y. and Endo, S. (1982) All night sleep polygraphic recording of healthy aged persons: REM and slow wave sleep. *Sleep*, **5**, 277–83.

Hayflick, L. (1977) The cellular basis for biological aging. In *Handbook of the Biology of Aging*, eds C.E. Finch and L. Hayflick, New York: Academic Press.

Hedgepeth, B.E. and Hale, W.D. (1983) Effect of a positive reminiscing intervention on affect, expectancy and performance. *Psychological Reports*, **53**, 867–70.

Henning, L.H. and Tirrell, F.J. (1982) Counsellor resistance to spiritual exploration. *Personnel and Guidance Journal*, **10,** 92–5.

Heppner, P.P. (1988) *The Problem Solving Inventory (PSI): Research Manual*, Palo Alto, CA: Consulting Psychologists Press.

Heppner, P.P. and Anderson, W.P. (1985) The relationship between problem-solving self-appraisal and psychological adjustment. *Cognitive Therapy and Research*, **9**, 415–27.

Heppner, P.P. and Hillerbrand, E.T. (1991) Problem-solving training: Implications for remedial and preventive training. In *Handbook of Social and Clinical Psychology*, eds C.R. Snyder and D.R. Forsyth, New York: Pergamon Press.

Heppner, P.P. and Krauskopf, C.J. (1987) An information processing approach to personal problem solving. *Counselling Psychologist*, **15**, 371–447.

Heppner, P.P., Hibel, J.H., Neal, G.W. *et al.* (1982) Personal problem solving: A descriptive study of individual differences. *Journal of Counselling Psychology*, **29**, 580–90.

Heppner, P.P., Reeder, B.L. and Larson, L.M. (1983) Cognitive variables associated with personal problem-solving appraisal: Implications for counselling. *Journal of Counselling Psychology*, **30**, 537–45.

Heppner, P.P., Baumgardner, A. and Jackson, J. (1985) Problem solving self-appraisal, depression and attribution styles: Are they related? *Cognitive*

Therapy and Research, **9**, 105–13.

Heppner, P.P., Kampa, M. and Bruning, L. (1987) The relationship between problem-solving self-appraisal and indices of physical and psychological health. *Cognitive Therapy and Research*, **11**, 155–68.

Herbst, K.G. (1982) *Social Attitudes to Hearing Loss and Elderly People*, Keele: Beth Johnson Foundation Publications.

Herr, J. and Weakland, J. (1979) *Counseling Elders and Their Families*, New York: Springer.

Hersen, M. and Bellak, A.S. (1981) *Behavioural Assessment: A Practical Handbook*, New York: Pergamon Press.

Hertzog, C., Dixon, R. and Hultsch, D. (1990) Relationships between meta-memory, memory predictions and memory task performance in adults. *Psychology and Aging*, **6**, 215–27.

Hill, R. (1970) *Family Development in Three Generations*, Cambridge, MA: Schenkman.

Hite, S. (1976) *The Hite Report*, New York: Macmillan.

Hofland, B. (1990) Autonomy and long-term care practice. *Generations*, **14**, 91–4.

Holmes, T.H. and Rahe, R.H. (1967) The social readjustment rating scale. *Journal of Psychosomatic Research*, **11**, 213–18.

Horn, J.L. (1970) Organization of data on life-span development of human abilities. In *Life-span Developmental Psychology. Research and Theory*, eds L.R. Goulet and P.B. Baltes, New York: Academic Press.

Horn, J.L. and Donaldson, G. (1976) On the myth of intellectual decline in adulthood. *American Psychologist*, **31**, 701–19.

Hoyt, D.R., Kaiser, M.A., Peters, G.R. and Babchuk, N. (1980) Life satisfaction and activity theory: A multidimensional approach. *Journal of Gerontology*, **35**(6), 935–41.

Hultsch, D.F. and Deutsch, F. (1981) *Adult Development and Aging: A Life Span Perspective*, New York: McGraw-Hill.

Hunt, T.L. (1978) *The Equity and Impact of Medicare and Medicaid with Respect to Mexican Americans in Texas*. Unpublished doctoral dissertation, Austin: University of Texas at Austin.

Ikels, C. (1982) Final progress report on 'cultural factors in family support for the elderly'. Mimeo. In Keith, J., Age in Anthropological Research. In Binstock, R. and Shanas, E. (1985) *Handbook of Aging and Social Sciences*, New York: Van Nostrand, Rheinhold Co.

Intrieri, R., Kelly, J., Brown, M. and Castilla, C. (1993) Improving medical students' attitudes toward and skills with the elderly. *Gerontologist*, **33**, 373–8.

Irish Department of Health (1987) *Vital Statistics*, Dublin: Stationery Office.

Irish Department of Health (1988) *Vital Statistics*, Dublin: Stationery Office.

Irish National Council for the Aged (1982) *Day Hospital Care*, Dublin: Irish National Council for the Aged.

Irish National Council for the Aged (1984) *An Analysis of the State's Contribution*, Dublin: Irish National Council for the Aged.

Irish National Council for the Aged (1987) *Attitudes of Young People to Ageing and the Elderly*, Report no 16, Dublin: Stationery Office.

Israel, B.A., Hogue, C.C. and Gorton, A. (1983) Social networks among elderly women: implications for health education. *Health Education Quarterly*, **10**, 173–203.

Ivester, C. and King, K. (1977) Attitudes of adolescents toward the aged. *Gerontologist*, **17**(1), 85–9.

Jarvik, L.F., Eisdorfer, I. and Blum, J.E. (eds) (1973) *Intellectual Functioning in Adults*, New York: Springer.

Jerrome, D. (1994) Family estrangement, parents and children who 'lose touch'. *Journal of Family Therapy*, **16**(3), 241–58.

Johnson, P. (1985) *The Economics of Old Age in Britain: A Long-Run View 1881–1981*. Discussion Paper 47, Centre for Economic Policy Research, London.

Johnson, W.Y. and Wilborn, B. (1991) Group counselling as an intervention in anger expression and depression in older adults. *Journal for Specialists in Group Work*, **16**, 133–42.

Jones, D.A., Victor, C.R. and Vetter, N.J. (1983) Careers for the elderly in the community. *Journal of the Royal College of General Practitioners*, **33**, 707–10.

Jung, C.G. (1965) *Memories, Dreams and Reflections,* New York: Vintage Books.

Kahn, R.L., Wethington, E. and Ingersoll-Dayton, B. (1987) Social support and social networks: Determinants, effects and interactions. In *Life-Span Perspectives and Social Psychology*, ed. R.P. Abeles, Hillsdale, NJ: Lawrence Erlbaum, pp.139–65.

Kalish, R. (1975) *Late Adulthood: Perspectives on Human Development*, Monterey, CA: Brooks Cole.

Kalish, R. (1976) Death and dying in a social context. In *Handbook of Aging and the Social Sciences*, eds R. Binstock and E. Shanas, New York: Van Nostrand Reinhold.

Kalish, R.A. and Reynolds, D.K. (1976) *Death and Ethnicity: A Psycho-Cultural Study*, Los Angeles: University of Southern California Press.

Karpf, R. (1992) Individual psychotherapy with the elderly. In *Mental Health Interventions for the Aging*, ed. A. Morton, New York: Praeger.

Kasi, S.V. and Rosenfield, S. (1980) The residential environment and its impact on the mental health of the aged. In *Handbook of Mental Health and Aging*, eds J.E. Birren and B. Sloane, Englewood Cliffs, NJ: Prentice-Hall.

Kastenbaum, R. (1971) Age: Getting there on time. *Psychology Today*, **5**(7), 52–4, 82–4.

Kastenbaum, R. (1975) Time, death and ritual in old age. In *The Study of Time*, eds J.T. Fraser and N. Lawrence, New York: Springer, pp. 20–38.

Kastenbaum, R. (1981) *Death, Society and Human Experience*, 2nd edn, St Louis: C.V. Mosby.

Kastenbaum, R. (1992) Death, suicide and the older adult. *Suicide and Life-Threatening Behaviour*, **22**, 1–14.

Keating, N. and Cole, P. (1980) What do I do with him 24 hours a day? Changes in the housewife's role after retirement. *Gerontologist*, **20**, 84–9.

Kellehear, A. and Lewin, T. (1988–89) Farewells by the dying: A sociological study. *Omega, Journal of Death and Dying*, **19**, 275–93.

Kelliher, A.T. (1991) *Conjugal Bereavement: Theory and Practice*, Unpublished M.Coun Thesis, University College, Cork.

Kemp, B. (1988) *The Older Health and Mood Index: Development and Use*, Donney, CA: Rehabilitation Research and Training Center on Aging.

Kemp, B.J., Corgiat, M. and Gill, C. (1992) Effects of brief cognitive–behavioural group psychotherapy on older persons with and without disabling illness. *Behaviour, Health and Aging*, **2**, 21–8.

Kiesler, D. (1966) Some myths of psychotherapy research and the search for a paradigm. *Psychological Bulletin*, **65**, 110–36.

Kimmel, D. (1974) *Adulthood and Aging*, New York: John Wiley.

Kimmel, D. (1988) Ageism, psychology and public policy. *American Psychologist*, **43**, 175–8.

Kimmel, D. (1990) *Adulthood and Aging*, 3rd edn, New York: Wiley.

King, P.H.M. (1980) The life cycle as indicated by the nature of the transference in the psychoanalysis of the middle-aged and elderly. *International Journal of*

Psychoanalysis, **61**, 153–60.

Kinsey, A.C. and Gebhard, P.H. (1953) *Sexual Behaviour in the Human Female*, Philadelphia: W.B. Saunders.

Kinsey, A.C., Pomeroy, W.B and Martin, C.E. (1948) *Sexual Behaviour in the Human Male*, Philadelphia: W.B. Saunders.

Kiyak, M. *et al.* (1982) Dentists' attitudes toward and knowledge of the elderly. *Journal of Dental Education*, **46**, 266–73.

Klein, M.H., Mathieu, P.L., Kiesler, D.P. and Gendlin, E.T. (1970) *The Experiencing Scale Manual,* Madison, WI: University of Wisconsin Press.

Koenig, H.G., George, L.K. and Siegler, I.C. (1988) The use of religion and other emotion-regulating coping strategies among older adults. *Gerontologist*, **28**(3), 303–10.

Kogan, N. (1961) Attitudes toward old people: The development of a scale and examination of correlates. *Journal of Abnormal and Social Psychology*, **62**, 616–22.

Kornhaber, A. and Woodward, K.L. (1981) *Grandparent/grandchildren: The vital connection*, Garden City, NJ: Anchor.

Kozma, A. and Stones, J.J. (1980) The measurement of happiness: Development of the Memorial University of Newfoundland Scale of Happiness (MUNSH) *Journal of Gerontology*, **35**, 906–12.

Krause, N. (1993) Measuring religiosity in later life. *Research on Aging*, **15**, 170–97.

Krause, N. and Liang, J. (1992) Cross-cultural variations in depressive symptoms in later life. *International Psychogeriatrics*, **4**, 185–202.

Kubler-Ross, E. (1969) *On Dying and Death: What the Dying Have to Teach Doctors, Nurses, Clergy and Their Own Families*, London: Macmillan.

Kubler-Ross, E. (1974) *Questions and Answers on Death and Dying*, New York: Macmillan.

Kubler-Ross, E. (1975) *Facing Death: Modern Perspectives in the Psychiatry of Old Age*, Churchill: Howells.

Kucharski, L. T., White, R. and Schratz, M. (1979) Age bias, referral for psychological assistance and the private physician. *Journal of Gerontology*, **34**, 423–8.

Kymissis, P. (1976) Observations on the use ofsynallactic group image technique in an after care group. *Journal of Art Psychotherapy*, **3**(1), 23–6.

Labouvie-Vief, G. (1985) Intelligence and cognition. In *Handbook of the Psychology of Aging*, 2nd edn, eds J.E. Birren and K.W. Schaie, New York: Van Nostrand Reinhold, pp. 500–30.

LaForge, R. (1963) *Research Use of ICL*, Oregon Research Institute Technical Report 3, No. 4, Eugene, Oregon.

LaForge, R. and Suczek, R.F. (1955) The interpersonal dimension of personality III. An interpersonal checklist. *Journal of Personality*, **24**, 94–112.

Landau, J. (1980) Loneliness and creativity. In *The Anatomy of Loneliness*, eds J. Hartzog, J.R. Audy and Y. Cohen, New York: International Universities Press.

Langer , E.J. and Rodin, J. (1976) The effects of choice and enhanced personal responsibility for the aged: A field experiment in an institutional setting. *Journal of Personality and Social Psychology*, **34**, 191–8.

Larson, L.M. (1984) *Training Self-Appraised Effective and Ineffective Problem Solvers in Assertion.* Unpublished Master's thesis, University of Missouri, Columbia.

Larson, R., Tuzanek, J. and Mannell, R. (1985) Being alone versus being with people: Disengagement in the daily experience of older adults. *Journal of Gerontology*, **40**(3), 375–81.

La Rue, A., Dessonville, C. and Jarvick, L. (1985) Aging and mental disorders. In

Handbook of the Psychology of Aging, eds J.E. Birren and K.W. Schaie, New York: Van Nostrand Reinhold.

Lazare, A. (1979) Unresolved grief. In *Outpatient Psychiatry: Diagnosis and Treatment*, ed. A. Lazare, Baltimore: Williams and Wilkins, pp. 498–512.

Leszcz, M., Feigenbaum, E., Sadavoy, J. and Robinson, A. (1985) A men's group: Psychotherapy of elderly men. *International Journal of Group Psychotherapy*, **35**, 177–96.

Leszcz, M.A. (1985) Characterizing adolescents, middle-aged and elderly adults: Putting the elderly into perspective. *International Journal of Aging and Human Development*, **22**(2), 105–21.

Leventhal, E. (1991) Biological aspects. In *Comprehensive Review of Geriatric Psychiatry*, eds J. Sadavoy, L. Lazarus and L. Jarvik, Washington: American Psychiatric Press.

Levin, W.C. (1988) Age stereotyping: College student evaluations. *Research on Aging*, **10**, 134–48.

Levinson, D.J. (1978) *The Seasons of a Man's Life*, New York: Ballantine Books.

Levy, S.M., Derogatis, L.R., Gallagher, D. and Gatz, M. (1980) Intervention with older adults and the evaluation of outcome. In *Aging in the 1980s*, ed. L.W. Poon, Washington DC: American Psychological Association.

Lewinsohn, P.M., Biglan, A. and Zeiss, A.M. (1976) Behavioural treatment of depression. In *The Behavioural Management of Anxiety, Depression and Pain*, ed. P.O. Davidson, New York: Brunner/Mazel.

Lewinsohn, P.M., Munoz, R.F., Youngren, M.A. and Zeiss, A.M. (1978) *Control your Depression*, Englewood Cliffs, NJ: Prentice-Hall.

Lewis, M.I. and Butler, R.N. (1974) Life review therapy. *Geriatrics*, **29**, 165–73.

Lewis, M.I. and Johansen, K.M. (1982) Resistances to psychotherapy with the elderly. *American Journal of Psychotherapy*, **36**, 497–504.

Lidz, T. (1983) *The Person: His and Her Development Throughout the Life Cycle*, New York: Basic Books.

Lieberman, M.A. and Gourash, N. (1979) Evaluating the effects of change groups on the elderly. *International Journal of Group Psychotherapy*, **29**, 283–304.

Livson, F.B. (1981) Paths to psychological health in the middle years: Sex differences. In *Present and Past in Middle Life*, eds D.H. Eichorn, J.A. Clauson, N. Haan *et al.*, New York, Academic Press.

Loftus, E. (1980) *Memory*, Reading, MA: Addison-Wesley.

Longino, C.F. and Kitson, G.C. (1976) Parish clergy and the aged: Examining stereotypes. *Journal of Gerontology*, **31**, 340–5.

Lopata, H.Z. (1973) *Widowhood in an American City*, Cambridge, MA: Schenkman.

Lopez, M.A. and Silber, S.L. (1981) Counseling the elderly: A training program for professionals. *Educational Gerontology*, **7**, 363–74.

Lovinger, R.J. (1984) *Working with Religious Issues in Therapy*, New York: Jason Aronson.

Lowenthal, M., Thurner, M. and Chiriboga, D. (1975) *Four Stages of Life*, San Francisco, CA: Jossey-Bass.

Lowy, L. (1979) *Social Work with the Aging: the Challenge and Promise of the Later Years,* New York: Harper and Row.

Ludeman, K. (1981) The sexuality of the older person: Review of the literature. *Gerontologist*, **21**, 203–8.

Luft, J. and Ingram, H. (1955) *The Johari Window: A Graphical Model for Interpersonal Relations*. University of California at Los Angeles, Extension Office. Western Training Laboratory in Group Development. August.

McGoldrick, M. and Pearce, J.K. (1981) Family therapy with Irish-Americans. *Family Process*, **20**, 223–41.

McMahon, A.W. and Rhudick, P.J. (1964) Reminiscing: Adaptational significance in the aged. *Archives of General Psychiatry*, **10**, 292–8.

McNair, D., Lorr, M. and Droppleman, L. (1971) *Manual for the Profile of Mood States*, San Diego: Educational Testing Services.

McNeil, D. (1986) *Mood: Measurement, Dimenal Variation and Age Effects.* Unpublished doctoral dissertation, Memorial University of Newfoundland, Canada.

Maddox, G.L. (1968) Persistence of lifestyle among the elderly. In *Middle Age and Aging*, ed. B. Neugarten, Chicago: University of Chicago Press.

Maddox, G.L. (1970) Adaptation to retirement. *Gerontologist*, **10**, 14–18.

Malde, J. (1988) Guided autobiography: A counselling tool for older adults. *Journal of Counselling and Development*, **66**, 290–3.

Mancini, J.A. (1980) Friend interaction, competence and morale in old age. *Research and Aging*, **2**(4), 416–31.

Manfredi, C. and Pickett, M. (1987) Perceived stressful situations and coping strategies utilized by the elderly. *Journal of Community Health Nursing*, **4**, 99–110.

Manthei, R. and Matthews, D. (1982) Helping the reluctant client to engage in counselling. *British Journal of Guidance and Counselling*, **1**, 44–50.

Marshall, V. (1980) Dominant and emerging paradigms in the social psychology of aging. In *Later Life: The Social Psychology of Aging*, ed. V. Marshall, Beverly Hills: Sage.

Martin, L.J. (1944) *A Handbook for Old Age Counsellors*, San Francisco, CA: Geertz.

Martin, V. and DeGrunchy, C. (1930) *Salvaging Old Age*, New York: Macmillan.

Masters, W.J. and Johnson, V.E. (1966) *Human Sexual Response*, Boston: Little, Brown.

Matatesta, C. and Kalnok, M. (1984) Emotional experiences in younger and older adults. *Journal of Gerontology*, **39**, 301–8.

Medley, M. (1976) Satisfaction with life among sixty-five years and older: A causal model. *Journal of Gerontology*, **31**, 448–55.

Meer, B. and Baker, J. (1966) The Stockton Geriatric Rating Scale. *Journal of Gerontology*, **41**, 85–90.

Meerloo, J.A.M. (1955a) Psychotherapy with elderly people. *Geriatrics*, **10**, 538–87.

Meerloo, J.A.M. (1961) Modes of psychotherapy in the aged. *Journal of the American Geriatric Society*, **9**, 225–34.

Mellinger, G., Balter, M.Z. and Uhlenhuth, E. (1985) Insomnia and its treatment. *Archives of General Psychiatry*, **42**, 225–32.

Mijuskovic, B. (1986) Loneliness: Counselling adolescents. *Adolescence*, **21**, 941–50.

Miles, L.E. and Dement, W.C. (1980) Sleep and aging. *Sleep*, **3**, 1-220.

Miller, J.F. (1985) Assessment of loneliness and spiritual well-being in chronically ill and healthy adults. *Journal of Professional Nursing*, **1**, 79–85.

Miller, M. (1978) Geriatric suicide: The Arizona study. *Gerontologist*, **18**, 488–96.

Miller, S., Blalock, J. and Ginsburg, H. (1984–85) Children and the aged: Attitudes, contact and discriminative ability. *International Journal of Aging and Human Development*, **19**, 47–53.

Minuchin, S. (1974) *Families and Family Therapy*, Cambridge, MA: Harvard University Press.

Moane, G. (1993) Dependency and caring needs among the elderly. *Irish Journal of Psychology*, **14**(1), 189–203.

Monge, R.H. (1975) Structure of the self-concept from adolescence through old age. *Experimental Aging Research*, **1**, 81–91.

Morin, C. and Azrin, N. (1988) Behavioural and cognitive treatment of geriatric insomnia. *Journal of Consulting and Clinical Psychology*, **56**, 748–53.

Morin, C.M. and Gramling, S.E. (1989) Sleep patterns and aging. Comparison of older adults with and without insomnia complaints. *Psychology and Aging*, **4**,290–4.

Morin, C.M., Kowatch, R.A., Barry, T. and Walton, E. (1993) Cognitive behaviour therapy for late life. *Journal of Consulting and Clinical Psychology*, **61**, 137–46.

Morrison, R. and Radtke, D.D. (1988) *Aging with Joy*, Mystic, CT: Twenty-Third Publications.

Murphy, G.J., Hudson, W.W. and Cheung, P.P.L. (1980) Marital and sexual discord among older couples. *Social Work Research and Abstracts*, **16**, 11–16.

Myers, J.E. (1988) The mid/late life generation gap. *Journal of Counselling and Development*, **66**, 331–5.

Myers, J.E. (1989) *Fusing Gerontological Counselling into Counsellor Preparation: Curricular Guide*, Alexandria, VA: American Association for Counselling and Development.

Natale, J.M. (1986) *Loneliness and the Aging Client: Psychotherapeutic Considerations*, Binghampton, Haworth Press NY: pp. 77–93.

National Council on the Aging (1975) *The Myth and Reality of Aging in America*, Washington DC: National Council on the Aging.

Neal, W.G. and Heppner, P.P. (1982) Personality correlates of effective personal problem solving. Symposium presented at the Meeting of the American Personnel and Guidance Association, Detroit.

Nelson-Jones, R. (1982) *The Theory and Practice of Counselling*, London: Holt Rinehart and Winston.

Nemiroff, R.A. and Colarusso, M. (1988)Frontiers of adult development in theory and practice. *Journal of Geriatric Psychiatry*, **21**(1), 7–27.

Netz, Y. and Ben-Sira, D. (1993) Attitudes of young people, adults and older adults from three generation families toward the concepts 'deaf person', 'youth', 'adult' and 'old person'. *Educational Gerontology*, **19**(7), 607–21.

Neugarten, B.L. (1964) *Personality in Middle and Later Life*, New York: Atherton Press.

Neugarten, B.L. (1971) Grow old along with me! The best is yet to be. *Psychology Today*, **5**(7), 45–8.

Neugarten, B.L. (1972) Personality and the aging process. *Gerontologist*, **12**(1), 9–15.

Neugarten, B.L. and Datan, N. (1973) Sociological perspectives on the life cycle. In *Life Span Developmental Psychology: Personality and Socialization*, eds P.B.Baltes and K.W. Schaie, New York: Academic Press.

Neugarten, B.L. and Peterson, W.A. (1957) A study of the American age grading system. Proceedings of the 4th Congress of the International Association of Gerontology, **16**, 134–43.

Neugarten, B.L. and Weinstein, K.K. (1964) The changing American grandparent. *Journal of Marriage and the Family*, **26**, 199–204.

Neugarten, B.L., Havighurst, R.J. and Tobin, S.S. (1966) The measurement of life satisfaction. *Journal of Gerontology*, **16**, 134–43.

Newman, G. and Nichols, C.R. (1974) Sexual activities and attitudes in older persons. *Journal of the American Medical Association*, **173**, 33–5.

Nezu, A.M. (1985) Differences in psychological distress between effective and ineffective problem solvers. *Journal of Counselling Psychology*, **32**, 135–8.

Nezu, A.M. and Ronan, G.F. (1988) Social problem solving as a moderator of stress-related depressive symptoms: A prospective analysis. *Journal of*

Personality and Social Psychology, **51**, 1277–92.

Nezu, A.M., Nezu, C.M., Saraydarian, L. *et al.* (1986) Social problem solving as a moderating variable between negative life stress and depressive systems. *Cognitive Therapy and Research*, **10**, 489–98.

Nidiffer, W.W. and Moore, A.B. (1985) Attitudes of university administrators toward older adults. *Educational Gerontology*, **11**, 387–99.

Norris, A. (1986) *Reminiscences with Elderly People*, London: Winslow Press.

Nowak, C.A., Karuza, J. and Namikas, J. (1976) Youth, beauty, and the midlife woman: the double whammy strikes again. Proceedings of Conference on Women in Midlife Crisis, Cornell University, Ithaca.

Nuessel, F. H. (1982) The language of ageism. *Gerontologist*, **22**, 3.

Oberleder, M. (1966) Psychotherapy with the aging: An art of the possible. *Psychotherapy*, **3**, 139–42.

O'Brien, C.R., Johnson, J.L. and Miller, B. (1979) Counseling the aging: Some practical considerations. *Personnel and Guidance Journal*, **57**(6), 288–91.

O'Connor, J., Ruddle, H. and O'Gallagher, M. (1989) *Sheltered Housing in Ireland: Its Role and Contribution in the Care of the Elderly*, Dublin: National Council for the Aged, Report No.20.

Ogilvie, D.M. (1987) Life satisfaction and identity structure in late middle-aged men and women. *Psychology and Aging*, **2**, 217–24.

O'Leary, E. (1986) *The Psychology of Counselling*, Cork: University Press.

O'Leary, E. (1990) Cultural differences between Ireland and the USA in the perception of friendship, the development of trust and problem solving behaviour: A phenomenological investigation with implications for counselling. *Cross Cultural Psychology Bulletin*, **24**, 9–12.

O'Leary, E. (1992) *Gestalt Therapy: Theory, Practice and Research*, London: Chapman & Hall.

O'Leary, E. and Kelly, B. (1990) *An Investigation of the Psychological and Social Needs and Physical Environment of the Elderly in an Inner City Parish*, Cork: South Parish Community Association.

Olsho, L., Harkins, S. and Lenhardt, M. (1985) Aging and the auditory system. In *Handbook of the Psychology of Aging*, 2nd edn, eds J.E. Birren and K.W. Schaie, New York: Van Nostrand Reinhold.

Osgood, N. (1991) Psychological factors in late-life suicide. *Crisis*, **12**, 18–25.

Owens, W.A. (1966) Age and mental abilities: A second adult follow-up. *Journal of Educational Psychology*, **57**, 311–25.

Page, R. and Berkow, D. (1994) *Creating Contact, Choosing Relationship*, San Francisco, CA: Jossey-Bass.

Palmore, E. and Maeda, D. (1985) *The Honorable Elders Revisited*, Durham, NC: Duke University Press.

Parker, E.S. and Noble, E.P. (1977) Alcohol consumption and cognitive functioning in social drinkers. *Journal of Studies on Alcohol*, **38**, 1224–32.

Parkes, C.M. (1972) *Bereavement: Studies of Grief in Adult Life*, New York: International Universities Press.

Parnes, M. and Nestel, G. (1981) The retirement experience. In *Work and Retirement: A Longitudinal Study of Men*, ed. M. Parnes, Cambridge, MA: MIT Press.

Pascarelli, E. and Fischer, W. (1974) Drug dependence in the elderly. *International Journal of Aging and Human Development*, **5**, 347–56.

Patterson, C.H. (1986) *Theories of Counseling and Psychotherapy*, 4th edn, New York: Harper and Row.

Patterson, L. and Eisenberg, S. (1983) *The Counselling Process*, 3rd edn, Boston: Houghton Mifflin.

Pattison, E.M. (1977) Ten years of change in alcoholism treatment and delivery systems. *American Journal of Psychiatry*, **134**(3), 261–6.

Pearlin, L. and Schooler, C. (1978) The structure of coping. *Journal of Health and Social Behaviour*, **19**, 2–21.

Peck, R.C. (1968) Psychological developments in the second half of life. In *Middle Age and Aging: A Reader in Social Psychology*, ed. B.L. Neugarten, Chicago: University of Chicago Press, pp. 88–92.

Peplau, L.A. and Perlman, D. (1982) *Loneliness: a Source of Current Theory, Research and Therapy*, New York: Wiley.

Perlick, D. and Atkins, A. (1984) Variations in the reported age of a patient: A source of bias in the diagnosis of depression and dementia. *Journal of Consulting and Clinical Psychology*, **52**, 812–20.

Perlmutter, M. and Hall, E. (1992) *Adult Development and Aging*, New York: Wiley.

Perls, F.S. (1969) *Gestalt Therapy Verbatim*, Toronto: Bantam.

Perls, F., Hefferline, R. and Goodman, P. (1951) *Gestalt Therapy*, New York: Julian Press.

Perrotta, P. and Meacham, J. (1981) Can a reminiscing intervention alter depression and self-esteem? *International Journal of Aging and Human Development*, **14**, 23–30.

Peterson, D. and Karnes, E. (1976) Older people in adolescent literature. *Gerontologist*, **16**, 225–31.

Peterson, J.A. (1980) Social–psychological aspects of death and dying and mental health. In *Handbook of Mental Health and Aging*, eds J.E. Birren and B. Sloane, Englewood Cliffs, NJ: Prentice-Hall, pp. 922–42.

Pfeiffer, E. (1975) Mental status questionnaire. *Journal of the American Geriatric Society*, **23**, 433–6.

Pfeiffer, E. (1980) The psychological evaluation of the elderly patient. In *Handbook of Geriatric Psychiatry*, eds E.W. Busse and D.G. Blazer, New York: Van Nostrand Reinhold, pp. 275–84.

Poggi, R.G. and Berland, D.I. (1985) The therapist's reactions to the elderly. *Gerontologist*, **25**(5), 508–13.

Polster, E. and Polster, M. (1973) *Gestalt Therapy Integrated*, New York: Vintage Books.

Porcino. J. (1985) Psychological aspects of aging in women. *Women and Health*, **10**, 115–22.

Porter, K. and O'Connor, N. (1978) Changing attitudes of university students to old people. *Educational Gerontology: An International Quarterly*, **3**, 139–48.

Power, B. (1980) *Old and Alone in Ireland*, Dublin: Society of St. Vincent de Paul.

Pratt, M.W. (1992) Older but wiser? A longitudinal study of mature adult thinking about the social domain. Paper presented at the international Congress of Psychology, Brussels, July .

Pratt, M.W. and Norris, J.E. (1994) *The Social Psychology of Aging*, Oxford: Blackwell.

Rabins, P.V. (1982) The impact of dementia on the family. *Journal of the American Medical Association*, **248**, 333–5.

Rattenberg, C. and Stones, M.J. (1989) A controlled evaluation of reminiscence and current topics discussion groups in a nursing home context. *Gerontologist*, **29**, 768–71.

Ray, D., Raciti, M.A. and Ford, C.V. (1985) Ageism in psychiatrics: Associations with gender, certification and theortical orientation. *Gerontologist*, **25**(5), 495–500.

Reichard, S., Livson, F. and Peterson, P.G. (1962) *Aging and Personality*, New York: Wiley.

Renshaw, D. (1981) Pharmacotherapy and female sexuality. *British Journal of Sexual Medicine*, **71**, 34–7.

Renshaw, D. (1991) Sexuality. In *Comprehensive Review of Geriatric Psychiatry*, eds J. Sadavoy, L. Lazarus and L. Jarvik, Washington DC: American Psychiatric Press.

Reynolds, C.F., Kupfer, D.J., Hoch C.C. *et al.* (1986) Sleep deprivation in healthy elderly men and women: effects on mood and on sleep during recovery. *Sleep*, **9**(4), 492–501.

Richardson, C.A., Gilleard, J., Lieberman, S. and Peeler, R. (1994) Working with older adults and their families: A review. *Journal of Family Therapy*, **16**(3), 225–40.

Richardson, I.M. (1964) *Age and Need*, Edinburgh: E. and S. Livingstone.

Richardson, R., Lowenstein, A. S. and Weissberg, M. (1989) Coping with the suicidal elderly: A physician's guide. *Geriatrics*, **44**, 43–7.

Richman, J. (1977) The foolishness and wisdom of age: Attitudes towards the elderly as reflected in jokes. *Gerontologist*, **17**, 210–19.

Rodin, J. and Langer, E. (1980) Aging labels: The decline of control and the fall of self-esteem. *Journal of Social Issues*, **36**(2), 12–29.

Rogers, C.R. (1961) *On Becoming a Person*, London: Constable.

Rogers, C.R. (1980) *A Way of Being*, Boston, MA: Houghton Mifflin.

Rokach, A. (1989) Antecedents of loneliness: A factorial analysis. *Journal of Psychology*, **123**(4), 369–84.

Rose, A.M. (1965) The subculture of the aging: A framework for research in social gerontology. In *Older People and Their Social World*, eds A.M. Rose and W.A. Peterson, Philadelphia: F.A. Davis.

Rose, A.M. (1968) The subculture of the aging: A topic for sociological research. In *Middle Age and Aging*, ed. B. Neugarten, Chicago: University of Chicago Press, pp. 29–34.

Rose, A.M. and Peterson, W.A. (1965) *Older people and Their Social World*, Philadelphia, PA: F.A. Davis.

Rosen, C. (1982) Ethnic differences among impoverished rural elderly in use of religion as a coping mechanism. *Journal of Rural Community Psychology*, **3**, 27–34.

Rosenbaum, W.A. and Button, J. (1989) Is there a gray peril? *Gerontologist*, **29**, 300–6.

Rosenberg, M. (1965) *Society and the Adolescent Self-Image*, Princeton, NJ, Princeton University Press.

Rosner, A. (1968) *Stress and Maintenance of Self-concept in the Aged*. Unpublished doctoral dissertation, University of Chicago.

Roth, L.H., Meisel, A. and Lidz, C. (1977) Tests of competency to consent to treatment. *American Journal of Psychiatry*, **134**, 279–84.

Rowe, J.W. (1985) Health care of the elderly. *New England Journal of Medicine*, **312**, 827–35.

Roybal, E. (1988) Mental health and aging. *American Psychologist*, **43**(3), 189–94.

Rubenstein, C. and Shaver, P. (1982) *In Search of Intimacy*, New York: Delacorte Press.

Rubin, K. (1973) *Decentration skills in institutionalized and non-institutionalized elderly*. Proceedings of the 81st Annual Convention of the American Psychological Association, Montreal, Canada.

Rubin, R. (1977) Learning to overcome reluctance for psychotherapy with the elderly. *Journal of Geriatric Psychiatry*, **10**(2), 215–27.

Ryan, E.B. and Capadano, H.L. (1978) Age perceptions and evaluate reactions toward adult speakers. *Journal of Gerontology*, **33**, 98–102.

Ryan, M. and Peterson, J. (1987) Loneliness in the elderly. *Journal of Gerontological Nursing*, **13**(5), 6–12.

Ryff, C.D. and Heincke, S.G. (1983) Subjective organization of personality in adulthood and aging. *Journal of Personality and Social Psychology*, **44**(4), 807–16.

Sadavoy, J., Lazarus, L. and Jarvik, L. (eds) (1991) *Comprehensive Review of Geriatric Psychiatry*, Washington DC: American Psychiatric Press.

Safford, F. (1988) Value of gerontology for occupational social work. *Social Work*, Jan–Feb, 33(1).

Salkovskis, P.M. and Clark, D.M. (1991) Cognitive therapy for panic attacks. *Journal of Cognitive Psychotherapy*, **5**, Special Issue: Panic Disorders, 215–26.

Sargent, S.S. (ed.) (1980) *Non-traditional Therapy and Counselling With the Aging*, New York: Springer.

Satir, V. (1967) *Conjoint Family Therapy*, Palo Alto, CA: Science and Behaviour Books.

Schaie, K.W. (1977–78) Toward a stage theory of adult cognitive development. *Journal of Aging and Human Development*, **8**, 129–38.

Schaie, K.W. (1983) *Longitudinal Studies of Adult Psychological Development*, New York: Guilford Press.

Schaie, K.W. and Labouvie-Vief, G. (1974) Generational versus ontogenic components of change in cognitive behaviour: A fourteen-year cross-sequential study. *Developmental Psychology*, **10**, 305–20.

Schaie, K.W. and Strother, C.R. (1968) A cross-sequential study of age changes in cognitive behaviour. *Psychological Bulletin*, **70**, 671–80.

Schaie, K.W., Labouvie-Vief, G. and Beuch, B.V. (1973) Generational and cohort-speech differences in adult cognitive functioning: A 14 year study of independent samples. *Developmental Psychology*, **9**, 151–66.

Schellenberg, R., Knorr, W., Beyer, H. *et al.* (1989) Repeated acoustic stimulation of acute schizophrenic patients and the habituation of EEG power changes. *International Journal of Psychophysiology*, **7**(1), 55–63.

Scher, M. (1981) Men in hiding: A challenge for the counsellor. *Personnel and Guidance Journal*, **60**, 199–202.

Schick, F.L. (1984) *Statistical Handbook of Aging Americans*, Phoenix, AZ: Oryx Press.

Schmidt, D.F. and Boland, S.M. (1986) Structure of perceptions of older adults: Evidence for multiple stereotypes. *Psychology and Aging*, **1**(3), 255–60.

Schonfield, D. (1982) Who is stereotyping who and why? *Gerontologist*, 22.

Schuckit, M. and Miller, P. (1975) Alcoholism in elderly men: A survey of a general medical ward. *Annals of the New York Academy of Sciences*, **273**, 551–71.

Scrutton, S. (1989) *Counselling Older People - a Creative Response to Aging*, London: Edward Arnold.

Segerberg, O. (1982) *Living to be 100: 1,200 Who Did and How They Did It*, New York: Scribners.

Seltzer, M.M. (1977) Differential impact of various experiences on breaking down age stereotypes. *Educational Gerontology: An International Quarterly*, **2**, 183–9.

Seltzer, M. and Atchley, R. (1971) The concept of old: Changing attitudes and stereotypes. *Gerontologist*, **11**, 226–30.

Shanas, E. and Streib, G.F. (eds) (1965) *Social Structure and the Family: Generational Relations*, Englewood Cliffs, NJ: Prentice Hall.

Shanas, E., Townsend, P., Wedderburn, D. *et al.* (eds) (1968) *Old People in Three Industrial Societies*, New York: Atherton.

Sheehan, N.W. and Nuttall, P. (1988) Conflict, emotion and personal strain among family caregivers. *Family Relations*, **37**, 92–8.

Sherman, E. (1981) *Counseling the Aging: An Integrative Approach*, New York: Free Press.

Sherman, E. (1987) Reminiscence groups for community elderly. *Gerontologist*, **27**(5), 569–72.

Sherman, E. (1991) Reminiscentia: Cherished objects as memorabilia in late-life reminiscence. *International Journal of Aging and Human Development*, **33**, 89–100.

Shlien, J. (1984) Secrets and the psychology of secrecy. In *Client-Centred Therapy and the Person-Centred Approach*, eds R. Levant and J. Shlien, New York: Praeger.

Shneidman, E.S. (1970) You and death. *Psychology Today*, August, 67–72.

Shneidman, E.S. (1973) Suicide notes. *Psychiatry*, **36**, 379–94.

Shostrom, E.L. (1974) *The Personal Orientation Inventory Manual,* San Diego: EDITS.

Shulman, B. and Berman, R. (1988) *How to Survive Your Aging Parents*, Chicago: Surrey Books.

Shulman, B.H. and Sperry, L. (1992) Consultation with adult children of aging parents. *Individual Psychology*, **48**, 427–31.

Shulman, S.C. (1985) Psychodynamic group therapy with older women. *Journal of Contemporary Social Work*, December, 579–86.

Shura, S. (1974) *Aging: An Album of People Growing Old,* New York: Wiley.

Skinner, B.F. (1983) Intellectual self-management in old age. *American Psychologist*, **38**(3), 239–44.

Smith, P.L., Kendall, L. and Hulin, L. (1969) *The Measure of Satisfaction in Work and Retirement: A Strategy for the Study of Attitudes*, Chicago: Rand McNally.

Smyer, M.A. (1984) Life transitions and aging: Implications for counselling older adults. *Counselling Psychologist*, **12**(2), 17–28.

Snaith, R.P., Ahmed, S., Mehta, S. and Hamilton, M. (1971) Assessment of the severity of depressive illness. *Psychological Medicine*, **1**, 143–9.

Solnick, R.L. and Birren, J.E. (1977) Age and male erectile responsiveness. *Archives of Sexual Behavior*, **6**, 1–9.

Solnick, R.L. and Corby, N. (1983) Human sexuality and aging. In *Aging: Scientific Perspectives and Social Issues*, eds D.S. Woodruff and J.E. Birren, Monterey, CA: Brooks Cole.

Sparacino, J. (1978) Individual psychotherapy with the aged: A selective review. *International Journal of Aging and Human Development*, **9**(3), 197–220.

Spence, D. (1968) Medical student attitudes toward the geriatric patient. *Journal of the American Geriatrics Society*, **16**(9), 976–83.

Spero, M.H. (1985) *Psychotherapy of the Religious Patient*, Springfield, Ill: C.C. Thomas.

Spielberger, C., Gorusch, R. and Lushere, R. (1983) *The State Trait Anxiety Inventory Manual*, Palo Alto, CA: Consulting Psychologists Press.

Spitzer, R. and Endicott, J. (1977) *The SADS - Change Interview*, New York: New York State Psychiatric Institute.

Spitzer, R., Endicott, J. and Robins, E. (1978) Research diagnostic criteria: Rationale and reliability. *Archives of General Psychiatry*, **35**, 773–82.

Srole, L. (1956) Social integration and certain corollaries: An exploratory study. *American Social Review*, **21**, 709–16.

Starr, B.D. (1985) Sexuality and aging. In *Annual Review of Gerontology and Geriatrics*, Vol 5, eds M.P. Lawton and G.L. Maddox, New York: Springer.

Sterns, H.L., Weis, D.M. and Perkins, S.E. (1984) A conceptual approach to counseling older adults and their families. *Counselling Psychologist*, **12**(2), 55–61.

Steuer, J., Mintz, J., Hammen, C.L. *et al.* (1984) Cognitive–behavioural and psychodynamic group psychotherapy in treatment of geriatric depression. *Journal of Consulting and Clinical Psychology*, **52**, 180–9.

Stevens-Ratchford, R.G. (1993) The effect of life review reminiscence activities on depression and self-esteem in older adults. *American Journal of Occupational Therapy*, **47**, 413–20.

Stones, M.J. and Kozma, A. (1986) Happiness and activities as properties. *Journal of Gerontology*, **41**, 85–90.

Storandt, M. (1983) *Counseling and Therapy With Older Adults*, Boston: Little, Brown.

Stotsky, B.A. (1968) *The Elderly Patient*, New York: Grune and Stratton.

Strachey, J. (1978) *Complete Psychological Works*, London: Hogarth Press.

Streib, G.F. and Schneider, C.J. (1971) *Retirement in American Society*, Ithaca, NY: Cornell University.

Stroebe, M. and Stroebe, W. (1989) Who participates in bereavement research? A review and empirical study. *Omega, Journal of Death and Dying*, **20**, 1–30.

Stroebe, W., Stroebe, M. and Domittner,G. (1988) Individual and situational differences in recovery from bereavement: A risk group identified. *Journal of Social Issues*, **44**, 143–58.

Stuart-Hamilton, I. (1994) *The Psychology of Aging*, London: Jessica Kingsley.

Swan, G.E., Dame, A. and Carmelli, D. (1991) Involuntary retirement, Type A behaviour and current functioning in elderly men: A 27 year follow-up of the Western Collaborative Group Study. *Psychology and Aging*, **6**, 384–91.

Szapocznik, J., Santisteban, D. and Kurtines, W. (1982) Life enhancement counselling and the treatment of depressed Cuban American elders. *Hispanic Journal of Behavioural Sciences*, **4**, 487–502.

Tatai, K and Tatai, K. (1991) Suicide in the elderly: A report for Japan. *Crisis*, **12**(2), 40–4.

Tellis-Nayak, Y. (1982) The transcendent standard: The religious ethos of the rural elderly. *Gerontologist*, **22**, 359–61.

Tesch, S., Whitbourne, S.K., Nehrke, M.F. (1981) Friendship, social interaction and subjective well-being of older men in an institutional setting. *International Journal of Aging and Human Development*, **13**(4), 317–28.

Thomas, E.C. and Yamamoto, K. (1975) Attitudes toward age: An exploration in school-age children. *International Journal of Aging and Human Development*, **6**, 117–29.

Thompson, L.W., Breckenridge, J.S. and Gallagher, D.E. (1983) Effects of bereavement on self-perceptions of physical health in elderly widows and widowers. *Journal of Gerontology*, **39**(3), 309–14.

Thompson, L.W., Gallagher, D.E. and Breckenridge, J.S. (1987) Comparative effectiveness of psychotherapies for depressed elders. *Journal of Consulting and Clinical Psychology*, **55**, 385–90.

Thoresen, C. (1992) Foreword. In *Gestalt Therapy: Theory, Research and Practice*, ed. E. O'Leary, London: Chapman and Hall.

Thorne, B. (1984) Person-centered therapy. In *Individual Therapy in Britain*, ed. W. Dryden, London: Harper and Row.

Thorson, J.A., Whatley, L. and Hancock, K. (1974) Attitudes towards the aged as a function of age and education. *Gerontologist*, **19**, 10–20.

Tibbitts, C. (1979) Can we invalidate negative stereotypes in aging? *Gerontologist*, **19**, 10–20.

Tobin, S.S. and Lieberman, M.A. (1976) *Last Home for the Aged: Critical Implications of Institutionalization*, San Francisco, CA: Jossey-Bass.

Townsend, P. (1981) The structural dependency of the elderly: creation of social policy in the 20th century. *Aging and Society*, **1**(1), 6–28.

Tracey, T.J., Sherry, P. and Keital, M. (1986) Distress and help seeking as a function of person–environment fit and self-efficacy: A causal model. *American Journal of Community Psychology*, **14**, 657–76.

Traxler, A. (1971) Intergenerational differences in attitudes toward old people. Paper presented at the Annual Meeting of the Gerontological Society, Houston.

Treas, J. (1975) Aging and the family. In *Aging: Scientific Perspectives and Social Issues*, eds D.S. Woodruff and J.E. Birren, New York: Van Nostrand.

Tuckman, J. and Lorge, J. (1953) Attitudes toward old people. *Journal of Social Psychology*, **37**, 249–60.

Tuckman, J. and Lorge, E. (1958) Attitudes towards aging of individuals with experiences with the aged. *Journal of Genetic Psychology*, **92**, 199–204.

US Bureau of the Census (1982) *Current Population Reports*. Washington DC: Government Printing Office.

US Bureau of the Census (1986) *Statistical Abstract of the United States, 1986*, Washington DC: United States Department of Commerce.

Vayhinger, M.M. (1980) The approach of patriarchal psychology. In *Non-Traditional Therapy and Counselling with the Aging*, Vol. 6, ed S. Sargent, New York: Springer.

Venkoba Rao, A. (1991) Suicide in the elderly: A report from India. *Crisis*, **12**, 33–40.

Victor, C.R. (1987) *Old Age in Modern Society: A Textbook in Gerontology*, London: Croom Helm.

Walker, A. (1981) Towards a political economy of old age. *Aging and Society*, **1**(1).

Walsh, W. (1992) *The Complete Answer to Male Impotence*, Dublin and London: Dublin Medical Centre and London Diagnostic Centre.

Walton, C., Schultz, C., Beck, C. and Walls, R. (1991) Psychological correlates of loneliness in the older adult. *Archives of Psychiatric Nursing*, **5**, 165–70.

Ward, R.A. (1979) *The Aging Experience. An Introduction to Social Gerontology*, Philadelphia: Lippincott.

Ward, R.A. (1984) *The Aging Experience: an Introduction to Social Gerontology*, 2nd edn, New York: Harper and Row.

Wass, H. (1977) Views and opinions of elderly persons concerning death. *Educational Gerontology*, **2**, 15–26.

Waters, E. (1984) Building on what you know: Techniques for individual and group counseling with older people. *Counselling Psychologist*, **12**(2), 63–74.

Waters, E., Weaver, A. and White, B. (1980) *Gerontological Counseling Skills: A Manual for Training Service Providers*, Rochester, MI: Continuum Center, Oakland University.

Watkins, C. (1983) Transference phenomena in the counselling situation. *Personnel and Guidance Journal*, **62**, 206–10.

Watkins, E.C. (1992) Developing and writing the life-style report. *Individual Psychology*, **48**, 462–72.

Watson, M.A. and Ager, C.L. (1991) The impact of role valuation and performance as life satisfaction in old age. *Physical and Occupational Therapy in Geriatrics*, **10**, 27–62.

Webb, W.B. (1982) Sleep in older persons: Sleep structures of 50 to 60 year old men and women. *Journal of Gerontology*, **327**, 581–6.

Weeks, D.J. (1994) A review of loneliness concepts with particular reference to old age. *International Journal of Geriatric Psychiatry*, **9**, 345–55.

Weg, R.B. (1983a) *Sexuality in the Later Years: Roles and Behavior*, New York: Academic Press.

Weinberg, J. (1951) Psychiatric techniques in the treatment of older people, In *Growing in the Older Years*, eds W. Donahue and C. Tibbits, Ann Arbor, University of Michigan Press.

Weinberger, L.E. and Millham, J. (1975) A multi-dimensional, multiple method analysis of attitudes toward the elderly. *Journal of Gerontology*, **30**, 343–8.

Wellman, F.E. and McCormack, J. (1984) Counseling with older persons: A review of outcome research. *Counselling Psychologist*, **12**(2), 81–95.

West, R. (1992) *Memory Fitness after Forty*, Gainesville: Triad Press.

Westcott, N.A. (1983) Application of the structured life-review technique in counselling elders. *Personnel and Guidance Journal*, **62**, 180–1.

Whelan, C.T. and Whelan, B.J. (1988) *The Transition to Retirement*, Dublin: Economic and Social Research Institute.

Whitaker, C. and Keith, D. (1981) Symbolic experiential family therapy. In *Handbook of Family Therapy*, eds A. Gurman and D. Kniskern, New York: Brunner/Mazel.

Whitbourne, S.K. (1985) *The Aging Body*, New York: Springer.

Whitbourne, S. and Hulicka, I. (1990) Ageism in undergraduate psychology tests. *American Psychologist*, **45**, 1127–36.

White, C. (1975) Sexuality in the institutionalised elderly. Paper presented at the meeting of the New York State Public Health Association, Buffalo, NY.

Whitehead, E. E. and Whitehead, J. D. (1982) *Christian Life Patterns*, New York: Image Books.

Wiedeman, G. and Matison, S. (1975) *Personality, Development and Deviation: Textbook for Social Work*, New York: International Universities Press.

Wilkie, F.L. and Eisdorfer, I. (1973) Systemic disease and behavioural correlates. In *Intellectual Functioning in Adults*, eds L. Jervick, I. Eisdorfer and J.E. Blum, New York: Springer.

Williamson, J., Evans, L. and Munley, A. (1980) *Aging and Society*, New York: Holt, Rinehart and Winston.

Wingard, J., Heath, R. and Himelstein, S. (1982) The effects of contextual variation on attitudes toward the elderly. *Journal of Gerontology*, **37**, 475–82.

Winn, R.L. and Newton, N. (1982) Sexuality in ageing: a study of 106 cultures. *Archives of Sexual Behaviour*, **11**, 283–98.

Wolpe, J. (1969) *The Practice of Behaviour Therapy*, New York: Pergamon.

Wood, V., Wylie, M.L. and Shaefor, B. (1969) An analysis of a short self-report measure of life satisfaction: Correlation with rater judgements. *Journal of Gerontology*, **24**, 465–9.

Woodruff, D. (1985) Arousal, sleep and aging. In *Handbook of the Psychology of Aging*, 2nd edn, eds J.E. Birren and K.W. Schaie, New York: Van Nostrand Reinhold.

Woodruff, D.S. (1975) Relationships between EEG alpha frequency reaction time and age: a biofeedback study. *Psychophysiology*, **13**, 673–81.

Woodruff, D.S. and Birren, J.E. (1975) *Aging: Scientific Perspectives and Social Issues*, New York: Van Nostrand.

Worden, W.J. (1983) *Grief Counselling and Grief Therapy*, London: Tavistock.

Working Party on Services for the Elderly in Ireland (1988) *The Years Ahead: A Policy for the Elderly*. Dublin: Stationery Office.

Worthington, E.L. (1988) Understanding the values of religious clients: A model and its application to counselling. *Journal of Counselling Psychology*, **35**(2), 166–74.

Yalom, I.D. (1975) *The Theory and Practice of Group Psychotherapy*, New York: Bain Books.

Yesavage, J., Brink, T., Rose, R. *et al.* (1983) Development and validation of a geriatric depression screening scale: A preliminary report. *Journal of Psychiatric Research*, **17**, 37–49.

Zarit, S.H. (1980) *Aging and Mental Disorders: Psychological Approaches to Assessment and Treatment*, New York: Free Press.

Zelin, M.L. Adler, G. and Meyerson, P.G. (1972) cited in *Anger and Hostility in Cardiovascular and Behavioural Disorders,* M.A. Chesney and R.H. Rosenman, New York: Hemisphere Publishing Corporation.

Zepelin, H., McDonald, C.S. and Zamit, G.K. (1984) Effects of age on auditory awakening thresholds. *Journal of Gerontology*, **39**(3), 294–300.

Zuckerman, M. and Lubin, B. (1965) *Manual for the Multiple Affect Adjective Check List*, San Diego: Educational and Industrial Testing Service.

Zung, W. (1965) A self-rating depression scale. *Archives of General Psychiatry*, **12**, 63–70.

Index